100 GAME THEORIES AND DECISION MODELS

GAME THEORY

BY DAN WAITE

MUTUALLY ASSURED DESTRUCTION	DOLLAR AUCTION	HAWK-DOVE GAME
VOLUNTEER'S DILEMMA	SILENT DUEL	AI ALIGNMENT GAME
BAYESIAN GAME	TIPPING POINT GAME	SOCIAL INFLUENCE
TIT-FOR-TAT IN EVOLUTION	DIVIDE THE DOLLAR GAME	MONTY HALL PROBLEM
DIFFUSION OF RESPONSIBILITY	FREE RIDER PROBLEM	FLOCKING BEHAVIOUR
PARASITE-HOST GAME	CYBERSECURITY GAME	PREDATOR-PREY GAME

100 GAME THEORIES

RATIONAL DECISION-MAKING IN COMPETITIVE SITUATIONS

EVOLUTIONARILY STABLE STRATEGY	LIMITED WAR GAME	SECURITY DILEMMA
TRUST GAME	SUNK COST GAME	SHAPLEY VALUE
TERRORIST VS. GOVERNMENT	SPY VS. SPY GAME	DETERRENCE THEORY GAME
COLONEL BLOTTO GAME	WAR OF ATTRITION	MARKET FOR LEMONS
MORAL HAZARD GAME	PRINCIPAL-AGENT PROBLEM	JOB MARKET SIGNALLING
SOCIAL MEDIA VIRALITY GAME	SPAM DETECTION GAME	ADVERSE SELECTION GAME
BERTRAND COMPETITION	CASCADING FAILURE GAME	EL FAROL BAR PROBLEM
SELF-DRIVING CAR DILEMMA GAMES	MECHANISM DESIGN THEORY	AND MANY, MANY MORE

100 GAME THEORIES AND DECISION MODELS FOR RATIONAL DECISION MAKING IN COMPETITIVE SITUATIONS

100 GAME THEORIES AND DECISION MODELS FOR RATIONAL DECISION MAKING IN COMPETITIVE SITUATIONS

BY DAN WAITE

Published by LOCO TEMPUS LIMITED 2025

Copyright Dan Waite 2025

Cover design by Dan Waite

British Library Cataloguing in Publication Data

A catalogue record for this book is available from the British Library

ISBN: 978-1-0683958-3-3

ISBN   978-1-0683958-3-3

9 781068 395833 >

Dan Waite here, CEO of Better Noise Music. I still remember my 10th Birthday when for my birthday party, my friends came over to watch WAR GAMES on VHS. They film had been release a year earlier but in was now available for film rental.

The topic of the film is M.A.D. Mutually Assured Destruction by nuclear war. The film title gives the fact away that this is a Game Theory, but as a ten year old I didn't know how many similar theories there are.

As I mentioned in my last book '100 Cognitive and Mental Models' a good friend of mine Ade Adeluwoye and I regularly swap inspirational book ideas and have suggestions on what to read to develop personally and within our careers.

Unlike the Mental Models book, researching this Game Theories book has brought me into contact with many theories that I had not come across before, and that have given me a new perspective to models that can help solve problems with ease.

I hope these are in a digestible and easily understood format, and look out for the next books in the series.

Best of Luck, Dan

This is dedicated to my wife Irena, my family & friends and work colleagues, present and past.

With thanks to Ade Adeluwoye, Nicolas Bate, Sir Richard Branson, Allen Kovac for your trust and guidance as a boss and mentor and Napolean Hill for the advice in spotting opportunity in hard work.

Thank you to inspirational contacts who as a result of their books and classes have me thinking differently, they are Rory Sutherland and Will Page.

In memory of my father David Waite.

10

CHAPTERS

13

14

Coordination & Bargaining Games

1 Schelling's Coordination Game

Schelling's Coordination Game in Game Theory

Breakdown of the Theory

Schelling's Coordination Game, developed by **Thomas Schelling**, examines how individuals or groups coordinate their choices **without direct communication**. Unlike competitive games where players have conflicting interests, **coordination games require players to align their decisions to achieve mutual benefits**.

The challenge in this game is that there are **multiple equilibria**—different successful coordination points. Players must rely on **shared expectations, social norms, or common knowledge** to make the same decision. A **focal point (Schelling point)** is the solution people naturally gravitate toward when no explicit instructions are given.

Example of Schelling's Coordination Game

Imagine **two travellers, Alex and Jordan**, in **New York City** who need to meet but cannot communicate. They must independently choose a meeting place from:

1. **Times Square**

2. **Central Park**

3. **Empire State Building**

4. **Brooklyn Bridge**

While any location could work, **Times Square** is the most **widely recognized landmark**. Without prior discussion, both travellers are most likely to pick **Times Square**, making it a **focal point** for coordination. If they both choose it, they meet (**coordination achieved**). If they choose differently, they fail to meet (**coordination failure**).

Why It Works

Schelling's game works because **people rely on mutual expectations** rather than communication. The key factors that influence coordination include:

- **Cultural conventions** (e.g., major landmarks).

- **Common knowledge** (e.g., universally accepted norms).

- **Logical reasoning** (e.g., picking the most prominent option).

Even though multiple equilibria exist, **focal points simplify decision-making** by offering a natural solution.

How It Works

- Players choose from multiple options but **only benefit if their choices match**.

- **There is no dominant strategy**—the best move depends on predicting what the other player will do.

- **Focal points emerge as natural equilibria**, guiding decisions without explicit coordination.

Applications of Schelling's Coordination Game

This game has widespread real-world applications:

1. **Driving Conventions** – People follow **right-hand or left-hand driving norms** depending on their country.

2. **Language Selection** – In international business, **English** often serves as a focal point.

3. **Market Standards** – Businesses adopt industry standards (e.g., **USB vs. Lightning cables**) for compatibility.

4. **Protests and Gatherings** – Demonstrators rally at **central squares or government buildings** as natural meeting points.

Key Insights

1. **Shared expectations drive coordination.**

2. **Focal points reduce uncertainty in decision-making.**

3. **Not all coordination games have clear solutions.**

4. **Past experiences reinforce coordination strategies.**

Final Thoughts

Schelling's Coordination Game highlights how **people align decisions based on logic and social norms**. Understanding this concept helps in **policymaking, business strategy, and everyday problem-solving**, ensuring **efficient and predictable** outcomes in complex decision-making environments.

2 Hawk-Dove Game

Hawk-Dove Game in Game Theory

Breakdown of the Theory

The **Hawk-Dove Game**, also known as **the Game of Chicken**, is a fundamental model in **game theory** that illustrates **conflict resolution, competition, and strategy in resource disputes**. It describes interactions between two players (or groups) who must decide between **aggressive (Hawk) or peaceful (Dove) behaviour** when competing for a shared resource.

The key takeaway is that **mutual aggression leads to costly conflict**, while mutual peace leads to **shared benefits**. However, an asymmetrical outcome—where one player fights while the other yields—favours the aggressive player. This model is widely used in **evolutionary biology, political standoffs, and business negotiations.**

Example of the Hawk-Dove Game

Imagine **two rival companies, AlphaTech and BetaCorp**, competing for dominance in the same market. They each have two strategic options:

1. **Play Hawk (Aggressive strategy)** – Engage in a **price war, aggressive advertising, or legal battles**.

2. **Play Dove (Cooperative strategy)** – Avoid conflict, focusing on their **own niche and long-term growth**.

Possible Outcomes:

AlphaTech's Move \ BetaCorp's Move	Hawk (Aggressive)	Dove (Cooperative)
Hawk (Aggressive)	**Both suffer losses** due to market competition (e.g., price war)	AlphaTech dominates while BetaCorp retreats
Dove (Cooperative)	BetaCorp dominates while AlphaTech retreats	**Both share the market peacefully** and maintain profits

- If **both companies play Hawk**, they enter a **destructive price war**, leading to **mutual losses**.

- If **one plays Hawk while the other plays Dove**, the aggressive company **wins market dominance**, while the cooperative one **loses market share**.

- If **both play Dove**, they **share profits and coexist peacefully**.

Why It Works

The **Hawk-Dove Game** works because it reflects **real-world competition**, where aggressive actions **carry risks and costs**, while cooperation may not always be the optimal choice.

- **If everyone fights (Hawk-Hawk), both lose**, making aggression a risky move.

- If one fights while the other concedes, the aggressor gains the upper hand.
- If both cooperate (Dove-Dove), stability and mutual benefit emerge.

How It Works

1. **Players independently decide** whether to act aggressively or peacefully.
2. **If both are aggressive, conflict leads to mutual losses.**
3. **If one concedes, the aggressor gains an advantage.**
4. **If both are peaceful, a fair and stable equilibrium is reached.**

Applications of the Hawk-Dove Game

1. **Evolutionary Biology** – Animals competing for food or territory must decide **whether to fight or retreat.**
2. **Business Competition** – Companies decide **whether to engage in aggressive tactics or coexist peacefully.**
3. **International Relations** – Countries engaging in military standoffs (e.g., **Cold War strategies**).
4. **Social Behaviour** – Individuals competing for leadership in groups must **balance aggression and cooperation.**

Key Insights

1. Mutual aggression leads to destructive outcomes.

2. A balance between cooperation and conflict is often the best strategy.

3. Players must assess risks before engaging in aggression.

4. Reputation and past interactions influence future decisions in repeated games.

Final Thoughts

The **Hawk-Dove Game** explains why competition can be destructive and why **compromise is often a better long-term strategy**. In **business, politics, and nature**, players must carefully **weigh the risks of aggression versus the benefits of cooperation** to maximize their success.

3 Volunteer's Dilemma

Volunteer's Dilemma in Game Theory

Breakdown of the Theory

The **Volunteer's Dilemma** is a **game theory model** that examines situations where a group benefits if **at least one person** takes action, but everyone **prefers that someone else** does it. Each individual faces a trade-off between:

1. **Acting (volunteering)** – Taking on the cost of effort but ensuring the group benefits.

2. **Not acting (free-riding)** – Avoiding personal effort but risking that no one volunteers, causing the group to suffer.

If no one volunteers, **everyone loses**, even though each person was trying to avoid personal cost. This dilemma appears in **social cooperation, emergency response, and workplace settings**, where collective benefit depends on at least one participant stepping up.

Example of the Volunteer's Dilemma

Imagine **four employees in a tech startup** working on a major project. A last-minute software bug is discovered, and it must be fixed overnight before launch.

- The bug **must be fixed by at least one person** for the project to succeed.

- If **no one volunteers**, the company **suffers reputational and financial damage**.

- The employee who volunteers **loses personal time** but **ensures success**.

Possible Outcomes:

Employee Choice	Consequence
One employee volunteers	The project succeeds, but the volunteer sacrifices personal time.
More than one volunteer	The project succeeds, but multiple employees take unnecessary effort.
No one volunteers	The project fails, and everyone faces consequences (e.g., layoffs, bad reviews).

This dilemma captures the reality that while **volunteering is essential, individuals have an incentive to wait for someone else to step up.**

Why It Works

The **Volunteer's Dilemma** works because **it models real-world situations where responsibility is uncertain:**

- **If one person acts, the group succeeds**, but individuals may hesitate to take on costs.

- **If too many volunteer, resources are wasted**, showing that **over-participation can be inefficient**.

- **If no one acts, everyone suffers**, demonstrating the **risk of collective inaction**.

How It Works

1. **Players independently decide whether to volunteer or not.**

2. **If no one volunteers, everyone suffers.**

3. **If one player volunteers, the problem is solved, but they bear the cost.**

4. **If multiple players volunteer, unnecessary effort is wasted.**

The game demonstrates that **volunteering is a strategic decision based on group size, perceived costs, and expectations about others' behaviour**.

Applications of the Volunteer's Dilemma

1. **Emergency Situations** – A person must call 911 in an accident, but everyone assumes someone else will.

2. **Corporate Responsibility** – Companies rely on one competitor to take the lead on **sustainability or ethical practices**.

3. **Military and Public Service** – Societies depend on volunteers for **military service, community work, and civic duties.**

4. **Workplace Team Projects** – Employees must decide **who takes on extra work** when no one else wants to.

Key Insights

1. **The larger the group, the less likely an individual will volunteer** (diffusion of responsibility).

2. **People hesitate to act if they believe someone else will do it** (bystander effect).

3. **Incentives and recognition increase volunteering** (e.g., bonuses, awards).

4. **Social norms and repeated interactions encourage long-term cooperation.**

Final Thoughts

The **Volunteer's Dilemma** highlights the **tension between self-interest and group benefit**. It explains **why people hesitate in crises, why businesses delay action on collective issues, and how incentives can improve participation.** Addressing this dilemma often requires **social norms, leadership, or external incentives** to encourage proactive behaviour.

4 El Farol Bar Problem

El Farol Bar Problem in Game Theory

Breakdown of the Theory

The **El Farol Bar Problem**, introduced by **W. Brian Arthur**, is a **game theory model** that explores how individuals make decisions under **uncertainty and limited information**. The problem illustrates **adaptive behaviour** in complex systems where players must **predict the choices of others** to maximize their own benefit.

It falls under the category of **minority games**, where the best outcome for a player depends on **not choosing what the majority chooses**. This contrasts with typical coordination games, where success often relies on **conforming** rather than **differentiating**.

Example of the El Farol Bar Problem

Imagine that **100 people** in a small town like to visit **El Farol Bar** every Thursday.

- The bar is **enjoyable if it's not too crowded**, meaning attendance should be ≤ **60 people** for a good experience.

- If **more than 60 people** show up, it becomes **overcrowded and unpleasant**.

- If **too few people** go, those who stayed home **missed an enjoyable evening** unnecessarily.

Each person **must independently decide whether to go,** knowing that their decision depends on **predicting how many others will also go**.

Possible Outcomes:

Scenario	Outcome
Fewer than 60 people go	All attendees have a great experience.
Exactly 60 people go	The bar is at **optimal capacity**.
More than 60 people go	Overcrowding occurs, making the night unpleasant.
Few people go due to fear of overcrowding	Many regret staying home.

No **single equilibrium** exists because if too many expect overcrowding and stay home, the bar will be empty causing them to **regret their decision and go next time**. Over time, people **adapt strategies** based on past observations.

Why It Works

The **El Farol Bar Problem** works because it captures **real-world decision-making under uncertainty**:

- **People must predict the behaviour of others without direct communication.**

- **Over-reliance on patterns can lead to fluctuating attendance** (self-fulfilling prophecies).

- **Diverse decision-making strategies emerge** as people try to outguess one another.

How It Works

1. **Players make independent decisions** without coordination.

2. **If too many go, the experience is poor**—next time, more will stay home.

3. **If too few go, more will be tempted to attend next time.**

4. **Over time, an adaptive balance emerges**, but **attendance keeps fluctuating** rather than stabilizing.

This is an example of a **complex adaptive system**, where **no single strategy dominates**, but players continuously adjust based on past experience.

Applications of the El Farol Bar Problem

1. **Traffic Congestion** – Drivers must decide whether to take the **highway or an alternate route**, knowing that if too many take one option, it will become congested.

2. **Stock Market Trading** – Investors must predict **whether others will buy or sell** to maximize profits.

3. **Shared Resources** – Farmers using a **common water supply** must balance usage, so it **doesn't run dry**.

4. **Internet Bandwidth Usage** – People using **Wi-Fi networks** experience slow speeds when too many log on at once.

Key Insights

1. **Decentralized decision-making can lead to cyclical patterns of overuse and underuse.**

2. **Predicting the majority's behaviour is difficult and leads to strategic diversity.**

3. **No single "optimal" strategy exists—adaptive behaviour prevails.**

4. **Systems like traffic, finance, and network bandwidth share similar unpredictability.**

Final Thoughts

The **El Farol Bar Problem** shows how **adaptive decision-making and strategic diversity** emerge in environments where people must **anticipate the actions of others**. It provides insights into **traffic flow, financial markets, and resource management**, proving that **self-organizing behaviour can lead to fluctuating yet functional equilibrium**.

5 Silent Duel

Silent Duel in Game Theory

Breakdown of the Theory

The **Silent Duel** is a **game theory model** that represents a **zero-sum conflict** where two players must act strategically under uncertainty, without knowing the exact timing of their opponent's actions. It is a model of **decision-making under risk**, commonly applied in **military strategy, business competition, and sports psychology**.

The game is particularly interesting because it introduces **asymmetric information**—neither player knows when or if the opponent will act. The goal is to **strike at the right moment** to maximize success while minimizing risk.

Example of the Silent Duel

Imagine **two snipers, Alex and Jordan**, stationed in opposing hideouts.

- Each has **one bullet** and must **decide when to shoot**.

- If a sniper **shoots too early**, they risk **missing and revealing their position**.

- If they **wait too long**, the opponent might **shoot first and win**.

- **If both fire at the same time and miss**, the game resets to a tense standoff.

Possible Outcomes:

	Jordan Waits	Jordan Shoots Early	Jordan Shoots Late
Alex Waits	Standoff continues	Alex loses if Jordan shoots accurately	Alex wins if Jordan hesitates
Alex Shoots Early	Jordan loses if Alex is accurate	Both might miss, resetting the game	Alex loses if Jordan reacts perfectly
Alex Shoots Late	Alex loses if Jordan shoots first	Alex wins if Jordan hesitates	Both fire at peak accuracy, high risk for both

This game highlights **risk-reward dynamics—waiting increases accuracy but also increases vulnerability.**

Why It Works

The **Silent Duel** works because it reflects **real-world decision-making under uncertainty**:

- **Timing is crucial**—players must balance patience with the **risk of acting too late.**

- **Predicting the opponent's strategy** is key—if one player **anticipates hesitation**, they can strike first.

- **Risk and reward trade-offs shape decisions**— delaying improves **precision but exposes vulnerability**.

How It Works

1. **Both players start at equal positions**, deciding when to act.

2. **If one player acts first and succeeds, they win**— but if they fail, they reveal their strategy.

3. **If both wait, tension increases**, making the decision harder.

4. **Repeated games lead to adaptive strategies**, where players change tactics to counter their opponent's behaviour.

Applications of the Silent Duel

1. **Military Strategy** – Submarines or fighter pilots must **decide when to fire**, balancing **stealth vs. engagement**.

2. **Corporate Competition** – Companies launching **new technology or pricing strategies** must decide **when to strike first**.

3. **Political Strategy** – Nations in **diplomatic standoffs** must decide **when to act** without escalating conflict.

4. **Sports Psychology** – Boxers or tennis players must **decide when to attack**, knowing hesitation or early aggression carries risks.

Key Insights

1. **The fear of acting too soon or too late creates high tension.**

2. **Delaying increases precision but exposes vulnerability.**

3. **Predicting the opponent's behaviour is crucial.**

4. **In repeated duels, adaptive strategies emerge.**

Final Thoughts

The **Silent Duel** illustrates how **timing, risk, and decision-making under uncertainty** shape competition. It applies to **military engagements, corporate battles, and sports strategies**, proving that **success depends on balancing patience with decisive action.**

6 Dollar Auction

Dollar Auction in Game Theory

Breakdown of the Theory

The **Dollar Auction**, introduced by **Martin Shubik**, is a paradox in **game theory** that demonstrates **escalation of commitment** and the **sunk cost fallacy**. It is a non-cooperative, zero-sum game where players rationally begin with the expectation of profit but often end up **overpaying due to competitive escalation.**

The game highlights how **small investments can trap players in a cycle of increasing bids**, leading to **irrational behaviour** where both the winner and loser can end up worse off than when they started.

Example of the Dollar Auction

Imagine an auctioneer selling a **$1 bill** with the following rules:

1. **Bidding starts at $0.01**, and players must increase bids in **$0.01 increments.**

2. **The highest bidder wins the dollar** but must **pay their final bid.**

3. **The second-highest bidder also pays their final bid** but wins **nothing.**

   At first, it seems logical to bid up to **$0.99**, as the winner still profits. However, once the bid reaches

$1.00, the second-highest bidder, who has invested **$0.99**, has a choice:

- **Quit and lose $0.99**

- **Bid $1.01 and win, but overpay for the dollar.**

This escalation **continues beyond the dollar's value**, with both players trapped in a **battle to minimize their losses**.

Possible Outcomes:

Player 1's Bid	Player 2's Bid	Outcome
$0.99	$1.00	Player 2 wins, Player 1 loses $0.99
$1.01	$1.02	Player 2 now risks a bigger loss if they quit
$1.50	$1.51	Both players are now in a losing position
$2.00	$2.01	Players have lost double the prize value

This cycle can continue indefinitely, illustrating **irrational decision-making under competitive pressure**.

Why It Works

The **Dollar Auction** works because it exploits **human psychology** and **game dynamics**:

- **Sunk cost fallacy**—Players feel compelled to continue bidding to recover past investments.

- **Loss aversion**—Fear of losing money motivates continued bidding.

- **Escalation of commitment**—The more a player invests, the harder it becomes to walk away.

How It Works

1. Players start by bidding rationally, aiming for a **profit**.

2. As the bid approaches **$1.00**, the risk of loss **increases**.

3. Once over **$1.00**, both players are trapped—bidding continues **not to win, but to minimize losses**.

4. Eventually, one player **quits, suffering a loss**, while the winner **overpays for the prize**.

Applications of the Dollar Auction

1. **Corporate Takeover Bidding Wars** – Companies overbid for acquisitions, paying beyond an asset's value.

2. **Political Campaign Spending** – Candidates escalate advertising budgets, unable to back down once invested.

3. **Stock Market Speculation** – Traders hold onto **losing stocks**, believing they can recover losses.

4. **Military Conflicts** – Nations escalate wars, unwilling to retreat despite high costs.

Key Insights

1. **Small investments can escalate into large losses.**

2. **Sunk cost fallacy keeps players trapped in the game.**

3. **Competitive rivalry leads to irrational decision-making.**

4. **Recognizing escalation early is key to avoiding losses.**

Final Thoughts

The **Dollar Auction** illustrates the dangers of **commitment bias, escalation, and competitive irrationality**. It applies to **business, politics, finance, and military strategy**, proving that **rational players can make irrational choices when trying to avoid losses.** The best strategy? **Recognize the trap early and walk away.**

7 Rubinstein Bargaining Model

Rubinstein Bargaining Model in Game Theory

Breakdown of the Theory

The **Rubinstein Bargaining Model**, developed by **Ariel Rubinstein**, is a **game theory model** that describes how two players negotiate over the division of a surplus (e.g., money, resources, or profits) when they make **alternating offers over time**. Unlike one-shot bargaining games, the **Rubinstein model accounts for time preference**, meaning that players **value immediate payoffs more than delayed ones**.

Key assumptions of the model:

1. **Two rational players negotiate** over how to split a resource.

2. **Players make alternating offers**—one player proposes a split, and the other accepts or rejects it.

3. **If rejected, the proposer changes** in the next round, but waiting imposes a cost (time discounting).

4. **Players prefer earlier agreements**, so they are incentivized to reach a deal quickly.

The **equilibrium solution** in this model shows that the player who **values time the least (more patient player)** tends to **get a better deal**, while the more impatient player concedes more.

Example of the Rubinstein Bargaining Model

Imagine **two companies, SoftTech and CodeWave**, negotiating a **$10 million partnership**.

- **SoftTech makes the first offer**: They propose **$7M for themselves and $3M for CodeWave**.

- **CodeWave rejects the offer** and counteroffers: **$5M–$5M split**.

- If SoftTech **waits too long**, the deal may become **less valuable** due to market changes.

- If both parties delay excessively, **the total value may shrink** (e.g., competitors may enter the market).

Eventually, both parties recognize that continued bargaining **reduces the total benefit** and settle at a division where the more patient player (who can afford to wait) gets a larger share.

Why It Works

The **Rubinstein Bargaining Model** works because it reflects **real-world negotiation dynamics**:

- **Time preference influences decision-making—** players who can afford to wait secure better deals.

- **Concessions emerge strategically**—both parties weigh the cost of waiting versus the benefit of holding out.

- **Players cannot demand too much**, as rejection leads to a counteroffer where they may receive less.

How It Works

1. **One player makes an offer**, deciding how to split a resource.

2. **The second player accepts or rejects.**

3. **If rejected, the second player proposes a counteroffer**, and the game continues.

4. **Time discounting reduces the overall benefit** the longer negotiations continue.

5. **Equilibrium is reached when neither player wants to delay further**, considering time costs.

Applications of the Rubinstein Bargaining Model

1. **Labor Negotiations** – Unions and employers negotiate wages, with the **more patient side gaining better terms.**

2. **Mergers and Acquisitions** – Companies bargaining over **ownership percentages** must consider how long they can afford to negotiate.

3. **International Trade Agreements** – Countries negotiating tariffs and trade deals adjust offers based on **how urgently they need an agreement.**

4. **Real Estate Transactions** – Buyers and sellers counteroffer based on **how desperate they are to close the deal.**

Key Insights

1. **Patience is a key advantage in negotiations.**

2. **Delays reduce total value**, making quick agreements preferable.

3. **A rational equilibrium exists**, where neither player has an incentive to continue bargaining.

4. **More bargaining power belongs to the side that can afford to wait.**

Final Thoughts

The **Rubinstein Bargaining Model** provides a **realistic and structured approach** to understanding **negotiation behaviour**. It explains why some parties **secure better deals based on time preference and strategic patience.** Whether in **business, labour disputes, or international politics**, the ability to wait and apply time pressure is often the key to **winning negotiations.**

8 Coase Bargaining Solution

Coase Bargaining Solution in Game Theory

Breakdown of the Theory

The **Coase Bargaining Solution**, based on the work of **Ronald Coase**, is a game theory model that explains how parties can efficiently resolve disputes over externalities through **private negotiation**, rather than relying on government intervention. The **Coase Theorem** states that if:

1. **Property rights are well-defined,**

2. **Transaction costs are low**, and

3. **Parties can negotiate freely,**

then **an efficient outcome will be reached, regardless of the initial allocation of rights**. This means that as long as negotiation is possible, resources will be allocated to their most valuable use, leading to an optimal solution.

Example of the Coase Bargaining Solution

Consider a **factory** that emits pollution near a **fishing business** operating downstream. The pollution harms the fish population, reducing the fishing company's revenue.

- **Scenario 1: The Factory Has the Right to Pollute**

  - The fishing company can **pay the factory** to reduce pollution.

  - If the fishing company values clean water more than the factory values polluting, a **negotiated settlement** occurs.

- **Scenario 2: The Fishing Business Has the Right to Clean Water**

  - The factory can **pay the fishing company** for the right to pollute.

  - If the factory values polluting more than the fishing company values clean water, a **financial agreement is reached**.

In both cases, as long as **negotiation is possible**, the factory and the fishing company **can find a mutually beneficial arrangement without government intervention**.

Why It Works

The **Coase Bargaining Solution** works because it emphasizes **voluntary agreements over regulation**:

- **Mutual benefit** – Both parties negotiate to reach the most efficient solution.

- **Flexibility** – The solution adapts to **different property rights structures**.

- **Avoids inefficiencies** – Government-imposed solutions (like taxes or bans) may be **less effective** than direct negotiation.

How It Works

1. **Determine property rights** – Who has the right to pollute or to clean water?

2. **Assess the value of externalities** – What is the cost of pollution vs. the cost of reducing it?

3. **Negotiate a settlement** – The party who benefits more pays the other to adjust behaviour.

4. **Efficient allocation occurs** – Resources are used in the way that maximizes value.

Applications of the Coase Bargaining Solution

1. **Environmental Agreements** – Companies negotiate pollution reduction **instead of relying on government-imposed limits**.

2. **Intellectual Property** – Businesses settle disputes over **patent rights and licensing** through deals rather than lawsuits.

3. **Land Disputes** – Homeowners compensate each other over **noise complaints, fences, or shared property boundaries**.

4. **Workplace Flexibility** – Employees and employers negotiate **remote work agreements** instead of following rigid company-wide policies.

Key Insights

1. **Clear property rights are essential for efficient bargaining.**

2. **Low transaction costs make negotiation feasible.**

3. **Without legal or administrative barriers, private agreements lead to optimal solutions.**

4. **Regulation should focus on reducing transaction costs rather than imposing rigid rules.**

Final Thoughts

The **Coase Bargaining Solution** shows that **market-based negotiation can resolve externalities efficiently**, provided transaction costs are low, and property rights are well-defined. It applies to **business, environmental policy, and legal disputes**, reinforcing the idea that **cooperation often leads to better outcomes than regulation**.

9 Zeuthen Strategy

Zeuthen Strategy in Game Theory

Breakdown of the Theory

The **Zeuthen Strategy**, developed by **Frederik Zeuthen**, is a **bargaining model** in **game theory** that explains how two parties negotiate when they have conflicting interests. It is particularly useful in situations where both players must decide **how much to concede to avoid conflict or breakdown in negotiations**.

The key idea is that the player **who has the most to lose from negotiation failure** will be the one to **make a concession first**. Over time, both players make strategic concessions until an agreement is reached. The strategy ensures that neither party **gives up too much too soon**, leading to a **rational and optimal bargaining outcome**.

Example of the Zeuthen Strategy

Imagine two companies, **GreenTech** and **SolarX**, negotiating a **joint venture** to develop a new solar panel. They must decide how to split **$10 million in expected profits**.

- **GreenTech wants a 70-30 split** in their favour.
- **SolarX insists on a 50-50 split**.

Each company must decide whether to **stand firm or make concessions**, knowing that if negotiations fail, both walk away **with nothing**.

Using the Zeuthen Strategy:

1. **Assess the Risk of Breakdown:**

    o   If GreenTech insists on 70%, but SolarX refuses, they risk losing the deal.

    o   If SolarX pushes too hard, GreenTech may walk away.

2. **Who Has the Most to Lose?**

    o   If GreenTech believes it **needs the deal more**, it should **make a concession first** (e.g., offer a 60-40 split).

    o   If SolarX also sees value in the deal, it might counter with **55-45**, moving closer to agreement.

3. **Agreement Reached:**

    o   Both companies **gradually adjust their demands** until they reach a **mutually acceptable compromise** (e.g., a 55-45 split).

Why It Works

The **Zeuthen Strategy** works because it forces rational decision-making:

- **Players consider the cost of negotiation failure** before making a move.

- **Concessions happen gradually**, preventing one player from taking advantage of the other.

- **Each side signals willingness to cooperate**, making agreement more likely.

How It Works

1. **Each player evaluates the risk of no agreement.**

2. **The player who faces the highest risk makes the first concession.**

3. **The other player assesses the new offer and decides whether to counter.**

4. **This process repeats until both parties find an acceptable compromise.**

Applications of the Zeuthen Strategy

1. **Labor Negotiations** – Unions and employers decide **who concedes first** based on the cost of a strike.

2. **Business Mergers** – Companies negotiate ownership shares, adjusting based on **who needs the deal more**.

3. **International Diplomacy** – Countries negotiating **trade agreements or ceasefires** use similar strategies.

4. **Salary Negotiations** – Employees and employers adjust demands based on **who benefits more from the deal**.

Key Insights

1. **The player with more to lose concedes first.**

2. Negotiation is a step-by-step process—sudden large concessions are rare.

3. Mutual concessions lead to optimal agreements.

4. Players must strategically balance standing firm vs. making gradual concessions.

Final Thoughts

The **Zeuthen Strategy** explains how rational players **navigate negotiations without unnecessary conflict**. By gradually adjusting demands based on **risk assessment**, both parties can reach a **mutually beneficial deal**, making it a powerful tool in **business, politics, and everyday negotiations**.

10 Shapley Value

Shapley Value in Game Theory

Breakdown of the Theory

The **Shapley Value**, developed by **Lloyd Shapley**, is a **solution concept in cooperative game theory** used to fairly distribute **payoffs among players** who contribute differently to a collective effort. It is widely applied in **economics, political science, and business negotiations**, where multiple participants work together and need an **equitable way to divide rewards**.

The **Shapley Value formula** calculates each player's contribution by considering all possible **coalitions** (subsets of players) and their **marginal contributions** to those coalitions. It ensures that each player receives a **fair share** of the total benefit based on their actual impact on the outcome.

The formula is:

$$\phi_i = \sum_{S \subseteq N \setminus \{i\}} \frac{|S|!(|N| - |S| - 1)!}{|N|!} \times (v(S \cup \{i\}) - v(S))$$

where:

- ϕ_i is the Shapley Value for player i,
- $v(S)$ is the value of coalition S,
- N is the total set of players,
- S represents all possible coalitions excluding player i.

This method guarantees that **each player's contribution is accounted for across all possible scenarios.**

Example of the Shapley Value

Consider a **startup company** with three co-founders:

- **Alice (Tech Expert)** – Develops the core product.
- **Bob (Investor)** – Provides funding.
- **Charlie (Marketer)** – Drives customer adoption.

The startup generates **$10 million** in revenue. How should the profit be divided based on contributions?

1. **Alone, none of them could create a successful company → $0 value individually.**
2. **Alice + Bob (Tech + Funding) create $6M value.**
3. **Alice + Charlie (Tech + Marketing) create $5M value.**

4. **Bob + Charlie (Funding + Marketing) create $4M value**.

5. **All three together create $10M**.

Using the **Shapley Value**, each member gets a fair share based on their **marginal contributions across all coalitions**.

Why It Works

The **Shapley Value** works because it:

- **Ensures fairness** by considering all possible coalitions.

- **Prevents disputes** by offering a structured way to divide profits.

- **Encourages cooperation** by fairly rewarding contributions.

How It Works

1. **List all coalitions and their values**.

2. **Calculate each player's marginal contribution** to every coalition.

3. **Compute the average contribution across all coalitions** to determine each player's share.

Applications of the Shapley Value

1. **Revenue Sharing** – Splitting ad revenue among content creators and platforms.

2. **Political Power Distribution** – Measuring influence in **coalition governments**.

3. **Cost Allocation** – Dividing **joint business expenses** among departments.

4. **Machine Learning & AI** – Assessing **feature importance in predictive models**.

Key Insights

1. **The Shapley Value ensures a fair, mathematically sound distribution of payoffs.**

2. **It considers all possible coalitions to prevent over- or under-compensation.**

3. **It applies to diverse fields, from business to artificial intelligence.**

4. **Fair allocation encourages long-term cooperation and trust.**

Final Thoughts

The **Shapley Value** is a powerful tool in **cooperative game theory** for ensuring **fair and logical profit-sharing**. It applies to **business, politics, machine learning, and economics**, proving that **equitable contributions lead to sustainable collaboration**.

Voting & Political Game Theory

11 Median Voter Theorem

Median Voter Theorem in Game Theory

Breakdown of the Theory

The **Median Voter Theorem (MVT)** is a concept in **game theory and political science**, introduced by **Duncan Black** and later expanded by **Anthony Downs**. It states that in a **majority-rule voting system**, the candidate or policy closest to the **median voter's preference** is most likely to win.

The model assumes:

1. **Voter preferences are distributed along a one-dimensional spectrum** (e.g., left to right in politics).

2. **Each voter has a single-peaked preference**, meaning they prefer policies closest to their ideal point.

3. **Candidates or parties seek to maximize votes** by adjusting their positions.

This leads to **policy convergence**—politicians and parties **move toward the centre** to capture the **median voter**, as voters on the extremes have fewer options.

Example of the Median Voter Theorem

Consider a **presidential election** in a country where voters are evenly spread across the **political spectrum**, from **left-wing (L) to right-wing (R)**.

- **Candidate A** (left-wing) starts at **L = 25** on a scale from 0 (far left) to 100 (far right).

- **Candidate B** (right-wing) starts at **R = 75**.

- The **median voter is at M = 50**, representing the centre.

To maximize votes:

- **Candidate A shifts right** (closer to M).

- **Candidate B shifts left** (closer to M).

Eventually, both candidates **position themselves near the median voter**, as **any further deviation risks losing centrist support.**

Why It Works

The **Median Voter Theorem** works because:

- **Candidates need 50%+1 votes to win**, so they move toward the largest voter segment.

- **Extreme positions alienate moderate voters**, reducing electability.

- **Voters prefer candidates closest to their views**, creating a pull toward the centre.

How It Works

1. **Candidates assess voter distribution** on a political or policy spectrum.

2. **They adjust policies and rhetoric** to align with the median voter's preference.

3. **Parties converge toward the centre**, making elections competitive.

4. **Voters choose the candidate closest to their preference**, reinforcing the strategy.

Applications of the Median Voter Theorem

1. **Political Elections** – Explains why candidates in **two-party systems** (e.g., U.S. Democrats vs. Republicans) adopt **moderate policies**.

2. **Legislative Policy-Making** – Politicians craft policies that **appeal to the median voter** to gain majority support.

3. **Market Competition** – Businesses design products to attract the **largest consumer base**, avoiding niche extremes.

4. **Public Opinion & Media** – News outlets may moderate content to **appeal to mainstream audiences**.

Key Insights

1. Majority-rule systems naturally favour moderate policies.

2. Extreme candidates struggle unless voter distribution is highly polarized.

3. Third-party candidates disrupt the median voter balance, often shifting elections.

4. Policy convergence reduces ideological diversity in competitive elections.

Final Thoughts

The **Median Voter Theorem** explains why **political parties shift toward the centre** in majority-rule democracies. It applies beyond politics, influencing **business, media, and public policy**, showing how **competition leads to moderate, widely acceptable choices**.

12 Gerrymandering Game

Gerrymandering Game in Game Theory

Breakdown of the Theory

The **Gerrymandering Game** is a **game theory model** that explains how political parties manipulate **electoral district boundaries** to maximize their advantage in elections. By redrawing district maps strategically, a party can **concentrate or dilute opposition votes**, influencing outcomes **without changing the total number of votes cast**.

Gerrymandering follows two primary strategies:

1. **Packing** – Concentrating **opposing voters into a few districts**, allowing them to win those while losing everywhere else.

2. **Cracking** – Splitting **opposing voters across multiple districts**, preventing them from forming a majority in any of them.

The party controlling redistricting plays a **strategic game** against the opposition, **manipulating district lines to maintain power** while avoiding legal challenges.

Example of the Gerrymandering Game

Imagine **State X**, where **two political parties, Party A (Blue) and Party B (Red),** compete for **10 legislative seats**. The **voter population is evenly split 50-50**, meaning in a fair system, each party should win **5 seats each**.

Scenario 1: Fair Districting

If districts are drawn **fairly**, each party wins **5 districts each**, creating a balanced government.

Scenario 2: Party A (Blue) Uses Gerrymandering

If Party A controls redistricting, they **manipulate district boundaries**:

- **Packing**: They place **most Party B voters** into **2 districts**, ensuring huge victories there (e.g., **80%-20%** wins for Party B).

- **Cracking**: They **spread the remaining Party B voters** across the other **8 districts**, ensuring **Party A wins narrowly (55%-45%)**.

- **Final result**: Party A **wins 8 districts**, and Party B wins only **2**, despite the **total votes being 50-50**.

This illustrates how **manipulating electoral maps distorts democratic representation,** making election outcomes **less about voter preference and more about strategic districting**.

Why It Works

The **Gerrymandering Game** works because:

- **Voters cannot easily change districts**, making manipulation highly effective.

- **Even small boundary adjustments can flip election results**.

- **Once in power, a party can redraw districts repeatedly**, ensuring long-term dominance.

How It Works

1. **Party in control draws new district maps.**

2. **They use "packing" and "cracking" to weaken the opposition.**

3. **The manipulated maps ensure an electoral advantage** despite equal total votes.

4. **Elections occur under the new districts, favouring the controlling party**.

Applications of the Gerrymandering Game

1. **U.S. Congressional Elections** – Political parties manipulate **district maps** to secure seats.

2. **Corporate Board Elections** – Shareholders may **structure voting groups** to maintain control.

3. **Union Negotiations** – Employers may **divide workers** strategically to weaken union votes.

4. **International Politics** – Governments may **redraw provincial or district lines** to favour ruling parties.

Key Insights

1. **Manipulating voting districts can significantly alter election results.**

2. **Packing and cracking are the primary strategies for maximizing power.**

3. **Even in a fair system, strategic redistricting can distort democracy.**

4. **Reforms (like independent commissions) are needed to prevent abuse.**

Final Thoughts

The **Gerrymandering Game** shows how **strategic manipulation of voting districts can override majority preference**. While it is an effective political tool, it **undermines democratic fairness**, emphasizing the need for **neutral redistricting processes** to ensure truly representative elections.

13 Condorcet Paradox

Condorcet Paradox in Game Theory

Breakdown of the Theory

The **Condorcet Paradox**, named after **Marquis de Condorcet**, is a concept in **game theory and social choice theory** that demonstrates how **majority voting can lead to inconsistent and cyclic preferences**. It challenges the assumption that **majority rule always produces a clear and rational winner.**

The paradox occurs when **collective preferences become non-transitive**, meaning that even if a majority prefers **Option A over Option B** and **Option B over Option C**, it is possible that the same majority prefers **Option C over Option A**, creating a **voting cycle** with no clear winner.

This paradox highlights a fundamental flaw in **simple majority voting systems**, showing that **group decisions do not always reflect consistent individual preferences.**

Example of the Condorcet Paradox

Imagine an election with **three candidates**:

- **Alice (Progressive)**

- **Bob (Centrist)**

- **Charlie (Conservative)**

Voters have **different preferences**, distributed as follows:

Voter Group (33%)	1st Choice	2nd Choice	3rd Choice
Group 1	Alice	Bob	Charlie
Group 2	Bob	Charlie	Alice
Group 3	Charlie	Alice	Bob

Now, we compare pairwise votes:

1. **Alice vs. Bob → Alice wins** (66% prefer Alice over Bob).

2. **Bob vs. Charlie → Bob wins** (66% prefer Bob over Charlie).

3. **Charlie vs. Alice → Charlie wins** (66% prefer Charlie over Alice).

Even though a majority prefers **Alice over Bob**, **Bob over Charlie**, and **Charlie over Alice**, the cycle continues indefinitely. **There is no clear winner**, despite each individual voter having a logical preference.

Why It Works

The **Condorcet Paradox** works because **voter preferences are not always structured in a linear or transitive way**. Key factors contributing to the paradox include:

- **Diverse voter preferences**, leading to contradictory majority outcomes.

- **Strategic voting**, where groups shift support based on expectations.

- **Multi-option elections**, which make it difficult to reach a clear majority winner.

How It Works

1. **Voters rank multiple choices based on personal preference.**

2. **Pairwise comparisons are made** between each option.

3. **If a cycle forms, no option is the clear winner**, revealing the paradox.

Applications of the Condorcet Paradox

1. **Presidential Elections** – When multiple candidates split the vote, making a **clear majority winner difficult.**

2. **Policy Decisions** – Legislators may face cyclic preferences when choosing **between multiple policy options.**

3. **Corporate Decision-Making** – Board members ranking projects may **fail to reach a clear investment decision.**

4. **Sports Rankings** – In competitions, **Team A beats Team B, Team B beats Team C, but Team C beats Team A**, creating **ranking inconsistencies.**

Key Insights

1. Majority rule does not always produce a rational outcome.

2. Cyclic preferences create voting instability.

3. Alternative voting systems (e.g., ranked-choice or Condorcet methods) help resolve these issues.

4. Strategic voting can manipulate election results in paradoxical ways.

Final Thoughts

The **Condorcet Paradox** reveals a fundamental flaw in **majority voting systems,** where **group preferences can become irrational and cyclic.** It emphasizes the need for **alternative decision-making methods,** such as **ranked-choice voting or Condorcet methods,** to **ensure fairer and more consistent electoral outcomes.**

14 Banzhaf Power Index

Banzhaf Power Index in Game Theory

Breakdown of the Theory

The **Banzhaf Power Index**, developed by **John F. Banzhaf III**, is a **game theory measure** that quantifies the **voting power of individuals or groups** in a decision-making system. It is widely used in **weighted voting systems**, where not all voters have equal influence. The index determines how often a voter is **critical** in turning a losing coalition into a winning one.

A **critical voter** is someone whose support is **necessary** for a coalition to win. The **Banzhaf Power Index** calculates the probability of each voter being in this **pivotal position**, ensuring a **fair assessment of voting power**.

Example of the Banzhaf Power Index

Imagine a **corporate board** making a decision. The board has **four members** with different voting weights:

- **Alice: 40 votes**
- **Bob: 35 votes**
- **Charlie: 20 votes**
- **Dana: 5 votes**
- **Majority required: 51 votes**

Step 1: Identify Winning Coalitions (Total Votes ≥ 51)

Winning coalitions include:

- **Alice + Bob (40 + 35 = 75 votes)**
- **Alice + Charlie (40 + 20 = 60 votes)**
- **Bob + Charlie + Dana (35 + 20 + 5 = 60 votes)**
- **Alice + Bob + Charlie (40 + 35 + 20 = 95 votes)**

Step 2: Identify Critical Voters

- **Alice is critical** in (Alice + Charlie), (Alice + Bob), and (Alice + Bob + Charlie).

- **Bob is critical** in (Alice + Bob) and (Bob + Charlie + Dana).

- **Charlie is critical** in (Alice + Charlie) and (Bob + Charlie + Dana).

- **Dana is never critical**, as removing her from (Bob + Charlie + Dana) still results in a win.

Using the **Banzhaf Power Index**, we calculate each voter's **relative influence** based on how often they are critical in winning coalitions.

Why It Works

The **Banzhaf Power Index** works because:

- **Raw vote count doesn't always equal power—** small voters can be crucial in coalitions.

- **It reflects real-world decision-making,** where alliances determine outcomes.

- **It prevents misrepresentation** in systems where simple majority rules fail to show actual influence.

How It Works

1. **List all possible coalitions.**

2. **Identify which voters are critical** in each winning coalition.

3. **Count the number of times each voter is pivotal.**

4. **Divide each voter's count by the total pivotal instances** to calculate power.

Applications of the Banzhaf Power Index

1. **Political Elections** – Evaluating **swing states** in U.S. presidential elections.

2. **Corporate Board Decisions** – Assessing **shareholder influence** based on stock ownership.

3. **Legislative Voting** – Understanding power distribution in **coalition governments.**

4. **International Organizations** – Determining the influence of countries in **UN voting systems.**

Key Insights

1. **Not all voters have equal power, even if they have similar vote counts.**

2. **Swing voters and pivotal players hold the most influence.**

3. **Coalition-building determines real decision-making power.**

4. **Smaller players can still be powerful if they join strategic alliances.**

Final Thoughts

The **Banzhaf Power Index** provides a **fair and mathematical way to measure influence in voting systems**. It is widely used in **politics, corporate governance, and international organizations**, ensuring that **decision-making power reflects true influence rather than just vote counts**.

15 Spatial Voting Model

Spatial Voting Model in Game Theory

Breakdown of the Theory

The **Spatial Voting Model** is a **game theory framework** used to analyse how voters and candidates position themselves on a **political spectrum**. Developed from the work of **Anthony Downs** in his **Economic Theory of Democracy (1957)**, it assumes that:

1. **Voters and candidates exist in a policy space**, usually represented as a left-right (liberal-conservative) spectrum.

2. **Each voter has an ideal point**, meaning they prefer candidates whose policies are closest to their own.

3. **Candidates strategically adjust their positions** to maximize votes.

4. **The Median Voter Theorem often applies**, predicting that in a two-party system, candidates will **move toward the centre** to appeal to the majority.

Example of the Spatial Voting Model

Imagine an election in a town where three candidates— **Alice (Liberal), Bob (Centrist), and Charlie (Conservative)**—compete for votes. The town's **voter preferences** are distributed as follows:

Political Position	% of Voters
Liberal (0-30)	30%
Moderate (31-70)	40%
Conservative (71-100)	30%

- **Alice** starts at **position 20** (liberal).

- **Bob** starts at **position 50** (centrist).

- **Charlie** starts at **position 80** (conservative).

Since **Bob is closest to the median voter (50)**, he has the highest chance of winning. To stay competitive:

- **Alice moves toward 40**, capturing moderate voters.

- **Charlie shifts left to 60**, appealing to centrists.

As both extreme candidates move toward the centre, the **spatial model explains why political parties often moderate their positions to win elections.**

Why It Works

The **Spatial Voting Model** works because:

- **Voters choose candidates closest to their preferences**, leading to **predictable voting patterns.**

- **Candidates adjust policies to maximize votes**, resulting in **policy convergence**.
- **It explains real-world political dynamics**, especially in **two-party democracies**.

How It Works

1. **Voters are placed on a policy spectrum** based on ideology.
2. **Candidates position themselves strategically** to attract the most voters.
3. **If a candidate moves too far from the median voter, they risk losing majority support**.
4. **Over time, competition drives candidates toward centrist positions** to gain electoral advantage.

Applications of the Spatial Voting Model

1. **Presidential Elections** – Explains why U.S. candidates shift toward the centre during general elections.
2. **Legislative Decision-Making** – Politicians adjust policies based on their constituency's position on the spectrum.
3. **Corporate Strategy** – Businesses target **broad customer preferences** rather than niche extremes.

4. **Public Opinion Analysis** – Media and policymakers predict **how the public will respond to policy shifts**.

Key Insights

1. **Political candidates tend to converge toward the centre** in competitive elections.

2. **Extreme positions are risky**, as they alienate median voters.

3. **Voter distribution affects how much candidates shift policies.**

4. **Third-party candidates disrupt the balance**, pulling major candidates away from the centre.

Final Thoughts

The **Spatial Voting Model** provides a structured way to understand **political competition, voter behaviour, and electoral strategy**. It explains **why centrist positions dominate in major elections**, making it a **powerful tool in political science and economics**.

16 Logrolling

Logrolling in Game Theory

Breakdown of the Theory

Logrolling is a **game theory concept** that describes a form of **strategic vote-trading** where individuals or groups exchange support for each other's proposals to maximize their personal gains. It is commonly used in **political negotiations, legislative decision-making, and corporate governance**.

The key idea is that **players prioritize their most valued issues** while making concessions on less important matters. This helps build **coalitions** and ensures **mutual benefits**, even if the overall outcome is not optimal for society.

Types of logrolling include:

1. **Explicit Logrolling** – Direct vote exchanges (e.g., "I'll vote for your policy if you vote for mine").

2. **Implicit Logrolling** – Indirect support-building through broader agreements (e.g., legislators bundling multiple policies into one bill).

3. **Distributive Logrolling** – Favor-trading where different regions or interest groups benefit (e.g., funding projects in multiple states to gain support).

Example of Logrolling in Game Theory

Imagine a **legislative body** with three politicians—**Alice, Bob, and Charlie**—voting on three separate policies:

- **Alice supports renewable energy subsidies.**

- **Bob supports agricultural subsidies.**

- **Charlie supports military expansion.**

Each policy **only benefits its supporter** and lacks a majority to pass. However, through logrolling:

- **Alice agrees to support Bob's farm bill** in exchange for his vote on energy subsidies.

- **Bob then supports Charlie's military expansion** in return for his vote on the farm bill.

This way, **all three policies pass**, even if **some voters would have opposed them individually**.

Voting Scenario Before Logrolling:

Policy	Alice's Vote	Bob's Vote	Charlie's Vote	Result
Renewable Energy	✅ Yes	❌ No	❌ No	❌ Fails
Agricultural Subsidies	❌ No	✅ Yes	❌ No	❌ Fails
Military Expansion	❌ No	❌ No	✅ Yes	❌ Fails

Voting Scenario After Logrolling:

Policy	Alice's Vote	Bob's Vote	Charlie's Vote	Result
Renewable Energy	✓ Yes	✓ Yes	✗ No	✓ Passes
Agricultural Subsidies	✓ Yes	✓ Yes	✓ Yes	✓ Passes
Military Expansion	✗ No	✓ Yes	✓ Yes	✓ Passes

This shows how **logrolling turns losing policies into winning ones** through vote-trading.

Why It Works

Logrolling works because:

- **Players prioritize their most valued outcomes** and trade away issues of lower importance.

- **It builds coalitions** and enables policies to pass that would otherwise fail.

- **Mutual gains ensure all parties benefit**, even if the overall outcome is inefficient.

How It Works

1. **Players identify their strongest priorities.**

2. **They negotiate support for each other's policies.**

3. **Votes are exchanged to form a winning coalition.**

4. **Policies pass that may not have succeeded individually.**

Applications of Logrolling

1. **Legislative Politics** – Politicians trade votes to pass bills (e.g., U.S. Congress funding bills).

2. **Corporate Decision-Making** – Board members support each other's budget priorities.

3. **International Agreements** – Countries exchange policy favours in trade deals.

4. **Union & Labor Negotiations** – Workers and employers make mutual concessions.

Key Insights

1. **Logrolling enables deals that would otherwise fail** by bundling multiple policies together.

2. **It can lead to excessive spending** (e.g., pork-barrel politics, where unnecessary projects are funded).

3. **Strategic negotiation determines who benefits most** from the agreements.

4. **While efficient for individuals, it may not always be optimal for society**.

Final Thoughts

The **logrolling strategy** highlights the **power of coalition-building and negotiation** in decision-making. While it helps individuals achieve their goals, it also **risks inefficiency and waste** when used excessively in politics or business.

17 Pork Barrel Game

Pork Barrel Game in Game Theory

Breakdown of the Theory

The **Pork Barrel Game** is a **game theory model** that explains how legislators strategically allocate government funds to **local projects** to secure political support. It highlights the **trade-offs between individual and collective interests**, showing how **rational politicians prioritize local gains over national efficiency** to maximize **re-election chances**.

This game demonstrates the problem of **distributive politics**, where politicians prefer **funding projects in their own districts** rather than making **cost-effective national investments**. While this benefits local constituents, it often leads to **wasteful government spending and budget inefficiencies**.

Example of the Pork Barrel Game

Imagine a **10-member legislative body** voting on a **$100 million national budget**. Each legislator wants a portion allocated to **local projects** to please voters, even if the projects **do not benefit the nation as a whole**.

Legislator	Proposed Project	Cost ($ Million)	Benefit (to Nation)
Alice	Local Road	10	Low
Bob	Bridge in His District	20	Low
Charlie	Stadium	15	Low
David	Research Facility	25	High
Emma	Park Renovation	10	Low
Other 5 Legislators	Various Projects	20	Mixed

Scenario 1: No Pork Barrel Spending (National Interest First)

- Funds are spent **only on high-benefit projects** (e.g., the research facility).
- Some districts receive **no direct funding**, making their legislators vulnerable in the next election.

Scenario 2: Pork Barrel Spending (Vote Trading Occurs)

- Legislators **trade votes** to ensure each district gets a project, regardless of efficiency.

- The **stadium, park, and bridge** get funding, even though they **offer little national benefit**.

- **Each legislator secures their own re-election**, but national economic efficiency suffers.

Why It Works

The **Pork Barrel Game** works because:

- **Politicians prioritize re-election over national interest.**

- **Voters reward legislators who secure local benefits, even at national expense.**

- **Logrolling (vote trading) ensures all legislators support each other's projects.**

How It Works

1. **Legislators propose local projects**, regardless of their national value.

2. **They form coalitions through vote-trading**, ensuring each district gets funding.

3. **Pork barrel projects are funded**, even if they waste national resources.

4. **Legislators secure re-election by pleasing local voters.**

Applications of the Pork Barrel Game

1. **Government Budgets** – National spending on **unnecessary projects** to win votes.

2. **Corporate Decision-Making** – Departments push for funding, even if **other projects have higher returns**.

3. **University Grants** – Professors lobby for **department-specific funding**, even if another program needs it more.

4. **International Politics** – Countries demand **regional benefits** in global trade agreements, even at economic costs.

Key Insights

1. **Pork barrel spending benefits local districts but harms national efficiency.**

2. **Vote trading encourages irrational spending.**

3. **Politicians focus on short-term electoral gains over long-term national interests.**

4. **Reforms like independent budget commissions can help reduce waste.**

Final Thoughts

The **Pork Barrel Game** reveals how **politicians use strategic spending to maintain power**, often at the expense of **national economic efficiency**. While it benefits **individual**

districts, excessive pork barrel spending can lead to **ballooning national debt and inefficient public policies**.

18 Agenda Control Game

Agenda Control Game in Game Theory

Breakdown of the Theory

The **Agenda Control Game** is a **game theory model** that explains how the ability to **set the order of decisions** influences outcomes. The game highlights the power of the **agenda setter**, who controls **what is voted on and in what order**, ultimately shaping the final decision. This is crucial in **politics, corporate strategy, and policy-making**, where controlling the decision-making process can be as powerful as having the majority vote.

Key aspects of the game:

1. **Agenda Setter** – The individual or group that determines the sequence of votes.

2. **Voters or Decision-Makers** – Those who must choose between options.

3. **Strategic Sequencing** – The agenda setter **structures the vote order** to push their preferred outcome.

Example of the Agenda Control Game

Consider a **city council** voting on how to allocate a **$10 million budget** among three projects:

- **Public Transportation (PT)**

- **Public Schools (PS)**

- **Lower Taxes (LT)**

There are **three council members**, each with different preferences:

Council Member	1st Choice	2nd Choice	3rd Choice
Alice	PS	PT	LT
Bob	LT	PT	PS
Charlie	PT	PS	LT

Scenario 1: Fair Voting (All Options Considered at Once)

- Each member votes for their **first choice**, leading to a **split vote with no majority**.

- **No clear winner emerges**, requiring a **runoff** or further negotiations.

Scenario 2: Agenda Control (Strategic Voting Order)

Suppose **Bob is the agenda setter** and prefers **lower taxes (LT)**. He **controls the voting sequence**:

1. **First, he sets a vote between PT vs. PS.**

   - **Charlie votes for PT, Alice votes for PS, and Bob votes PT → PT wins.**

2. **Next, he sets a final vote between PT vs. LT.**

○   **Charlie sticks with PT, but Bob and Alice now vote for LT → LT wins.**

By structuring the vote order strategically, Bob ensures his **least preferred option (PS) is eliminated first** and that his **top preference (LT) wins**, despite the initial vote distribution.

Why It Works

The **Agenda Control Game** works because:

- **Voters react differently depending on the order of decisions.**

- **By eliminating alternatives sequentially, the agenda setter manipulates the final outcome.**

- **Even if a majority prefers another option, a strategic order of votes can override their preference.**

How It Works

1. **The agenda setter decides the voting sequence.**

2. **Each vote eliminates one option, influencing the next decision.**

3. **The final choice is often different from what would have been selected in a fair, simultaneous vote.**

Applications of the Agenda Control Game

1. **Legislative Politics** – Parliamentary leaders set the order of amendments to influence laws.

2. **Corporate Board Meetings** – Executives structure votes on budgets and acquisitions.

3. **Jury Deliberations** – The order in which charges are considered affects verdicts.

4. **Public Referendums** – Governments determine how ballot measures are worded and voted on.

Key Insights

1. **Controlling the agenda is as powerful as having the majority.**

2. **Vote sequencing manipulates decision-making.**

3. **Even unpopular policies can pass through strategic order-setting.**

4. **Awareness of agenda control can help counter manipulation.**

Final Thoughts

The **Agenda Control Game** shows how **decision-making can be shaped by those who control the voting process**. Whether in **politics, business, or public policy,** understanding agenda control is essential to ensuring **fair and democratic outcomes.**

19 Legislative Bargaining Game

Legislative Bargaining Game in Game Theory

Breakdown of the Theory

The **Legislative Bargaining Game**, introduced by **Baron and Ferejohn (1989)**, is a **game theory model** that explains how legislators negotiate and form coalitions to **divide resources, pass policies, or allocate budgets**. Since no single legislator usually has complete power, they must **bargain strategically** to secure enough votes for their preferred policies.

The model assumes:

1. **A legislature with multiple members** who must decide how to divide a budget or pass laws.

2. **A proposer (agenda setter)** who suggests a division of resources.

3. **Other legislators who accept or reject the proposal.**

4. **Majority rule (simple or supermajority)** determines the outcome.

The key insight is that the **agenda setter has significant power** in shaping outcomes, as legislators must **weigh personal benefits against potential losses if they reject a proposal**.

Example of the Legislative Bargaining Game

Imagine a **five-member legislature** deciding how to allocate a **$100 million national budget** among **three major projects**:

- **Infrastructure (I)**
- **Healthcare (H)**
- **Education (E)**

Each legislator has a different priority:

Legislator	1st Choice	2nd Choice	3rd Choice
Alice	H	I	E
Bob	E	H	I
Charlie	I	E	H
Dave	I	H	E
Eve (Agenda Setter)	H	E	I

Scenario: Eve as the Agenda Setter

- Eve **proposes: $50M for Healthcare, $30M for Education, $20M for Infrastructure.**
- Alice and Bob benefit **directly**, so they **support** the deal.
- Charlie and Dave, who prefer infrastructure, **oppose the proposal.**

- The proposal **passes with a 3-2 majority**.

By strategically **offering just enough to secure a majority**, Eve ensures her preferred policy (**Healthcare**) dominates, even though **Infrastructure had broad support**.

Why It Works

The **Legislative Bargaining Game** works because:

- **Agenda setters shape policy outcomes** by structuring proposals to secure just enough votes.

- **Rational legislators accept deals** if rejecting them means getting nothing.

- **Coalition formation is critical**, as legislators must trade support for future benefits.

How It Works

1. **A proposer suggests a policy or budget allocation.**

2. **Legislators vote to accept or reject it.**

3. **If accepted, the policy is implemented; if rejected, a new round begins.**

4. **Over time, legislators adjust strategies to maximize their own benefits.**

Applications of the Legislative Bargaining Game

1. **National Budgets** – Legislators negotiate spending priorities.

2. **Corporate Decision-Making** – Board members distribute funding among departments.

3. **Coalition Governments** – Parties negotiate power-sharing agreements.

4. **International Trade Agreements** – Countries decide economic policies through bargaining.

Key Insights

1. **Agenda control gives significant power to those who set the terms of negotiation.**

2. **Legislators must accept trade-offs to secure policy wins.**

3. **Coalitions form based on strategic interests, not just ideology.**

4. **Minority groups can still gain benefits through negotiation and alliances.**

Final Thoughts

The **Legislative Bargaining Game** highlights how **policy-making is driven by strategic negotiation** rather than pure majority rule. Understanding how **agenda control, coalition-building, and vote-trading** work is key to predicting legislative outcomes in **politics, business, and international diplomacy.**

20 Re-election Game

Re-election Game in Game Theory

Breakdown of the Theory

The **Re-election Game** is a **game theory model** that examines how **incumbent politicians make strategic decisions** to maximize their chances of being re-elected. It explores the **trade-offs between short-term popularity and long-term policy effectiveness**, showing how politicians **balance voter expectations, policy choices, and campaign strategies** to maintain power.

The game assumes:

1. **Politicians (incumbents) seek re-election** and make decisions based on voter preferences.

2. **Voters respond to short-term outcomes**, often valuing **immediate benefits over long-term policies**.

3. **Challengers compete by offering alternative policies**, forcing incumbents to adjust strategies.

4. **Election cycles repeat**, meaning **past actions affect future electoral success**.

A rational incumbent **optimizes their decisions** by considering:

- **How voters react to policies** (e.g., tax cuts vs. infrastructure spending).

- **How opponents position themselves** in the race.

- **The role of campaign spending and messaging**.

Example of the Re-election Game

Imagine a **governor, Laura**, running for re-election in **State X**. She faces a challenger, **Mark**, who criticizes her economic policies.

Governor Laura's Strategic Choices:

- **Option 1: Implement short-term tax cuts** → Boosts immediate voter support but increases long-term debt.

- **Option 2: Invest in long-term infrastructure projects** → Strengthens the economy in the future but has no immediate voter impact.

- **Option 3: Focus on campaign spending** → Uses ads and social media to improve her image without major policy changes.

Possible Outcomes:

Laura's Decision	Voter Response	Election Outcome
Tax Cuts	Short-term approval increases	Higher chance of re-election, but future debt grows
Infrastructure Spending	Voters don't see immediate benefits	Risk of losing election despite good long-term policy
Campaign Focus	Public perception improves	Increased chance of re-election without major policy impact

If voters **prioritize immediate gains**, Laura may **choose tax cuts**, even if they harm the economy long-term. If voters **value future growth**, she may invest in infrastructure. The game **repeats every election cycle**, influencing how politicians govern.

Why It Works

The **Re-election Game** works because:

- **Politicians make calculated decisions** to **maximize votes, not necessarily long-term prosperity**.

- **Voters often prioritize short-term benefits**, affecting policy choices.

- **Challengers force incumbents to adjust strategies,** creating a dynamic competition.

How It Works

1. **The incumbent chooses policies and campaign strategies** based on voter preferences.

2. **Voters evaluate performance** and compare alternatives.

3. **Election results determine whether the incumbent stays or a new leader takes over.**

4. **The cycle repeats, influencing policy decisions over multiple terms.**

Applications of the Re-election Game

1. **Presidential & Parliamentary Elections** – Leaders make decisions to boost election chances.

2. **Corporate Governance** – CEOs prioritize **short-term stock performance** to satisfy investors.

3. **Local Government Policy** – Mayors invest in visible projects (e.g., parks, roads) before elections.

4. **International Relations** – Leaders sign short-term trade deals to win domestic support.

Key Insights

1. Incumbents prioritize policies that maximize short-term voter approval.

2. Voter behaviour influences whether long-term policies are implemented.

3. Challengers shape election dynamics by forcing incumbents to adjust strategies.

4. Election cycles create repetitive strategic decision-making.

Final Thoughts

The **Re-election Game** explains why **politicians often focus on short-term gains over long-term solutions**. It highlights the **strategic nature of electoral politics** and how **voter psychology shapes governance**. Understanding this game helps explain **why certain policies are prioritized in election years**.

Economic & Business Games

21 Bertrand Competition

Bertrand Competition in Game Theory

Breakdown of the Theory

The **Bertrand Competition** is a fundamental model in **game theory and industrial economics** that describes how firms compete by **setting prices** rather than output levels. Named after **Joseph Bertrand (1883)**, the model shows that when firms sell identical products and compete on price, they drive prices down to **marginal cost**, leading to a **perfectly competitive outcome** even in an oligopoly.

Key assumptions of the **Bertrand model**:

- **Two or more firms produce identical goods** (perfect substitutes).

- **Firms compete by setting prices**, not output.

- **Consumers buy from the firm offering the lowest price.**

- **If prices are equal, demand is split evenly among firms.**

- **Firms have constant marginal costs** (e.g., producing one more unit costs the same amount).

The surprising conclusion of Bertrand Competition is that even if there are only **two firms (duopoly)**, the **market**

behaves like perfect competition, with firms pricing at marginal cost and making **zero economic profit**.

Example of Bertrand Competition

Imagine **two airlines, AirBlue and SkyJet**, competing on a direct route between two cities. They have identical costs of **$100 per ticket**.

Scenario 1: Both Set High Prices

Airline	Ticket Price	Passengers	Profit (per ticket)
AirBlue	$200	50% of customers	$100 per ticket
SkyJet	$200	50% of customers	$100 per ticket

Since both charge the same price, they **split the market evenly**.

Scenario 2: Price Undercutting Begins

Airline	Ticket Price	Passengers	Profit (per ticket)
AirBlue	$180	100% (all customers switch)	$80 per ticket
SkyJet	$200	0%	No revenue

SkyJet loses all customers, so to regain them, it **lowers its price to $170**. This **price war** continues until prices fall to marginal cost **($100 per ticket)**.

Scenario 3: Equilibrium at Marginal Cost

Airline	Ticket Price	Passengers	Profit (per ticket)
AirBlue	$100	50%	$0
SkyJet	$100	50%	$0

At **$100 per ticket**, neither airline can lower prices further without making a loss. This is the **Bertrand equilibrium**, where firms **compete away all profit**.

Why It Works

The **Bertrand model** works because:

- **Price competition is more aggressive than quantity competition** (as seen in Cournot competition).

- **Identical products mean consumers always pick the cheaper option**, driving firms to lower prices.

- **Even a small price difference can shift all demand**, making undercutting a dominant strategy.

How It Works

1. **Each firm sets a price**, aiming to maximize profit.

2. **Consumers choose the cheapest option**, making firms lower prices to attract demand.

3. **The price war continues until prices reach marginal cost**, where firms earn zero economic profit.

Applications of Bertrand Competition

1. **Retail Industry** – Supermarkets competing on identical products lower prices aggressively.

2. **Airline Pricing** – Airlines on the same route often engage in price wars.

3. **Telecom Industry** – Mobile providers undercut each other on call and data plans.

4. **Online Shopping** – E-commerce sites like Amazon and Walmart match or beat competitor prices.

Key Insights

1. **Even a duopoly can behave like perfect competition if firms compete on price.**

2. **Price wars drive profits to zero when products are identical.**

3. **Introducing product differentiation (brand loyalty, quality differences) can prevent price erosion.**

4. **Real-world firms often avoid Bertrand-style competition by forming price agreements or using loyalty programs.**

Final Thoughts

The **Bertrand Competition model** demonstrates how **intense price competition eliminates profit margins**, even in markets with few firms. However, **real-world companies differentiate products, create brand loyalty, or use pricing strategies** to avoid the **race to the bottom** seen in pure Bertrand competition.

22 Cournot Competition

Cournot Competition in Game Theory

Breakdown of the Theory

Cournot Competition, introduced by **Antoine Augustin Cournot (1838)**, is a **game theory model** that describes how firms compete by **choosing quantities of output rather than setting prices**. Unlike **Bertrand Competition**, where firms compete on price, in Cournot Competition, firms decide **how much to produce**, and the **market price is determined by total industry output**.

Key assumptions of the **Cournot Model**:

1. **Two or more firms produce identical goods** (perfect substitutes).

2. **Firms simultaneously decide output levels**, knowing that total supply affects market price.

3. **Each firm aims to maximize profit**, considering the expected output of rivals.

4. **Higher total output leads to lower prices**, meaning firms must strategically balance quantity vs. profitability.

5. **Firms cannot collude**, but they adjust strategies over time based on competitors' actions.

Unlike Bertrand Competition, where price wars drive prices down to **marginal cost**, Cournot Competition **leads to**

positive economic profits, though not as high as in monopolistic markets.

Example of Cournot Competition

Imagine **two firms, AquaPure and FreshFlow**, competing in the bottled water industry. Each firm must decide how many units to produce.

Step 1: Market Demand and Revenue

- **Total market demand:** Q=100−PQ = 100 - P (where QQ is total quantity and PP is price).

- **Each firm's profit depends on its own output and the other firm's output.**

Step 2: Firms Make Quantity Decisions

Scenario	AquaPure's Output	FreshFlow's Output	Market Price	Profits
Monopoly (only AquaPure)	50	0	$50	High
Cournot Equilibrium	33	33	$34	Moderate
Competitive Outcome	50	50	$0	No Profit

If **AquaPure produces 50 units and FreshFlow produces nothing**, AquaPure **enjoys monopoly profits**. However, if **both firms produce 50 units**, the price falls to **zero**, and neither makes a profit.

At **Cournot equilibrium**, both firms choose **moderate output levels (33 units each)**, balancing **profit maximization and competition**.

Why It Works

The **Cournot model** works because:

- **Each firm reacts strategically** to its competitor's output.

- **Unlike Bertrand Competition**, price does not fall to marginal cost because firms limit supply.

- **Firms adjust production over time**, leading to a stable **Cournot-Nash equilibrium**, where neither firm benefit by changing output alone.

How It Works

1. **Firms independently choose output levels** based on expected competitor production.

2. **Total output determines market price**, affecting profits.

3. **If one firm increases output, prices drop, reducing profit for both firms.**

4. **A stable equilibrium is reached where neither firm has an incentive to change production.**

Applications of Cournot Competition

1. **Oligopoly Markets** – Industries with a few dominant firms, such as oil, steel, and cement.

2. **Telecommunications** – Network providers adjust investment in bandwidth and coverage.

3. **Agricultural Markets** – Competing farms decide production levels to avoid oversupply.

4. **Manufacturing Industry** – Firms producing similar products (e.g., car manufacturers) decide production strategies.

Key Insights

1. **Cournot Competition results in stable but imperfect competition**—firms earn more than in perfect competition but less than in a monopoly.

2. **Firms must balance supply to avoid price collapse** while still maximizing profit.

3. **Unlike Bertrand Competition, prices stay above marginal cost**, allowing firms to sustain profits.

4. **The more firms enter the market, the closer the outcome resembles perfect competition.**

Final Thoughts

The **Cournot Model** explains how firms compete on quantity rather than price, creating **strategic interdependence** in **oligopoly markets**. Unlike Bertrand Competition, **firms maintain positive profits**, making Cournot a **realistic model for industries with limited competition**.

23 Stackelberg Competition

Stackelberg Competition in Game Theory

Breakdown of the Theory

Stackelberg Competition, introduced by **Heinrich von Stackelberg (1934)**, is a **game theory model** of **sequential competition** where one firm (the **leader**) moves first by setting its output level, and the other firm (the **follower**) reacts accordingly. Unlike Cournot Competition, where firms choose output simultaneously, Stackelberg's model introduces an element of **strategic advantage** for the leader.

Key assumptions of the **Stackelberg Model**:

1. **Two firms produce identical goods** (perfect substitutes).

2. **The leader firm moves first**, choosing an output level.

3. **The follower observes the leader's choice** and sets its output accordingly.

4. **Both firms seek to maximize profit**, knowing their decisions affect market price.

5. **The follower behaves rationally**, responding optimally to the leader's decision.

This model demonstrates how **first-mover advantage** allows the leader to influence market conditions and **achieve higher profits** than in Cournot competition.

Example of Stackelberg Competition

Imagine **two firms, Alpha and Beta**, producing laptops. **Alpha is the leader**, setting its production first, while **Beta is the follower**, adjusting its output in response.

Step 1: Market Demand and Revenue

- **Total market demand:** $Q=100-P Q = 100 - P$ (where QQ is total quantity and PP is price).

- **If both firms produce 30 units each, the price is $40.**

- **If Alpha produces more, it forces Beta to reduce output to avoid excess supply.**

Step 2: Leader's Advantage

Scenario	Alpha's Output	Beta's Response	Market Price	Profits
Cournot Competition	33	33	$34	Moderate
Stackelberg Leader (Alpha)	50	25	$25	Higher for Alpha

Since **Alpha moves first**, it can **expand output aggressively** (e.g., 50 units), forcing **Beta to produce less (25 units)** because excess supply **lowers prices**. This gives **Alpha a profit advantage**.

Why It Works

The **Stackelberg model** works because:

- **The first-mover gains a strategic advantage**, setting a dominant market position.

- **The follower optimizes its response**, accepting a smaller market share.

- **The leader anticipates how the follower will react**, allowing for pre-emptive decision-making.

How It Works

1. **The leader sets its output first**, establishing market dominance.

2. **The follower observes the leader's decision** and optimizes its production.

3. **The leader benefits by constraining the follower's options**, securing a **higher share of total profit**.

Applications of Stackelberg Competition

1. **Tech Industry** – Companies like **Apple or Samsung** release new products first, forcing competitors to adjust.

2. **Automobile Manufacturing** – Market leaders **set production capacity**, influencing rival output.

3. **Retail and E-commerce** – Large retailers (e.g., Amazon) dominate pricing and inventory decisions.

4. **Telecom Industry** – First-movers in 5G technology force rivals to **adapt pricing and expansion strategies.**

Key Insights

1. **First-mover advantage allows firms to dominate markets.**

2. **Followers must strategically respond to leaders' choices.**

3. **Stackelberg Competition leads to higher profits than Cournot Competition for the leader.**

4. **Firms in competitive markets seek to become first-movers to shape industry dynamics.**

Final Thoughts

The **Stackelberg Model** explains how **sequential decision-making impacts competition**, showing that **first-mover advantage can shape market outcomes.** Unlike Cournot, where firms compete equally, **leaders in Stackelberg Competition strategically control the market**, giving them **higher long-term profits**.

24 Kreps-Scheinkman Model

Kreps-Scheinkman Model in Game Theory

Breakdown of the Theory

The **Kreps-Scheinkman Model** is a **game theory model** that examines how firms compete in two stages: **capacity choice (quantity competition) and price competition.** Developed by **David Kreps and Jose Scheinkman (1983)**, it challenges traditional **Cournot and Bertrand models** by showing that firms **first compete in capacity decisions, then in price setting.**

Key assumptions of the **Kreps-Scheinkman Model**:

1. **Firms make production capacity decisions first** (similar to Cournot competition).

2. **Once capacities are set, firms compete by setting prices** (like Bertrand competition).

3. **Firms cannot instantly adjust capacity**, meaning that supply is limited in the second stage.

4. **Consumers buy from the firm with the lowest price until that firm runs out of capacity.**

5. **If prices are equal, demand is split based on available capacity.**

The model's key result is that **even if firms compete in price (like Bertrand), they behave as if they are in a Cournot competition due to capacity constraints.** This means that even in industries with price competition, firms often **limit production strategically** to maintain profits.

Example of the Kreps-Scheinkman Model

Imagine **two bottled water companies, AquaFresh and PureFlow**, competing in a market.

Step 1: Capacity Decision (Cournot-Style Competition)

Each firm must **choose its production capacity** before knowing the final price competition outcome.

Firm	Chosen Capacity (Bottles)
AquaFresh	5,000
PureFlow	5,000

Step 2: Price Competition (Bertrand-Style)

After setting capacity, firms compete on price.

- If **AquaFresh sets a lower price**, it sells **all of its 5,000 bottles first**.

- If **PureFlow undercuts the price**, it sells first.

- If **both set the same price**, demand is split evenly.

Since firms **cannot exceed their capacity**, they **avoid extreme price undercutting** (unlike in pure Bertrand competition, where prices drop to marginal cost).

Why It Works

The **Kreps-Scheinkman Model** works because:

- **Capacity constraints prevent aggressive price competition**, leading to Cournot-like outcomes.

- **Firms behave strategically** in setting capacity, knowing it limits their pricing flexibility later.

- **It reflects real-world competition**, where firms invest in production before pricing decisions are made.

How It Works

1. **Firms first choose production capacity**, setting a limit on supply.

2. **Once capacity is fixed, firms compete by setting prices**.

3. **Consumers buy from the cheaper firm first, but only until its capacity runs out**.

4. **The result mimics Cournot competition, as price wars are avoided due to supply limitations**.

Applications of the Kreps-Scheinkman Model

1. **Manufacturing Industry** – Firms decide on production levels before competing on price.

2. **Retail and E-commerce** – Limited stock forces retailers to avoid extreme price undercutting.

3. **Airline Industry** – Airlines set seating capacity first, then adjust ticket prices.

4. **Energy Markets** – Power plants determine capacity before engaging in electricity pricing competition.

Key Insights

1. **Even with price competition, firms behave like Cournot competitors due to capacity constraints.**

2. **Firms strategically limit production to maintain profitability.**

3. **Real-world industries often face supply limits, making this model highly applicable.**

4. **Capacity decisions act as a pre-commitment, influencing later price competition.**

Final Thoughts

The **Kreps-Scheinkman Model** bridges the gap between **Cournot and Bertrand competition**, showing how **capacity constraints impact pricing behaviour**. It provides insights into **real-world industries where firms must first decide output levels before engaging in price competition**, proving that **strategic capacity decisions can prevent destructive price wars**.

25 Shapiro-Stiglitz Model

Shapiro-Stiglitz Model in Game Theory

Breakdown of the Theory

The **Shapiro-Stiglitz Model**, developed by **Carl Shapiro and Joseph Stiglitz (1984)**, is a **game theory model** in labour economics that explains **why unemployment exists even in competitive markets**. It introduces the concept of **efficiency wages**, where firms **pay above-market wages to reduce worker shirking and increase productivity**.

The model assumes:

1. **Workers decide whether to work hard or shirk** (exert low effort).

2. **Employers cannot perfectly monitor employees**, meaning shirking is possible.

3. **Firms can fire workers if caught shirking**, but workers may struggle to find a new job.

4. **Higher wages create an incentive for workers to stay productive**, as losing the job is costly.

The key result is that firms **voluntarily pay higher wages** to discourage shirking, which creates **involuntary unemployment** because firms **hire fewer workers than they would at lower wages**.

Example of the Shapiro-Stiglitz Model

Imagine a **retail company** managing its employees:

- **If the company pays a low wage ($10/hour),** workers have little to lose if fired, so they may **shirk responsibilities**.

- **If the company pays a high wage ($20/hour),** workers **fear losing a well-paying job** and are more likely to work hard.

Scenario 1: Low Wages (No Efficiency Wages)

Employee Action	Consequence
Work Hard	Low motivation, minimal effort
Shirk	High chance of getting caught, but job loss isn't severe

Scenario 2: High Wages (Efficiency Wages Applied)

Employee Action	Consequence
Work Hard	Keeps a well-paying job, avoids unemployment
Shirk	Risk of getting fired and struggling to find another high-wage job

By **paying above-market wages**, the firm **reduces shirking and increases overall productivity**, but it also **hires fewer workers**, leading to **unemployment** in equilibrium.

Why It Works

The **Shapiro-Stiglitz Model** works because:

- **Workers respond to incentives**—higher wages reduce motivation to shirk.

- **Firing is a real threat**—workers avoid shirking to keep a good job.

- **Firms optimize productivity**—they balance labour costs with performance.

How It Works

1. **Firms set wages above market level** to discourage shirking.

2. **Workers choose between effort or shirking,** knowing the consequences.

3. **Some workers are unemployed** because firms hire fewer employees at higher wages.

4. **Equilibrium unemployment emerges,** as firms need a reserve of job seekers to maintain discipline.

Applications of the Shapiro-Stiglitz Model

1. **Corporate Salaries** – Tech firms (e.g., Google) offer high salaries to attract and retain productive workers.

2. **Manufacturing Jobs** – Auto companies pay efficiency wages to ensure quality control.

3. **Finance & Banking** – Banks pay high wages to prevent fraud and misconduct.

4. **Public Sector Jobs** – Governments use high wages to reduce corruption in law enforcement and bureaucracy.

Key Insights

1. **Higher wages increase worker effort but also create unemployment.**

2. **Efficiency wages act as a tool to reduce monitoring costs.**

3. **Unemployment is necessary for discipline—if all workers had jobs, the threat of firing would be meaningless.**

4. **Government policies (like unemployment benefits) can influence labour market efficiency.**

Final Thoughts

The **Shapiro-Stiglitz Model** explains why **firms voluntarily pay above-market wages** and how **this leads to involuntary unemployment**. It provides insights into **labour markets, corporate wage policies, and worker productivity,** proving that **higher wages can sometimes be an investment in efficiency rather than just a cost.**

26 Principal-Agent Problem

Principal-Agent Problem in Game Theory

Breakdown of the Theory

The **Principal-Agent Problem** is a **game theory concept**
that describes situations where one party (**the principal**)
delegates a task to another party (**the agent**) who has
different incentives and access to more information. The
problem arises when:

1. **The agent's actions are difficult to monitor**,
   leading to potential **moral hazard** (opportunistic
   behaviour).

2. **The agent's goals differ from the principal's**,
   creating **conflicts of interest**.

3. **There is asymmetric information**, meaning the
   agent knows more about their actions than the
   principal.

This problem is common in **business, economics, and
politics**, where principals (e.g., shareholders, employers,
governments) must ensure agents (e.g., managers,
employees, policymakers) act in their best interest.

Example of the Principal-Agent Problem

Imagine a **company (the principal)** hiring a **CEO (the
agent)** to maximize profits.

- **The company (principal)** wants long-term growth and stable returns.

- **The CEO (agent)** wants high compensation and may take risky actions for short-term gains (e.g., inflating stock prices).

- **The CEO has more knowledge** about the firm's actual financial health than shareholders do.

Potential Issues:

1. **Moral Hazard** – The CEO might take **excessive risks** because they don't bear the full consequences of failure.

2. **Hidden Actions** – The CEO may **misreport earnings** to secure bigger bonuses.

3. **Conflict of Interest** – Instead of **long-term sustainability**, the CEO may focus on **short-term stock gains** to increase personal wealth.

Why It Works

The **Principal-Agent Problem** works because:

- **Information asymmetry gives agents an advantage** over principals.

- **Misaligned incentives lead to self-serving behaviour.**

- **It applies across various fields**, from corporate governance to politics.

How It Works

1. **The principal hires the agent** to perform a task.

2. **The agent has more information** about their own actions than the principal.

3. **The agent may act in self-interest**, deviating from the principal's goals.

4. **Mechanisms like contracts, incentives, and monitoring are needed** to align interests.

Applications of the Principal-Agent Problem

1. **Corporate Governance** – Shareholders (principals) monitor executives (agents) through stock options and audits.

2. **Employer-Employee Relationships** – Employers use **performance bonuses** to align incentives.

3. **Politics & Public Policy** – Citizens (principals) elect politicians (agents) who may pursue personal agendas instead of public welfare.

4. **Healthcare** – Patients rely on doctors, who may **prescribe unnecessary treatments** for financial gain.

Key Insights

1. **Asymmetric information creates inefficiencies and potential exploitation.**

2. Proper incentives (e.g., stock options, commissions) align interests.

3. Monitoring mechanisms (audits, transparency rules) help reduce agency problems.

4. Contracts should be designed to minimize conflicts while ensuring flexibility.

Final Thoughts

The **Principal-Agent Problem** is central to **organizational behaviour, economics, and governance**. Understanding it helps firms **design better contracts, improve corporate governance, and reduce conflicts of interest**, ensuring that agents act in the best interests of the principals they serve.

27 Moral Hazard Game

Moral Hazard Game in Game Theory

Breakdown of the Theory

The **Moral Hazard Game** is a **game theory model** that describes situations where one party (**the agent**) has an **incentive to take risks** because another party (**the principal**) bears the consequences. It occurs in environments with **asymmetric information**, where the agent's actions are difficult to monitor, leading to **opportunistic behaviour**.

This problem is common in **insurance, finance, employment, and policy-making**, where individuals or firms **alter their behaviour** when they don't bear the full cost of their decisions.

Key assumptions of the **Moral Hazard Game**:

1. **A principal-agent relationship exists**, where the agent acts on behalf of the principal.

2. **The agent's actions are not fully observable**, allowing hidden behaviour.

3. **The agent has an incentive to act in self-interest**, even if it harms the principal.

4. **Contracts, incentives, or monitoring can help mitigate the issue.**

Example of the Moral Hazard Game

Imagine an **insurance company (principal)** providing **car insurance** to a **driver (agent)**.

- Before insurance, the driver is **cautious** because they bear the full cost of accidents.

- After getting insurance, the driver **becomes reckless**, knowing the **insurance company will pay for damages**.

Scenario	Driver's Behaviour	Accident Risk	Who Bears the Cost?
No Insurance	Drives carefully	Low	Driver
With Insurance	Drives recklessly	High	Insurance Company

Because the driver **does not suffer the financial consequences of accidents**, they have an **incentive to take more risks**, creating **moral hazard**.

Why It Works

The **Moral Hazard Game** works because:

- **The agent's behaviour changes when they don't bear the full consequences.**

- Asymmetric information prevents the principal from knowing the agent's true actions.

- Without incentives or monitoring, agents exploit the system for personal gain.

How It Works

1. **The principal provides a contract or insurance,** expecting rational behaviour.

2. **The agent changes behaviour,** increasing risky actions.

3. **The principal incurs unexpected losses,** realizing the agent's actions are unobservable.

4. **To counteract moral hazard, the principal introduces incentives or monitoring** (e.g., deductibles, performance-based pay).

Applications of the Moral Hazard Game

1. **Insurance Industry** – Health or car insurance policyholders engage in **riskier behaviour** knowing the insurer will cover damages.

2. **Banking & Finance** – Banks take **high risks** knowing that governments will bail them out (**"Too Big to Fail"** problem).

3. **Employment Contracts** – Workers **reduce effort** if paid a fixed salary without performance monitoring.

4. **Government Bailouts** – Firms expect **government aid**, leading to excessive risk-taking in industries like airlines or finance.

Key Insights

1. **Moral hazard arises when agents don't fully bear the consequences of their actions.**

2. **Asymmetric information allows agents to exploit the system.**

3. **Incentive structures (e.g., deductibles, co-payments) help align behaviour.**

4. **Monitoring and penalties discourage excessive risk-taking.**

Final Thoughts

The **Moral Hazard Game** explains why **insurance companies, employers, and governments must carefully design incentives to prevent reckless behaviour**. It highlights the **importance of accountability and monitoring** in situations where agents might act irresponsibly if someone else bears the cost.

28 Adverse Selection Game

Adverse Selection Game in Game Theory

Breakdown of the Theory

The **Adverse Selection Game** is a **game theory model** that explains how **asymmetric information** leads to market inefficiencies. It occurs when one party in a transaction has **more information** than the other, leading to the selection of **lower-quality goods, services, or participants**.

The problem arises because:

1. **Buyers cannot distinguish high-quality from low-quality goods/services.**

2. **Sellers of low-quality goods have an incentive to stay in the market, while high-quality sellers exit.**

3. **This leads to a market dominated by low-quality goods, a phenomenon known as the "Lemons Problem" (Akerlof, 1970).**

Adverse selection occurs in **insurance, labour markets, financial markets, and product sales,** where buyers and sellers have **unequal access to information.**

Example of the Adverse Selection Game

Consider the **used car market**, where sellers know more about a car's quality than buyers.

- **High-quality cars (peaches)** are worth **$10,000**, but buyers are uncertain.

- **Low-quality cars (lemons)** are worth **$5,000**, but buyers can't tell them apart.

- **Buyers estimate the average car is worth $7,500** and offer that price.

What Happens?

Car Type	True Value	Buyer's Offer ($7,500)	Seller's Decision
Peach (Good Car)	$10,000	$7,500	Seller exits market
Lemon (Bad Car)	$5,000	$7,500	Seller stays in market

Since **peach owners won't sell at $7,500**, the market fills with **lemons**, reducing overall quality. Buyers, realizing this, **lower their offers further**, worsening the cycle.

Why It Works

The **Adverse Selection Game** works because:

- **Sellers have private information** that buyers lack.

- **Buyers lower their willingness to pay** due to uncertainty.

- **High-quality sellers exit the market, leaving only low-quality goods.**

How It Works

1. **The seller knows more about product quality than the buyer.**

2. **Buyers assume an average quality and lower their offers.**

3. **High-quality sellers refuse to sell, leaving only low-quality sellers.**

4. **The market fails or is dominated by poor-quality products.**

Applications of the Adverse Selection Game

1. **Health Insurance** – Unhealthy people buy insurance more than healthy people, raising costs.

2. **Job Market** – High-skilled workers may refuse jobs with low salaries, leaving only lower-skilled applicants.

3. **Financial Markets** – Risky borrowers apply for loans, increasing lender risk.

4. **Online Marketplaces** – Sellers of defective products stay, while honest sellers leave due to distrust.

Key Insights

1. Asymmetric information distorts market efficiency.

2. Without quality signals (warranties, ratings), buyers undervalue good products.

3. Markets dominated by adverse selection may collapse or underperform.

4. Solutions include screening, signalling, and third-party verification.

Final Thoughts

The **Adverse Selection Game** explains why **markets fail when buyers lack information about quality**. Effective solutions include **warranties, background checks, and transparency mechanisms**, helping restore market

29 Job Market Signalling

Job Market Signalling in Game Theory

Breakdown of the Theory

Job Market Signalling, introduced by **Michael Spence (1973)**, is a **game theory model** that explains how job applicants use **signals** (such as education or certifications) to convey their abilities to employers in a market with **asymmetric information.**

Key assumptions:

1. **Employers cannot directly observe a candidate's productivity.**

2. **Job seekers have private information about their own skills and effort levels.**

3. **Employers rely on observable signals (e.g., degrees, work experience) to infer ability.**

4. **Effective signals must be costly enough that only high-quality candidates choose to send them.**

This model helps explain **why education matters in hiring,** even when the degree itself does not directly contribute to job performance.

Example of Job Market Signalling

Imagine a job market with **two types of workers**:

- **High-skilled workers (Type A)** – Productive and efficient.

- **Low-skilled workers (Type B)** – Less productive but still seeking high wages.

Employers **cannot distinguish between Type A and Type B workers** based on appearance alone, so they use **education as a signal**:

- **Type A workers invest in higher education** because they can complete it more easily.

- **Type B workers avoid it because the effort and cost are too high for them.**

Possible Outcomes:

Worker Type	Education Cost	Salary Offered	Decision
Type A (High-Skilled)	Moderate	High Salary	Gets degree
Type B (Low-Skilled)	High	Low Salary	Skips degree

Since only **high-skilled workers** find it worthwhile to obtain a degree, **education effectively signals ability**, helping employers make hiring decisions.

Why It Works

The **Job Market Signalling Model** works because:

- **Education differentiates workers based on effort and cost.**

- **Employers respond to credible signals** rather than taking risks on unverified claims.

- **Signals help solve information asymmetry**, improving hiring efficiency.

How It Works

1. **Workers choose whether to obtain a costly signal (e.g., a degree).**

2. **Employers interpret the signal as an indicator of ability.**

3. **High-skilled workers benefit from sending signals,** while low-skilled workers do not.

4. **The labour market sorts candidates based on signals rather than unobservable ability.**

Applications of Job Market Signalling

1. **University Degrees** – Employers prefer candidates with degrees, assuming they are disciplined and capable.

2. **Certifications (e.g., CFA, PMP)** – Workers obtain credentials to demonstrate expertise.

3. **Internships & Experience** – Prior work experience signals competence to employers.

4. **Social Proof (LinkedIn, Awards)** – Online profiles and recommendations act as job market signals.

Key Insights

1. **Signals must be costly enough to deter low-quality candidates from using them.**

2. **Education does not necessarily increase productivity but helps employers identify skilled workers.**

3. **Effective signals reduce hiring risks and improve job matching.**

4. **Alternative signals (e.g., work samples, skills tests) may complement or replace traditional credentials.**

Final Thoughts

The **Job Market Signalling Model** explains why employers rely on **education, experience, and certifications** when hiring. It highlights how **workers strategically invest in signals** to differentiate themselves in competitive job markets.

30 Market for Lemons

Market for Lemons in Game Theory

Breakdown of the Theory

The **Market for Lemons**, introduced by **George Akerlof (1970)**, is a **game theory model** that explains how **asymmetric information** leads to market failure. It describes situations where sellers have **more information about product quality than buyers**, causing a decline in overall market quality. This is known as **adverse selection**, where bad products ("lemons") drive good products ("peaches") out of the market.

Key assumptions:

1. **Buyers cannot distinguish between high-quality ("peaches") and low-quality ("lemons") goods.**

2. **Sellers know more about the product's true condition.**

3. **Buyers set their willingness to pay based on average expected quality.**

4. **Sellers of high-quality goods exit the market if the price is too low.**

This results in a **negative feedback loop**, where the market becomes dominated by low-quality goods.

Example of the Market for Lemons

Consider a **used car market**, where:

- Good cars (peaches) are worth $10,000.

- Bad cars (lemons) are worth $5,000.

- Buyers cannot tell them apart and assume the average price should be $7,500.

What Happens?

Car Type	True Value	Buyer's Estimated Value	Seller's Decision
Peach (Good Car)	$10,000	$7,500	Seller exits market
Lemon (Bad Car)	$5,000	$7,500	Seller stays in market

Since good car sellers won't sell at $7,500, only lemons remain, reducing overall market quality. Buyers lower their willingness to pay further, making it even harder for good cars to stay in the market.

Why It Works

The Market for Lemons Model works because:

- Information asymmetry prevents buyers from making informed decisions.

- Sellers of high-quality goods exit the market, leaving only low-quality goods.

- **Buyers lower their expectations**, creating a downward spiral.

How It Works

1. **Sellers have private information about product quality.**

2. **Buyers assume an average quality and set prices accordingly.**

3. **High-quality sellers refuse to sell, leaving only bad products.**

4. **The market collapses or is dominated by low-quality goods.**

Applications of the Market for Lemons

1. **Used Car Sales** – Buyers hesitate due to hidden defects.

2. **Health Insurance** – Unhealthy individuals overuse insurance, raising costs.

3. **Online Marketplaces** – Fake or low-quality sellers dominate e-commerce.

4. **Financial Markets** – Risky firms attract investment while high-quality firms avoid undervaluation.

Key Insights

1. **Asymmetric information leads to market failure.**

2. **Buyers undervalue high-quality products due to uncertainty.**

3. **Sellers of good products exit the market, worsening quality.**

4. **Solutions include warranties, third-party verification, and transparency mechanisms.**

Final Thoughts

The **Market for Lemons** explains why **markets fail when buyers lack quality information**. Effective solutions like **certifications, reviews, and warranties** help restore trust and prevent adverse selection.

Military & Strategic Conflict Games

31 War of Attrition

War of Attrition in Game Theory

Breakdown of the Theory

The **War of Attrition** is a **game theory model** that describes **prolonged competition where players compete by enduring costs** until one concedes. The game was initially developed in **biology by John Maynard Smith (1974)** to explain how animals compete over resources, but it also applies to **economics, politics, and business strategy.**

Key assumptions:

1. **Two or more players compete for a valuable resource or prize.**

2. **The longer they stay in the game, the more costs they incur.**

3. **The game ends when one player concedes, allowing the other to win.**

4. **Players have no fixed time limit and must estimate when their opponent will give up.**

5. **The winner gains the prize, but both players pay the costs they incurred.**

The paradox of the War of Attrition is that **even a small reward can lead to high costs if players refuse to back down**.

Example of the War of Attrition

Imagine **two companies, AlphaTech and BetaCorp,** competing for a **valuable patent.**

- **Each company must bid for the patent**, but bidding incurs legal and research costs.

- **The patent is worth $50 million**, but every additional round of bidding costs each company **$5 million**.

- **If one company concedes, the other wins the patent, but both firms pay all costs incurred up to that point.**

Possible Outcomes:

Round	AlphaTech's Cost	BetaCorp's Cost	Outcome
1	$5M	$5M	Both continue
2	$10M	$10M	Both continue
3	$15M	$15M	One concedes
4	$20M	$20M	If neither concedes, they may spend more than the patent's value!

The game **ends when one company decides the costs outweigh the benefits.** If **neither company acts rationally,** they could **overpay for the patent,** turning a **profit opportunity into a loss.**

Why It Works

The **War of Attrition** works because:

- **Uncertainty about the opponent's endurance leads to excessive costs.**

- **Players engage in sunk-cost thinking,** refusing to back down after investing resources.

- **Commitment strategies influence the game**, as bluffing or appearing more determined can pressure the opponent into conceding first.

How It Works

1. **Players enter a contest, each incurring costs over time.**

2. **Both estimate the opponent's willingness to endure further costs.**

3. **One player eventually concedes when their costs exceed expected rewards.**

4. **The winner gains the prize, but both incur significant costs.**

Applications of the War of Attrition

1. **Business Price Wars** – Companies engage in aggressive pricing, leading to losses before one backs down.

2. **Military Conflicts** – Countries endure prolonged war, hoping the opponent will surrender first.

3. **Political Campaigns** – Candidates outspend rivals in elections, sometimes beyond the expected benefits.

4. **Labor Strikes** – Employers and unions sustain financial losses until one side concedes.

Key Insights

1. Endurance strategies can win but may be costly.

2. Rational players should avoid excessive costs relative to the prize.

3. Bluffing or signalling commitment can pressure opponents to concede first.

4. Understanding the opponent's cost tolerance is crucial for decision-making.

Final Thoughts

The **War of Attrition** highlights how **stubborn competition can lead to excessive costs,** making it a cautionary tale for **business, politics, and economics**. Knowing **when to concede** is just as important as knowing **when to persist**.

32 Blotto Game

Blotto Game in Game Theory

Breakdown of the Theory

The **Blotto Game**, first introduced by **Émile Borel (1921)**, is a **game theory model** that describes **how players allocate limited resources across multiple battlefields** to maximize their total advantage. The game is widely used to analyse **strategic decision-making in politics, military conflicts, business competition, and advertising campaigns.**

Key assumptions:

1. **Two or more players compete across multiple "battlefields" (contests).**

2. **Each player has a fixed budget (resources) to allocate strategically.**

3. **Whoever commits more resources to a given battlefield wins that contest.**

4. **The overall winner is the player who wins the most battlefields.**

5. **Players do not see the opponent's allocation until after committing their own.**

This game emphasizes **optimal allocation strategies**, unpredictability, and **strategic deception** to win as many contests as possible.

Example of the Blotto Game

Imagine two **political candidates, Alice and Bob,** competing in **five electoral districts**. Each candidate has **$100 million** to spend on their campaign but must decide **how to distribute their budget** across the districts.

District	Alice's Budget	Bob's Budget	Winner
1	$20M	$25M	Bob
2	$15M	$10M	Alice
3	$30M	$35M	Bob
4	$10M	$5M	Alice
5	$25M	$25M	Tie

Outcome:

- **Bob wins Districts 1 and 3.**
- **Alice wins Districts 2 and 4.**
- **District 5 is tied.**

Since **both candidates win two districts each,** the result **depends on tie-breaking rules,** showing how **resource allocation directly affects success.**

Why It Works

The **Blotto Game** works because:

- **Strategic resource allocation determines the winner.**
- **Players must anticipate their opponent's moves** without knowing them in advance.
- **Winning requires balancing aggressive and conservative spending.**

How It Works

1. **Players distribute their resources across multiple contests.**
2. **They compete without knowing the opponent's choices.**
3. **Each contest is won by the player who allocates more resources.**
4. **The player who wins the most contests is the overall winner.**

Applications of the Blotto Game

1. **Political Campaigns** – Candidates distribute funds across different states or voter demographics.
2. **Military Strategy** – Armies allocate troops across multiple battlefronts.

3. **Business Marketing** – Companies divide advertising budgets across different regions or media platforms.

4. **Cybersecurity** – Organizations allocate defences to protect against multiple threats.

Key Insights

1. **A uniform strategy is weak—adaptive allocation is key.**

2. **Players should use unpredictability to prevent easy counter-strategies.**

3. **Winning small contests with minimal resources can be more effective than overcommitting to major battles.**

4. **Knowing your opponent's tendencies provides a strategic edge.**

Final Thoughts

The **Blotto Game** demonstrates the importance of **strategic resource allocation, adaptability, and unpredictability** in competitive environments. Whether in **politics, business, or warfare**, success often depends on **how well resources are distributed across multiple fronts.**

33 Deterrence Theory Game

Deterrence Theory in Game Theory

Breakdown of the Theory

The **Deterrence Theory Game** is a **game theory model** that explains how **threats and the promise of retaliation prevent aggressive actions** by opponents. This model is widely used in **military strategy, international relations, and law enforcement**, demonstrating how **credible threats** can influence decision-making and maintain stability.

Key assumptions of the **Deterrence Theory Game**:

1. **Two or more players (nations, businesses, or individuals) interact in a strategic conflict.**

2. **One player (aggressor) decides whether to attack or challenge the other.**

3. **The other player (defender) must decide whether to retaliate or tolerate the aggression.**

4. **The game outcome depends on the credibility of threats and the cost of retaliation.**

Successful deterrence **prevents conflict** without requiring actual retaliation. However, if threats **lack credibility**, deterrence **fails, leading to conflict**.

Example of the Deterrence Theory Game

Consider two **rival nations, Nation A and Nation B**, where Nation A is considering invading Nation B.

Scenario	Nation A's Action	Nation B's Response	Outcome
1	Invades	Retaliates	War (both lose)
2	Invades	No retaliation	Nation A wins
3	Doesn't invade	-	Peace (both win)

If Nation B **credibly commits to retaliation**, Nation A is **deterred** from attacking, ensuring peace. However, if Nation B's **threat is weak or not credible**, Nation A **may attack, leading to conflict.**

Why It Works

The **Deterrence Theory Game** works because:

- **Rational players avoid costly conflicts if deterrence is credible.**

- **Commitment to retaliation increases the cost of aggression.**

- **Pre-emptive signalling (military build-up, alliances) strengthens deterrence.**

How It Works

1. **The aggressor evaluates potential gains vs. the cost of retaliation.**

2. The defender signals their willingness to retaliate.

3. If the threat is credible, the aggressor avoids aggression.

4. If deterrence fails, the conflict escalates.

Applications of Deterrence Theory

1. **Cold War Nuclear Strategy** – The US and USSR used **Mutually Assured Destruction (MAD)** to prevent war.

2. **Cybersecurity** – Governments threaten **cyber retaliation** to deter cyberattacks.

3. **Law Enforcement** – Harsh penalties deter **criminal behaviour**.

4. **Business Competition** – Companies threaten **price wars** to prevent market entry.

Key Insights

1. **Deterrence is effective only if threats are credible and enforceable.**

2. **Empty threats weaken deterrence, encouraging aggression.**

3. **Pre-emptive signalling (e.g., military alliances, economic sanctions) enhances deterrence.**

4. **Deterrence works best when both parties prefer avoiding conflict over escalation.**

Final Thoughts

The **Deterrence Theory Game** explains how **credible threats shape strategic decision-making**. Whether in **geopolitics, cybersecurity, or business strategy**, deterrence ensures stability by making aggression too costly to pursue.

34 Security Dilemma

Security Dilemma in Game Theory

Breakdown of the Theory

The **Security Dilemma** is a **game theory model** in **international relations** that explains how actions taken by one state to increase its security can unintentionally threaten other states, leading to an **arms race or conflict.** First conceptualized by **John Herz (1950)** and **Robert Jervis (1978)**, it highlights how **mutual distrust can escalate into unnecessary wars, even when no side desires conflict.**

Key assumptions of the **Security Dilemma**:

1. **States exist in an anarchic world (no central authority to enforce peace).**

2. **Each state prioritizes its own security and survival.**

3. **Defensive actions (e.g., military build-up) can be misinterpreted as aggression.**

4. **Fear and uncertainty lead states to adopt increasingly hostile postures.**

Because no state **fully trusts another**, even defensive measures **can provoke counteractions**, escalating tensions into potential conflict.

Example of the Security Dilemma

Consider **two rival nations, Alpha and Beta**, each seeking to protect itself:

1. **Alpha increases military spending**, believing this will deter Beta.

2. **Beta perceives Alpha's build-up as a potential future threat.**

3. **Beta responds by expanding its own military forces.**

4. **Alpha, now seeing Beta's actions, believes its fears were justified and further escalates its defences.**

5. **The cycle continues, leading to an arms race or even war.**

Nation	Initial Action	Perceived Threat	Response
Alpha	Builds military bases	Beta sees aggression	Beta expands military
Beta	Increases army size	Alpha sees escalation	Alpha deploys more forces
Alpha	Forms alliances	Beta feels encircled	Beta forms counter-alliances

Even if neither nation **intends to attack**, their actions **increase mutual insecurity**, making conflict more likely.

Why It Works

The **Security Dilemma** works because:

- States act in self-interest but unintentionally create hostility.

- Mutual distrust prevents cooperative solutions.

- Fear and misinterpretation lead to unnecessary escalation.

How It Works

1. A state increases its security through military, alliances, or technology.

2. Other states misinterpret these moves as aggressive rather than defensive.

3. They counter with their own security measures, creating a cycle of escalation.

4. Over time, distrust hardens, making de-escalation difficult.

Applications of the Security Dilemma

1. **Cold War Arms Race** – The US and USSR increased nuclear weapons, fearing each other's expansion.

2. **China-US Rivalry** – Military expansion in the South China Sea raises tensions.

3. **India-Pakistan Conflict** – Both nations stockpile nuclear weapons, fearing each other's intentions.

4. **AI & Cybersecurity** – Countries develop offensive cyber capabilities, escalating digital warfare risks.

Key Insights

1. **Even defensive actions can be perceived as aggressive.**

2. **Mutual distrust makes de-escalation challenging.**

3. **Communication and diplomacy can help break security spirals.**

4. **The dilemma is worsened in a world with no overarching authority to mediate conflicts.**

Final Thoughts

The **Security Dilemma** explains how **fear and uncertainty drive unnecessary conflict**, even among rational actors. In geopolitics, cybersecurity, and strategic business decisions, **misperception of threats often fuels escalation**, making trust-building and diplomacy essential for stability.

35 Mutual Assured Destruction (MAD) Game

Mutual Assured Destruction (MAD) in Game Theory

Breakdown of the Theory

Mutual Assured Destruction (MAD) is a **game theory model** that explains how two rational actors, possessing **nuclear weapons**, deter each other from launching an attack by ensuring **complete and catastrophic retaliation**. Developed during the **Cold War**, MAD is based on **deterrence theory**, where the threat of total destruction **prevents both sides from initiating conflict**.

Key assumptions of the **MAD game**:

1. **Two nuclear-armed states are in competition (e.g., U.S. vs. USSR).**

2. **Each state has the capability to destroy the other if attacked.**

3. **A first strike would trigger a second strike, ensuring mutual destruction.**

4. **Since survival is the ultimate goal, neither side initiates war.**

The paradox of MAD is that while **both sides prepare for war**, the **very existence of these weapons prevents war from occurring**.

Example of the MAD Game

Consider two rival nations, **Nation A and Nation B**, each possessing nuclear weapons.

Scenario	Nation A's Action	Nation B's Response	Outcome
1	Launches nuclear attack	Retaliates	**Both destroyed**
2	Does not attack	No retaliation	**Stable peace**
3	Launches attack	No response	**A wins, but unlikely**

- **If Nation A attacks first**, Nation B retaliates, leading to **total destruction**.

- **If neither attacks, peace is maintained** (even with high tensions).

- **If one side does not retaliate**, the other might win, but this is an **irrational assumption** because retaliation is expected.

Thus, the **only rational outcome is mutual deterrence**, where **neither side attacks** due to fear of annihilation.

Why It Works

The **MAD game works because:**

- **Both players have equal destructive capabilities, ensuring retaliation.**

- **Rational actors prioritize survival, making a first strike too risky.**

- **The presence of nuclear weapons discourages large-scale wars.**

How It Works

1. **Both nations maintain nuclear stockpiles to deter attacks.**

2. **Any attack guarantees a devastating counterattack.**

3. **Since neither side can "win" without being destroyed, war is avoided.**

4. **A fragile peace is maintained, relying on rational decision-making.**

Applications of MAD

1. **Cold War (U.S. vs. USSR)** – Nuclear stockpiling ensured neither side launched an attack.

2. **India-Pakistan Conflict** – Both nations maintain nuclear deterrence, preventing escalation.

3. **North Korea's Nuclear Strategy** – A small nuclear arsenal deters larger powers from intervention.

4. **Cybersecurity & AI Warfare** – Mutually destructive cyber-attacks deter large-scale hacking.

Key Insights

1. **MAD relies on rational decision-making; miscalculations can be catastrophic.**

2. **The presence of nuclear weapons prevents war but increases global tensions.**

3. **Peace under MAD is fragile and depends on continued deterrence.**

4. **Technology (missile defence, AI) could shift MAD dynamics in the future.**

Final Thoughts

The **MAD game theory model** explains how **fear of total destruction stabilizes international relations.** While it has **prevented nuclear wars so far,** it also highlights the dangers of **accidental conflicts, miscalculations, and emerging threats** in modern warfare.

36 Limited War Game

Limited War Game in Game Theory

Breakdown of the Theory

The **Limited War Game** is a **game theory model** that explains how conflicting parties engage in **controlled warfare** to achieve political or strategic objectives while avoiding total war. Unlike **Mutual Assured Destruction (MAD)**, where full-scale war leads to catastrophic consequences, the **Limited War Game** involves **measured military actions** to signal intent, exert pressure, or gain leverage without triggering full escalation.

This model is widely applied in **military conflicts, international relations, cyber warfare, and economic disputes**, where actors use **limited force or pressure** to achieve goals without the high costs of all-out war.

Key assumptions of the **Limited War Game**:

1. **Two or more players (nations, factions, corporations) are in conflict.**

2. **Each side prefers achieving objectives without full-scale war.**

3. **War costs increase with escalation, making limited actions preferable.**

4. **Players use calibrated military, economic, or cyber tactics to pressure opponents.**

5. **Both sides have incentives to keep conflict below a critical threshold.**

Since **escalation is costly,** players **balance aggression and restraint** to achieve strategic advantages without risking total destruction.

Example of the Limited War Game

Consider two nations, **Alpha and Beta,** disputing control over a border region.

Scenario	Alpha's Action	Beta's Response	Outcome
1	Limited military strikes	Retaliates with minor strikes	Ongoing limited conflict
2	Full-scale invasion	Total war	Catastrophic losses for both
3	Uses diplomacy	Negotiates	Peaceful resolution

- If **Alpha launches small-scale strikes,** Beta may **respond proportionally,** maintaining a controlled war.

- If **Alpha escalates to full war, Beta is forced to retaliate,** leading to **massive destruction.**

- If both use **diplomacy**, the conflict may be resolved **without military escalation**.

Since **neither side wants total war**, they engage in **calculated conflicts** to maximize their leverage while keeping escalation manageable.

Why It Works

The **Limited War Game works because**:

- It allows players to exert influence without full-scale destruction.

- Escalation costs often outweigh total war benefits.

- It enables strategic bargaining, where controlled force is a negotiation tool.

How It Works

1. One nation initiates a controlled action (military strike, economic sanction, cyberattack).

2. The opponent decides whether to escalate, retaliate proportionally, or negotiate.

3. Both sides evaluate whether further escalation is worth the cost.

4. Conflict continues in a controlled manner, or diplomacy resolves tensions.

Applications of the Limited War Game

1. **Cold War Proxy Wars** – U.S. and USSR engaged in conflicts (Vietnam, Afghanistan) without direct war.

2. **India-Pakistan Border Conflicts** – Periodic skirmishes avoid full-scale war.

3. **Cyber Warfare** – States launch cyberattacks instead of traditional military action.

4. **Trade Wars & Sanctions** – Economic pressures replace military force in global disputes.

Key Insights

1. **Limited war prevents full-scale destruction but still involves risks.**

2. **Nations use limited conflict as a bargaining tool.**

3. **Careful escalation management is required to prevent uncontrolled war.**

4. **Non-military tools (diplomacy, sanctions) often complement limited wars.**

Final Thoughts

The **Limited War Game** explains why **conflicts often remain controlled rather than escalating to total war**. It highlights **strategic restraint, cost-benefit calculations, and the role of diplomacy** in maintaining stability while achieving political objectives.

37 Terrorist vs. Government Game

Terrorist vs. Government Game in Game Theory

Breakdown of the Theory

The **Terrorist vs. Government Game** is a **game theory model** that analyses the strategic interactions between **governments and terrorist organizations**. It explains how **governments decide on counterterrorism strategies**, while **terrorists choose when and how to attack**. The model highlights how **deterrence, negotiation, and counterinsurgency efforts** shape the decisions of both actors.

Key assumptions of the **Terrorist vs. Government Game**:

1. **Two players (the government and a terrorist organization) engage in a strategic conflict.**

2. **The government seeks to minimize terrorist attacks while controlling costs.**

3. **The terrorist group seeks to maximize impact while avoiding elimination.**

4. **Both sides weigh the costs of escalation and retaliation.**

5. **The government can choose between suppression (military action), negotiation, or intelligence operations.**

The game reveals that **strict counterterrorism policies can sometimes increase radicalization**, while **negotiation may encourage further demands**. Governments must find a **balance between suppression and incentives** to reduce terrorist threats.

Example of the Terrorist vs. Government Game

Consider a government dealing with an insurgent terrorist group.

Scenario	Government's Action	Terrorist Response	Outcome
1	Heavy military crackdown	Increased attacks	Prolonged conflict
2	Negotiation	Ceasefire or increased demands	Possible peace but risks incentivizing terrorism
3	Intelligence operations	Disrupted terrorist plans	Reduced attacks

- If the government uses extreme military force, the terrorist group may **increase attacks** in retaliation.

- If the government negotiates, the terrorists might **pause attacks**, but they could also **increase demands**.

- If the government focuses on intelligence and strategic counterterrorism, it may **weaken the group over time**.

Since both players are **rational actors**, their choices depend on **cost-benefit analysis**.

Why It Works

The **Terrorist vs. Government Game works because**:

- **Both sides strategically adapt to the opponent's actions.**

- **Governments must balance deterrence with the risk of radicalization.**

- **Terrorist groups exploit weaknesses in counterterrorism strategies.**

How It Works

1. **The terrorist group decides whether to launch an attack, negotiate, or remain dormant.**

2. **The government chooses its response (military action, intelligence, negotiation).**

3. **Each action influences the opponent's next move.**

4. The cycle continues until one side is eliminated or a resolution is reached.

Applications of the Terrorist vs. Government Game

1. **U.S. War on Terror** – Balancing military intervention with diplomatic strategies.

2. **Israel-Palestine Conflict** – Military responses vs. negotiation efforts.

3. **Counterterrorism Intelligence** – Using surveillance and covert operations to prevent attacks.

4. **Cyberterrorism Defence** – Governments prevent cyber-attacks through cyber-intelligence.

Key Insights

1. **Over-aggressive counterterrorism can backfire, increasing radicalization.**

2. **Terrorist groups strategically choose between violence and negotiation.**

3. **A mix of military, intelligence, and diplomatic strategies is often most effective.**

4. **Understanding terrorist incentives helps governments design better counterterrorism policies.**

Final Thoughts

The **Terrorist vs. Government Game** explains how **governments and terrorist groups strategically adapt to each other's actions**. A **balanced approach** combining deterrence, intelligence, and diplomacy is often necessary to minimize long-term conflict and instability.

38 Spy vs. Spy Game

Spy vs. Spy Game in Game Theory

Breakdown of the Theory

The **Spy vs. Spy Game** is a **game theory model** that analyses strategic interactions between **competing intelligence agencies, rival spies, or nations engaging in espionage**. The game reflects how each side must choose between **covert operations, counterintelligence, deception, or direct confrontation** to gain an advantage while minimizing risks.

Key assumptions of the **Spy vs. Spy Game**:

1. **Two or more players (nations, intelligence agencies, or spies) compete in espionage.**

2. **Each side must choose between gathering intelligence, counterintelligence, misinformation, or sabotage.**

3. **Both players operate under uncertainty, not knowing the opponent's exact actions.**

4. **Success depends on a mix of deception, resource allocation, and strategic timing.**

5. **Over-escalation risks exposure, retaliation, or diplomatic consequences.**

This game highlights the **balance between intelligence gathering and secrecy**, where both players **seek to** outmanoeuvre the other without provoking full-scale conflict.

Example of the Spy vs. Spy Game

Consider two rival nations, **Nation A and Nation B,** engaged in espionage.

Scenario	Nation A's Action	Nation B's Response	Outcome
1	Conducts cyber espionage	Increases cyber defences	Reduced intelligence gain
2	Spreads disinformation	Exposes the deception	Public trust in Nation A decreases
3	Plants a double agent	Uses counterintelligence	Double agent is discovered
4	Engages in diplomatic negotiation	Exchanges intelligence	Peaceful outcome

- **If Nation A gathers intelligence, Nation B may increase counterintelligence efforts, making spying riskier.**

- If Nation A spreads misinformation, Nation B might expose it, damaging Nation A's credibility.

- If Nation A plants a spy, but Nation B is running a counterintelligence operation, the spy may be captured.

- If both nations agree to intelligence-sharing diplomacy, tensions may decrease.

Since both players **operate in secrecy and deception, uncertainty** plays a major role in decision-making.

Why It Works

The **Spy vs. Spy Game works because**:

- Espionage and counterintelligence require continuous adaptation.

- Success depends on deception, unpredictability, and strategic timing.

- Overuse of espionage increases exposure and retaliation risks.

How It Works

1. Each side selects espionage strategies (covert ops, counterintelligence, misinformation).

2. The opponent responds based on available intelligence.

3. Outcomes depend on the balance between secrecy and exposure.

4. The game continues indefinitely as intelligence warfare evolves.

Applications of the Spy vs. Spy Game

1. **Cold War Espionage** – U.S. vs. USSR intelligence operations (e.g., KGB vs. CIA).

2. **Cyber Espionage** – Nations hacking into rival governments (e.g., U.S.-China cyber warfare).

3. **Corporate Espionage** – Companies spying on competitors for trade secrets.

4. **Counterterrorism** – Intelligence agencies tracking terrorist cells.

Key Insights

1. **Intelligence operations require a mix of secrecy and deception.**

2. **Uncertainty forces players to anticipate and counter the opponent's moves.**

3. **Over-reliance on espionage can backfire if exposed.**

4. **Diplomacy and intelligence-sharing can sometimes reduce risks.**

Final Thoughts

The **Spy vs. Spy Game** illustrates how **nations, agencies, and corporations engage in intelligence warfare**. Success in espionage relies on **secrecy, counterintelligence, and strategic deception**, making it a **high-stakes, continuous game** with global consequences.

39 Insurgency & Counterinsurgency Model

Insurgency & Counterinsurgency Model in Game Theory

Breakdown of the Theory

The **Insurgency & Counterinsurgency (COIN) Model** in **game theory** explains the strategic interactions between **insurgent groups (rebels) and governments (counterinsurgents).** It describes how **insurgents use asymmetric warfare, guerilla tactics, and propaganda,** while **governments employ military force, intelligence, and political strategies** to suppress rebellion.

This model highlights how **insurgents exploit weaknesses in conventional military forces,** using **hit-and-run tactics, local support, and psychological warfare** to challenge a superior power. Conversely, **governments balance military force with political and social efforts** to **weaken insurgencies without alienating civilians.**

Key assumptions of the **Insurgency & Counterinsurgency Model:**

1. **Two players (insurgents and the government) engage in conflict over control and legitimacy.**

2. **Insurgents operate with lower resources but rely on secrecy, local support, and prolonged warfare.**

3. **Governments seek to eliminate insurgents while maintaining political stability.**

4. **Each side must carefully balance military actions, propaganda, and alliances.**

5. **Excessive force can backfire, strengthening insurgent recruitment.**

Since **insurgents rely on public perception**, governments must be cautious with **civilian casualties, human rights, and legitimacy** to prevent strengthening the insurgency.

Example of the Insurgency & Counterinsurgency Model

Consider a **nation facing an armed insurgency** in a rural region.

Scenario	Government's Action	Insurgent Response	Outcome
1	Heavy military crackdown	Insurgents gain sympathy & recruits	Conflict escalates
2	Targeted intelligence & policing	Insurgents weaken but continue operations	Partial success
3	Economic & political reforms	Insurgents lose public support	Peace & stability

- **If the government uses excessive force**, insurgents may gain **local and international support.**

- **If the government combines military action with intelligence and social programs**, insurgents may be **weakened over time.**

- **If the government prioritizes political and economic reforms**, it may **reduce insurgent recruitment and legitimacy.**

Since **both players adapt strategically**, the game involves **long-term decision-making rather than quick victories.**

Why It Works

The **Insurgency & Counterinsurgency Model works because**:

- **Asymmetric warfare forces governments to rethink traditional military strategies.**

- **Insurgents use unpredictability to challenge conventional forces.**

- **Governments must balance force with winning "hearts and minds" to succeed.**

How It Works

1. **Insurgents launch attacks, seeking to disrupt government control.**

2. **The government responds with military force, intelligence, or political measures.**

3. The population's reaction influences insurgent recruitment and legitimacy.

4. Both sides adjust strategies based on successes and failures.

Applications of the Insurgency & Counterinsurgency Model

1. **Vietnam War** – The Viet Cong used guerilla warfare against U.S. forces.

2. **Iraq & Afghanistan Conflicts** – U.S. and allied forces struggled against insurgencies.

3. **FARC in Colombia** – The Colombian government used a mix of military and peace talks to weaken insurgents.

4. **Cyber Insurgency** – Hacktivist groups (e.g., Anonymous) challenge governments using online tactics.

Key Insights

1. **Insurgencies succeed when they win public support and outlast the government.**

2. **Governments must avoid excessive force to prevent strengthening insurgent movements.**

3. **A mix of military, intelligence, and socio-political strategies is most effective.**

4. Insurgents adapt quickly, making flexibility key in counterinsurgency efforts.

Final Thoughts

The **Insurgency & Counterinsurgency Game** explains how governments and insurgents strategically adapt to each other's actions. A successful counterinsurgency strategy requires balancing military force, intelligence, diplomacy, and economic development to weaken insurgents without escalating conflict.

Psychological & Behavioural Game Theory's

40 Anchoring Game

Anchoring Game in Game Theory

Breakdown of the Theory

The **Anchoring Game** in **game theory** explains how **initial reference points (anchors) influence decision-making in negotiations, pricing, and strategic interactions.** This concept is closely related to **behavioural economics** and was popularized by **Daniel Kahneman and Amos Tversky** in their research on cognitive biases.

The **anchoring effect** occurs when the **first piece of information presented (the anchor) strongly influences subsequent decisions**, even if it is arbitrary or irrelevant. In strategic interactions, **players manipulate anchors** to steer negotiations or pricing in their favour.

Key assumptions of the **Anchoring Game**:

1. **Players use initial reference points to shape expectations.**

2. **Anchors create cognitive biases, leading opponents to adjust decisions based on the starting point.**

3. **Strong anchoring strategies influence negotiations, pricing, and competition.**

4. **Players must anticipate and counteract anchoring effects in order to maximize gains.**

Since **human decisions are rarely fully rational**, anchoring plays a **crucial role in bargaining, marketing, and behavioural strategy**.

Example of the Anchoring Game

Consider **a salary negotiation** between a company and a job applicant.

Scenario	Job Applicant's Initial Salary Demand	Employer's Counteroffer	Final Agreed Salary
1	$100,000	$80,000	$90,000
2	$80,000	$60,000	$70,000
3	$120,000	$95,000	$105,000

- **If the applicant starts with a high anchor ($120,000), the employer's counteroffer also increases.**

- **If the applicant sets a lower anchor ($80,000), the final agreed salary is lower.**

- **Anchoring works because people unconsciously adjust their decisions based on the first number presented.**

Since **anchors shape perception,** skilled negotiators use **strategic anchoring** to gain an advantage.

Why It Works

The **Anchoring Game works because:**

- **People rely on initial reference points, even if they are arbitrary.**

- **The first number in negotiations shapes the entire decision process.**

- **Anchors create a cognitive bias that limits rational adjustments.**

How It Works

1. **A player introduces a strong anchor (e.g., price, salary, or reference value).**

2. **The opponent subconsciously adjusts their expectations around the anchor.**

3. **Negotiations move within a range influenced by the anchor.**

4. **The final decision is closer to the initial anchor than it would be otherwise.**

Applications of the Anchoring Game

1. **Salary Negotiations** – Employees set high initial demands to pull final offers upward.

2. **Real Estate Pricing** – Sellers list properties at high prices to create high-value perception.

3. **Retail Discounts** – Stores mark items as "originally $500, now $300" to make discounts seem bigger.

4. **Legal Settlements** – Lawyers set extreme initial demands to influence settlement terms.

Key Insights

1. **First offers strongly influence final outcomes in negotiations.**

2. **Players should strategically set anchors to maximize their advantage.**

3. **Awareness of anchoring bias helps counteract manipulation.**

4. **Even irrelevant anchors affect decision-making, demonstrating cognitive bias.**

Final Thoughts

The **Anchoring Game** explains how **first offers, price points, and reference values shape decision-making in negotiations and pricing**. Understanding anchoring strategies **improves bargaining power, pricing tactics, and decision-making in competitive environments**.

41 Framing Effect Game

Framing Effect Game in Game Theory

Breakdown of the Theory

The **Framing Effect Game** in **game theory** explores how the **presentation of choices** influences decision-making. It is based on **behavioural economics**, particularly the work of **Daniel Kahneman and Amos Tversky**, who demonstrated that **people react differently depending on how options are framed**—even when the outcomes remain the same.

The key idea is that **people do not always make rational decisions**. Instead, their choices are shaped by whether options are framed **positively (as gains) or negatively (as losses)**.

Key assumptions of the **Framing Effect Game**:

1. **Players make decisions based on perceived gains or losses, not absolute outcomes.**

2. **The same information can lead to different choices depending on how it is presented.**

3. **Players are more risk-averse when choices are framed as gains.**

4. **Players are more risk-seeking when choices are framed as losses.**

Since **framing alters decision-making**, strategic players can use **language, context, and presentation** to influence choices in negotiations, politics, and marketing.

Example of the Framing Effect Game

Consider a **public health policy scenario** where a government must decide how to respond to a deadly virus outbreak.

Scenario	Positive Frame (Gains)	Negative Frame (Losses)	Player's Likely Decision
1	"Saving 200 out of 600 people"	"400 people will die"	Players prefer certainty (saving 200).
2	"90% success rate of treatment"	"10% failure rate of treatment"	Players prefer the success-frame option.
3	"Tax break for responsible spending"	"Penalty for overspending"	Players prefer the tax break.

- **When the choice is framed as saving lives, people prefer certainty (risk-averse).**
- **When framed as losing lives, people prefer risky options (risk-seeking).**

- The framing effect changes perception, even though the statistical outcomes are identical.

Since **players react based on perception rather than rational analysis,** framing can **nudge decisions toward desired outcomes.**

Why It Works

The **Framing Effect Game works because:**

- **Humans are psychologically wired to avoid losses more than they seek equivalent gains.**

- **Cognitive biases make perception more important than reality.**

- **Strategic framing influences how choices are evaluated.**

How It Works

1. **A player (government, business, negotiator) presents options in a specific frame.**

2. **The opponent reacts based on perceived gains or losses.**

3. **The decision shifts toward the option that appears most beneficial.**

4. **Players adjust framing strategies to maximize influence.**

Applications of the Framing Effect Game

1. **Political Messaging** – Policies are framed as "protecting jobs" instead of "preventing layoffs."

2. **Marketing & Sales** – "Buy one, get one free" is more effective than "50% off."

3. **Healthcare Decisions** – Doctors present surgery success rates instead of failure rates.

4. **Legal Strategy** – Lawyers frame settlements as "avoiding large risks" rather than "losing compensation."

Key Insights

1. **The way information is presented changes how people perceive risk and reward.**

2. **Players can strategically frame options to influence decisions.**

3. **Framing is especially powerful in politics, marketing, and negotiations.**

4. **Awareness of framing bias helps players make more rational choices.**

Final Thoughts

The **Framing Effect Game** explains how **language and presentation shape decision-making**. Understanding framing strategies **improves persuasion, negotiation, and marketing effectiveness**, proving that **perception is often more powerful than reality**.

42 Sunk Cost Game

Sunk Cost Game in Game Theory

Breakdown of the Theory

The **Sunk Cost Game** in **game theory** examines how **past investments influence present and future decision-making**, even when rationality suggests ignoring them. The **sunk cost fallacy** occurs when **players continue investing in a losing strategy simply because they have already spent resources on it**. This game highlights the tension between **rational economic behaviour and psychological biases** in decision-making.

Key assumptions of the **Sunk Cost Game**:

1. **Players have invested resources (money, time, effort) in a project or strategy.**

2. **The investment is non-recoverable (sunk cost).**

3. **Players must decide whether to continue or abandon the project.**

4. **Rational decision-making should consider only future costs and benefits, ignoring sunk costs.**

5. **Psychological commitment often causes players to escalate rather than cut losses.**

This model is applied in **business, politics, personal finance, and military strategy**, where decision-makers often struggle to **abandon failing projects** due to **emotional and reputational costs**.

Example of the Sunk Cost Game

Imagine a company, **TechCorp**, investing in a **new smartphone product**.

Scenario	Investment So Far	Future Costs	Expected Gains	Decision
1	$10M	$5M more	$3M	Rational choice: Abandon
2	$10M	$5M more	$12M	Rational choice: Continue
3	$10M	$10M more	$8M	Irrational choice: Continue due to sunk cost bias

- **If future gains exceed future costs, the project should continue.**
- **If future costs outweigh expected gains, rational players should cut losses.**

- Emotionally driven players may continue even when losses exceed gains, due to the sunk cost fallacy.

Since **human psychology resists "wasting" past investments**, players often **escalate their commitment**, leading to **greater losses over time**.

Why It Works

The **Sunk Cost Game works because**:

- **People overvalue past investments, even when they cannot be recovered.**

- **Players fear loss realization and reputational damage.**

- **Commitment bias makes it harder to accept failure and change course.**

How It Works

1. **A player makes an initial investment in a project or strategy.**

2. **New information reveals that continuing may not be beneficial.**

3. **The player must decide whether to persist or cut losses.**

4. **Irrational players continue investing, leading to more losses.**

5. **Rational players ignore sunk costs and focus on future benefits vs. costs.**

Applications of the Sunk Cost Game

1. **Business Investments** – Companies continue failing projects to justify past spending.

2. **Military Strategy** – Nations stay in prolonged wars to "honour past sacrifices."

3. **Personal Finance** – Investors hold onto failing stocks to avoid admitting loss.

4. **Relationships & Careers** – People stay in toxic situations due to past commitments.

Key Insights

1. **Sunk costs should not influence future decisions.**

2. **Players must focus on future costs and benefits, not past losses.**

3. **Avoiding escalation bias prevents long-term damage.**

4. **Rational decision-making requires emotional detachment from past investments.**

Final Thoughts

The **Sunk Cost Game** explains why **people and organizations struggle to abandon failing projects**. Recognizing the **sunk cost fallacy** improves **strategic decision-making, investment strategies, and resource management** by ensuring that **future actions are based on rational calculations, not emotional commitment**.

43 Hyperbolic Discounting Game

Hyperbolic Discounting Game in Game Theory

Breakdown of the Theory

The **Hyperbolic Discounting Game** in **game theory** explores how players **overvalue immediate rewards and undervalue long-term gains**, leading to **time-inconsistent decision-making**. Unlike standard economic models, where players discount future rewards at a constant rate (**exponential discounting**), hyperbolic discounting suggests that **people heavily Favor short-term benefits, even if waiting would lead to a higher payoff**.

This game highlights **self-control problems**, explaining why **people procrastinate, struggle with savings, or make impulsive decisions** despite knowing that long-term benefits outweigh short-term gratification.

Key assumptions of the **Hyperbolic Discounting Game**:

1. **Players prefer immediate rewards over larger future rewards.**

2. **The discount rate decreases over time (i.e., future rewards look more valuable the further they are).**

3. **Players exhibit time-inconsistency, meaning their preferences change as the decision point nears.**

4. **Self-control mechanisms, such as commitment devices, can help mitigate impulsive choices.**

Since **human perception of value is irrational over time,** this game explains **why people engage in behaviours that contradict their long-term interests.**

Example of the Hyperbolic Discounting Game

Imagine a person, **Alex**, deciding between two rewards:

Scenario	Immediate Reward	Delayed Reward (after 6 months)	Decision
1	$50 today	$100 in six months	Chooses $50 (hyperbolic discounting)
2	$50 in six months	$100 in 12 months	Chooses $100 (rational)

- **When both options are in the future (6 vs. 12 months), Alex makes the rational choice.**
- **When one option is immediate, Alex impulsively takes the smaller reward.**
- **Hyperbolic discounting explains why people prioritize instant gratification.**

Since **future rewards are undervalued when immediate alternatives exist,** players often **fail to act in their long-term best interest.**

Why It Works

The **Hyperbolic Discounting Game works because:**

- Humans are wired to prioritize present over future rewards.

- Delaying gratification requires self-control, which is mentally costly.

- As time passes, future rewards appear more valuable, leading to preference shifts.

How It Works

1. A player faces a choice between an immediate and a delayed reward.

2. The immediate reward is disproportionately tempting, leading to impulsive decisions.

3. Over time, future rewards become more attractive, but early decisions already locked in losses.

4. Commitment mechanisms (e.g., savings plans, penalties) help counteract short-term bias.

Applications of the Hyperbolic Discounting Game

1. **Personal Finance** – People prefer spending now over saving for retirement.

2. **Health & Fitness** – Dieting and exercise are postponed in Favor of instant comfort.

3. **Addiction & Habits** – Short-term pleasure (e.g., smoking) outweighs long-term health risks.

4. **Procrastination** – Delayed tasks feel less urgent until the deadline is near.

Key Insights

1. **People systematically undervalue future rewards when immediate options exist.**

2. **Time-inconsistency leads to self-control problems and poor long-term decisions.**

3. **Commitment strategies (automatic savings, deadlines, penalties) improve decision-making.**

4. **Understanding hyperbolic discounting helps in designing better policies and incentives.**

Final Thoughts

The **Hyperbolic Discounting Game** explains why **individuals and organizations struggle with long-term planning**. Recognizing this bias allows **better financial planning, habit formation, and self-discipline strategies,** ensuring that **decisions align with long-term well-being rather than short-term impulses.**

44 Endowment Effect Game

Endowment Effect Game in Game Theory

Breakdown of the Theory

The **Endowment Effect Game** in **game theory and behavioural economics** explains how **people assign greater value to things they own compared to identical things they do not own**. This psychological bias, first identified by **Richard Thaler (1980)**, contradicts classical economic models, which assume people value goods based on **market utility** rather than **ownership status**.

The endowment effect occurs because **ownership creates an emotional attachment**, leading individuals to **overestimate the value of their possessions**. This impacts **negotiations, pricing decisions, and market behaviour**, as individuals demand **higher prices to sell items than they would pay to acquire them**.

Key assumptions of the **Endowment Effect Game**:

1. **Players assign higher value to items they own compared to similar items they do not own.**

2. **Ownership creates a sense of loss aversion, making people reluctant to part with items.**

3. **Players demand higher compensation for giving up a possession than they would pay to acquire it.**

4. **The effect distorts rational decision-making in negotiations, markets, and consumer behaviour.**

Since **humans are loss-averse**, they tend to **overvalue owned items**, making exchanges and negotiations more complex.

Example of the Endowment Effect Game

Consider **a coffee mug experiment** where participants receive a free mug.

Scenario	Participant's Role	Willingness to Pay (WTP)	Willingness to Accept (WTA)
1	Buyer (no mug)	Offers $5 to buy	-
2	Seller (owns mug)	Wants $10 to sell	Rejects $5

- **Buyers (who do not own the mug) value it at $5.**

- **Sellers (who own the mug) demand $10 to part with it.**

- **The transaction does not occur because sellers overvalue their item due to the endowment effect.**

Since **ownership increases perceived value, market inefficiencies arise** due to mismatched expectations.

Why It Works

The **Endowment Effect Game works because**:

- People experience loss aversion, making ownership more valuable.

- Psychological attachment increases subjective valuation.

- Traditional economic models fail to account for emotional biases in valuation.

How It Works

1. A player acquires ownership of an item.

2. Their perceived value of the item increases compared to non-owners.

3. They demand a higher price to sell than they would pay to buy.

4. Trades become inefficient because of valuation mismatches.

Applications of the Endowment Effect Game

1. **Real Estate Pricing** – Homeowners overvalue their properties, leading to inflated prices.

2. **Stock Market Behaviour** – Investors hold on to losing stocks due to emotional attachment.

3. **Consumer Loyalty** – People overvalue brands they already use.

4. **Negotiations** – Sellers demand excessive compensation for parting with assets.

Key Insights

1. **Ownership distorts rational valuation and decision-making.**

2. **The endowment effect creates inefficiencies in negotiations and markets.**

3. **Awareness of this bias helps improve trading and pricing strategies.**

4. **Buyers and sellers must adjust expectations to reach fair market agreements.**

Final Thoughts

The **Endowment Effect Game** explains why **people irrationally overvalue their possessions,** leading to **pricing mismatches, negotiation failures, and market inefficiencies**. Recognizing this bias helps individuals and businesses **make better financial decisions, improve negotiations, and understand consumer behaviour more effectively**.

45 Prospect Theory Game

Prospect Theory Game in Game Theory

Breakdown of the Theory

The **Prospect Theory Game** in **game theory and behavioural economics** explains how individuals **perceive gains and losses differently,** leading to **irrational decision-making under risk**. Developed by **Daniel Kahneman and Amos Tversky (1979), Prospect Theory** challenges classical economic models that assume people always act rationally to maximize expected utility.

Instead, the theory suggests that:

1. **People fear losses more than they value equivalent gains (loss aversion).**

2. **They overweight small probabilities and underweight large probabilities.**

3. **Framing influences decision-making (gains vs. losses).**

4. **Risk attitudes depend on context—people are risk-averse in gains but risk-seeking in losses.**

This model is crucial in **finance, insurance, marketing, and political decision-making,** where risk perception affects choices.

Example of the Prospect Theory Game

Consider a decision-making scenario where **a player must choose between two options**:

Scenario	Option 1 (Sure Outcome)	Option 2 (Risky Outcome)	Decision
Gains Frame	$900 guaranteed	90% chance to win $1,000, 10% chance to win $0	Most people choose the guaranteed $900 (risk-averse).
Losses Frame	Lose $900 for sure	90% chance to lose $1,000, 10% chance to lose $0	Most people take the gamble (risk-seeking).

- **When framed as a gain, players prefer certainty and avoid risk.**

- **When framed as a loss, players prefer taking risks to avoid a definite loss.**

- **This violates expected utility theory, as logically identical choices lead to different decisions.**

Since **people react emotionally to perceived losses**, they make **inconsistent risk-based decisions**.

Why It Works

The **Prospect Theory Game works because:**

- Loss aversion makes people fear losing more than they enjoy winning.

- People do not weigh probabilities correctly, overestimating rare events.

- Framing biases influence decision-making, making perception more powerful than reality.

How It Works

1. A player evaluates choices based on perceived gains or losses.

2. They weigh probabilities irrationally, giving more importance to rare events.

3. If framed as a gain, they prefer certainty; if framed as a loss, they take risks.

4. The final decision depends on psychological biases rather than objective value.

Applications of the Prospect Theory Game

1. **Investment Decisions** – Investors hold losing stocks too long, fearing realized losses.

2. **Insurance Policies** – People overpay for rare-event insurance (e.g., airline crash coverage).

3. **Political Campaigning** – Candidates frame policies as preventing loss rather than creating gain.

4. **Marketing & Pricing** – Discounts are framed as "avoiding extra costs" rather than "gaining savings."

Key Insights

1. **People are risk-averse for gains and risk-seeking for losses.**

2. **Perceived losses feel more significant than equivalent gains.**

3. **Decision-making depends on how options are framed.**

4. **Understanding these biases helps in designing better policies, negotiations, and pricing strategies.**

Final Thoughts

The **Prospect Theory Game** explains why **people often make irrational choices under risk**. Recognizing this bias allows for **better financial decisions, strategic negotiations, and effective marketing strategies**, ensuring that **perception is managed to influence behaviour constructively**.

46 Reciprocity Game

Reciprocity Game in Game Theory

Breakdown of the Theory

The **Reciprocity Game** in **game theory and behavioural economics** explores how individuals or groups **respond to kind or unkind actions with similar behaviour**. Unlike classical economic models that assume pure self-interest, the **reciprocity principle** shows that **people reward generosity and punish unfairness, even at a personal cost**.

Reciprocity plays a key role in **cooperation, trust-building, and social norms**. It can be:

1. **Positive reciprocity** – Rewarding kind behaviour with kindness (e.g., returning a Favor).

2. **Negative reciprocity** – Punishing unfair or hostile behaviour (e.g., retaliating in negotiations).

Key assumptions of the **Reciprocity Game**:

1. **Players decide whether to cooperate or defect based on past actions.**

2. **Acts of generosity encourage further cooperation.**

3. **Unfair behaviour triggers retaliation, making conflict more likely.**

4. **Reputation and repeated interactions reinforce reciprocal behaviour.**

209

Since **people value fairness and trust**, reciprocity influences **business, politics, and personal relationships**.

Example of the Reciprocity Game

Imagine two businesses, **Company A and Company B**, negotiating a supply contract.

Scenario	Company A's Action	Company B's Response	Outcome
1	Offers fair pricing	Accepts and delivers high-quality goods	Long-term partnership
2	Overcharges unfairly	Refuses to renew contract	Lost business
3	Gives initial discount	Returns Favor with larger order	Increased cooperation
4	Delays payment	Demands stricter terms next time	Distrust grows

- **If Company A is fair, Company B reciprocates, fostering long-term collaboration.**

- **If Company A acts unfairly, Company B retaliates, damaging the relationship.**

- **When positive reciprocity exists, both parties gain; when negative reciprocity occurs, both suffer.**

Since **reputation and trust drive interactions,** businesses and individuals **weigh future consequences before acting unfairly.**

Why It Works

The **Reciprocity Game works because:**

- **People value fairness and punish unfairness, even at personal cost.**

- **Positive reciprocity leads to trust, strengthening cooperation over time.**

- **Negative reciprocity deters exploitation but can escalate conflict.**

How It Works

1. **A player initiates an action (fair or unfair).**

2. **The opponent evaluates whether to reciprocate positively or negatively.**

3. **The response shapes future interactions (trust vs. conflict).**

4. **Players develop reputations, influencing long-term relationships.**

Applications of the Reciprocity Game

1. **Business Negotiations** – Fair pricing and honest dealings lead to stronger partnerships.

2. **Workplace Culture** – Employers treating employees well get higher productivity in return.

3. **International Relations** – Diplomacy relies on mutual concessions and retaliatory sanctions.

4. **Social Norms & Relationships** – Acts of kindness strengthen communities, while betrayals lead to distrust.

Key Insights

1. **Trust and fairness encourage long-term cooperation.**

2. **People willingly punish unfairness, even at a cost.**

3. **Reputation plays a key role in shaping reciprocal behaviour.**

4. **Balancing positive reciprocity and deterrence prevents exploitation.**

Final Thoughts

The **Reciprocity Game** explains why **trust and fairness are essential in long-term interactions**. Understanding reciprocity helps in **business, diplomacy, and social relationships**, ensuring that **mutual cooperation leads to shared success** while **deterring unfair behaviour**.

47 Trust Game

Trust Game in Game Theory

Breakdown of the Theory

The **Trust Game** in **game theory** explores how **trust and reciprocity influence decision-making in economic and social interactions**. It highlights the **risk and uncertainty** involved when one player must decide whether to trust another, knowing the other party could either reciprocate or exploit that trust.

Unlike classical economic models that assume **rational self-interest**, the **Trust Game** incorporates **psychological and social factors**, showing that **trust fosters cooperation**, while **betrayal damages relationships and future interactions**.

Key assumptions of the **Trust Game**:

1. **Two players interact—a trustor (who decides to trust or not) and a trustee (who decides to reciprocate or betray).**

2. **The trustor must decide how much to trust the trustee, despite the risk of betrayal.**

3. **If trust is given, the trustee must choose between honouring or exploiting that trust.**

4. **Future interactions (reputation effects) influence trust and reciprocity.**

Since **trust is essential in relationships, business, and finance**, this game reveals how **individuals and institutions build or destroy trust over time**.

Example of the Trust Game

Imagine **an investor (trustor) and an entrepreneur (trustee)** in a startup deal.

Scenario	Investor's Action	Entrepreneur's Response	Outcome
1	Invests $100,000	Uses funds wisely, delivers profits	Long-term trust and success
2	Invests $100,000	Misuses funds, fails to deliver	Investor loses money, trust is broken
3	Does not invest	-	No partnership, missed opportunity

- If the investor trusts and the entrepreneur acts honestly, both benefit.

- If the investor trusts but the entrepreneur betrays, only the entrepreneur gains in the short term, but trust is lost.

- If the investor does not trust, no deal happens, even if a good opportunity exists.

Since **trust builds long-term cooperation,** rational players must **consider future consequences when making trust-based decisions.**

Why It Works

The **Trust Game works because:**

- **Trust creates economic and social value by enabling cooperation.**

- **Reputation and repeated interactions shape future trust decisions.**

- **Uncertainty forces players to weigh risk versus potential rewards.**

How It Works

1. **A trustor decides whether to trust or withhold trust.**

2. **If trust is given, the trustee decides to honour or betray the trust.**

3. **The outcome influences future interactions (positive or negative).**

4. **Repeated games reinforce trust or distrust, shaping long-term relationships.**

Applications of the Trust Game

1. **Banking & Finance** – Trust is key in loans, credit, and investments.

2. **Business & Partnerships** – Companies form alliances based on trust.

3. **Employer-Employee Relations** – Workers trust employers for fair wages and conditions.

4. **Online Transactions** – E-commerce platforms rely on trust and reviews to ensure fair exchanges.

Key Insights

1. **Trust enables long-term cooperation and success.**

2. **Betrayal damages reputation and reduces future opportunities.**

3. **Players must balance short-term gain with long-term trustworthiness.**

4. **Institutions use mechanisms (contracts, regulations) to reduce trust-related risks.**

Final Thoughts

The **Trust Game** explains why **trust is a critical factor in decision-making**. Understanding how trust develops, **how it is broken, and how it can be restored** helps individuals and businesses **build stronger, more reliable relationships**, ensuring **mutual success in the long run**.

48 Ultimatum Rejection Game

Ultimatum Rejection Game in Game Theory

Breakdown of the Theory

The **Ultimatum Rejection Game** is a variation of the **Ultimatum Game**, a classic **game theory experiment** that explores how individuals make decisions about **fairness, negotiation, and punishment**. It demonstrates that **people do not always act rationally in economic terms**, as they are willing to reject unfair offers—even at a personal cost—to punish perceived injustice.

Unlike traditional economic models, which assume that players maximize their own monetary gain, the **Ultimatum Rejection Game** highlights the role of **fairness, emotions, and social norms** in decision-making.

Key assumptions of the **Ultimatum Rejection Game**:

1. **Two players interact—one (the proposer) offers a split of a sum of money, while the other (the responder) accepts or rejects the offer.**

2. **If the responder accepts, both players receive their proposed amounts.**

3. **If the responder rejects, both players receive nothing.**

4. **Rational behaviour suggests accepting any non-zero offer, but fairness concerns often lead to rejection of "unfair" offers.**

Since **human behaviour is influenced by social and emotional factors,** players often **reject offers they perceive as unjust, even when doing so results in personal loss.**

Example of the Ultimatum Rejection Game

Consider a scenario where **two people must split $100:**

Scenario	Proposer's Offer	Responder's Decision	Outcome
1	$50 to each	Accepts	Both get $50 (fair outcome).
2	$70 to proposer, $30 to responder	Accepts	Proposer gets $70, responder gets $30.
3	$90 to proposer, $10 to responder	Rejects	Both get $0 (punishment for unfairness).

- **If the proposer offers a fair split (e.g., 50/50), the responder usually accepts.**

- **If the proposer offers an unfair split (e.g., 90/10), the responder may reject it to punish unfairness.**

- **This rejection contradicts rational choice theory but aligns with behavioural economics.**

Since **people value fairness and reciprocity**, they sometimes choose **punishment over personal gain**, discouraging future unfair behaviour.

Why It Works

The **Ultimatum Rejection Game works because**:

- **People care about fairness, even at a personal cost.**

- **Rejecting unfair offers discourages future exploitation.**

- **Social norms influence decision-making beyond pure self-interest.**

How It Works

1. **A proposer makes an offer on how to split a resource.**

2. **The responder evaluates the offer based on fairness perceptions.**

3. **If the offer is deemed fair, it is accepted; if unfair, it may be rejected.**

4. **Rejection leads to losses for both players but reinforces fairness norms.**

Applications of the Ultimatum Rejection Game

1. **Salary Negotiations** – Employees reject low salary offers, even if some income is better than none.

2. **Business Deals** – Unfair contract terms are often rejected to maintain market standards.

3. **Political Agreements** – Countries reject imbalanced treaties to uphold national interests.

4. **Consumer Behaviour** – Customers avoid businesses that price unfairly, even if alternatives are costlier.

Key Insights

1. **People are willing to sacrifice personal gain to uphold fairness.**

2. **Unfair behaviour is often punished, discouraging exploitation.**

3. **Social norms and emotions influence economic decisions.**

4. **Understanding fairness perceptions helps in negotiations and business strategy.**

Final Thoughts

The **Ultimatum Rejection Game** challenges traditional economic assumptions by **demonstrating that fairness, trust, and reciprocity shape decision-making**. Recognizing these psychological factors allows **businesses, policymakers, and negotiators to design better strategies that align with human behaviour**.

49 Fairness Norm Game

Fairness Norm Game in Game Theory

Breakdown of the Theory

The **Fairness Norm Game** in **game theory and behavioural economics** explores how individuals make decisions based on **social norms of fairness**, rather than purely rational self-interest. Traditional economic models assume that players seek to **maximize their own utility**, but the **Fairness Norm Game** demonstrates that **people often prioritize fairness, even at a personal cost.**

This game highlights how **fairness expectations shape cooperation, negotiations, and economic behaviour.** Players conform to fairness norms due to:

1. **Social expectations** – People expect fair treatment in interactions.

2. **Reputation concerns** – Violating fairness norms leads to social punishment.

3. **Emotional responses** – Feelings of injustice lead to retaliation, even when costly.

Key assumptions of the **Fairness Norm Game**:

1. **Players value fairness and reciprocity in decision-making.**

2. **Unfair actions result in retaliation or reduced cooperation.**

3. **People will accept lower individual payoffs if it means upholding fairness.**

4. **Reputation and future interactions influence adherence to fairness norms.**

Since **social norms are deeply ingrained in human behaviour**, fairness influences **business, politics, and personal relationships** beyond traditional economic incentives.

Example of the Fairness Norm Game

Consider two employees, **Alice and Bob**, who must split a bonus of **$1,000** from their manager.

Scenario	Alice's Proposal	Bob's Response	Outcome
1	$500 each	Accepts	Both receive $500 (fair outcome).
2	$800 to Alice, $200 to Bob	Accepts	Alice benefits more, but Bob resents unfairness.
3	$900 to Alice, $100 to Bob	Rejects	Both get $0 (fairness norm enforced).

- If Alice offers a fair split (50/50), Bob accepts, and cooperation continues.

- If Alice claims an unfair share (80/20), Bob may accept but feel resentment.

- If Alice is too unfair (90/10), Bob may reject, sacrificing money to uphold fairness.

Since **violating fairness norms leads to social punishment,** players often **prioritize fairness to maintain relationships and future cooperation.**

Why It Works

The **Fairness Norm Game works because:**

- **People value fairness beyond monetary gain.**

- **Retaliation enforces fairness norms and discourages exploitation.**

- **Fairness builds long-term cooperation and trust.**

How It Works

1. **One player proposes a distribution of resources.**

2. **The other player evaluates fairness based on social norms.**

3. **If the proposal is fair, cooperation continues; if unfair, punishment may follow.**

4. **Future interactions are influenced by the fairness of past decisions.**

Applications of the Fairness Norm Game

1. **Workplace Compensation** – Fair salaries promote employee satisfaction and retention.

2. **Business Partnerships** – Fair profit-sharing strengthens long-term relationships.

3. **Political Policies** – Equitable taxation and social policies maintain public trust.

4. **Market Transactions** – Consumers avoid businesses that engage in unfair pricing.

Key Insights

1. **Fairness norms shape economic and social interactions.**

2. **People enforce fairness, even at a personal cost.**

3. **Long-term cooperation depends on fair treatment.**

4. **Violating fairness norms leads to retaliation and reduced trust.**

Final Thoughts

The **Fairness Norm Game** explains why **people prioritize fairness over pure self-interest**. Understanding fairness norms helps in **negotiations, business ethics, and social policymaking**, ensuring **mutual cooperation and long-term stability in relationships**.

Biological & Evolutionary Game Theory

50 Evolutionarily Stable Strategy (ESS)

Evolutionarily Stable Strategy (ESS) in Game Theory

Breakdown of the Theory

The **Evolutionarily Stable Strategy (ESS)** is a **game theory concept** introduced by **John Maynard Smith (1973)** in the study of **evolutionary biology**. It explains how **certain strategies persist over time** because they are resistant to invasion by alternative strategies.

An **ESS is a strategy that, if adopted by most members of a population, cannot be easily replaced by a new, mutant strategy** because it provides a higher or equal fitness advantage. This concept helps explain **the stability of behaviours in competitive environments**, such as animal aggression, cooperation, and social structures.

Key assumptions of the **ESS model**:

1. **Players (organisms, individuals, or firms) interact repeatedly in a competitive environment.**

2. **Strategies evolve based on success in replication (biological fitness or economic gains).**

3. **A stable strategy dominates alternative (mutant) strategies.**

4. **If an alternative strategy emerges, it does not outperform the ESS and is eliminated over time.**

Since **natural selection favours behaviours that maximize survival and reproduction**, ESS helps explain why certain behaviours or strategies persist in populations.

Example of Evolutionarily Stable Strategy (ESS)

Consider the **Hawk-Dove Game**, where individuals compete for a shared resource.

Strategy	Hawk (Aggressive)	Dove (Passive)
Hawk vs. Hawk	Fights, risk of injury	Wins half, loses half
Hawk vs. Dove	Hawk always wins	Dove backs down
Dove vs. Dove	Shares resource	Both benefit

- **If all individuals are Hawks (aggressive), constant fighting reduces overall fitness.**

- **If all individuals are Doves (passive), they fail to compete effectively.**

- **A mix of Hawks and Doves reaches an ESS, where neither strategy can completely overtake the other.**

Since **no single strategy dominates completely**, an **optimal balance of aggression and cooperation** emerges as the ESS.

Why It Works

The **ESS model works because**:

- Stable strategies resist replacement by alternatives.

- Evolution selects behaviours that maximize survival and reproduction.

- Mutations or new strategies are eliminated if they do not provide an advantage.

How It Works

1. A strategy spreads in a population through natural selection or imitation.

2. If a new strategy emerges, it competes against the dominant strategy.

3. If the new strategy is weaker, it disappears; if stronger, it may replace the old strategy.

4. Over time, the population stabilizes at an evolutionarily stable equilibrium.

Applications of ESS

1. **Animal Behaviour** – Explains aggression, cooperation, and mating strategies in animals.

2. **Economic Competition** – Firms adopt stable pricing strategies to prevent undercutting.

3. **Cybersecurity** – Defensive strategies evolve to counter hacking threats.

4. **Political Strategy** – Stable government policies resist radical changes due to public adaptation.

Key Insights

1. **ESS explains why certain behaviours persist in nature and society.**

2. **Stable strategies resist invasion by alternative approaches.**

3. **Competition and cooperation shape long-term strategic evolution.**

4. **Understanding ESS helps predict outcomes in evolutionary biology, economics, and social systems.**

Final Thoughts

The **Evolutionarily Stable Strategy (ESS)** provides a **framework for understanding stable behaviours in competitive environments.** Whether in **biology, business, or politics**, ESS helps explain **why some strategies endure while others disappear**, shaping the evolution of societies, economies, and ecosystems.

51 Hawk-Dove-Bourgeois Game

Hawk-Dove-Bourgeois Game in Game Theory

Breakdown of the Theory

The **Hawk-Dove-Bourgeois Game** is an extension of the **Hawk-Dove Game**, incorporating a third strategy: **the Bourgeois strategy**. This game **models animal conflict resolution** and explains how **resource ownership influences aggressive and passive behaviours**. It was developed within **evolutionary game theory**, primarily through the work of **John Maynard Smith** in studying **animal competition and territoriality**.

The three strategies are:

1. **Hawk (Aggressive)** – Always fights for resources, risking injury but winning if the opponent is passive.

2. **Dove (Passive)** – Avoids conflict; shares with other Doves but always loses to Hawks.

3. **Bourgeois (Conditional)** – Acts as a **Hawk if it owns the resource** but as a **Dove if it does not**.

This model explains why **ownership and social rules reduce unnecessary conflict**, leading to a stable strategy in many animal species and human societies.

Example of the Hawk-Dove-Bourgeois Game

Consider three animals competing for territory:

Strategy	Against Hawk	Against Dove	Against Bourgeois
Hawk	50% chance of injury	Wins	50% chance of winning (if it owns territory)
Dove	Loses	Shares the resource	Loses if opponent owns the resource
Bourgeois	Wins if it owns the resource, retreats otherwise	Wins if it owns the resource, retreats otherwise	No conflict (ownership rule decides)

- **If two Hawks meet, they fight, causing injuries and energy loss.**
- **If a Hawk meets a Dove, the Hawk always wins.**
- **If two Doves meet, they share peacefully.**
- **The Bourgeois strategy reduces unnecessary fights by respecting ownership.**

Since **fighting is costly,** the **Bourgeois strategy stabilizes the population** by ensuring that conflict occurs only when necessary.

Why It Works

The **Hawk-Dove-Bourgeois Game works because:**

- It minimizes unnecessary conflicts, improving survival rates.

- Territorial ownership provides a clear rule for resolving disputes.

- It balances aggression and cooperation, leading to a stable evolutionary strategy.

How It Works

1. Players choose between aggression, passivity, or conditional (Bourgeois) behaviour.

2. If ownership is recognized, Bourgeois players avoid conflict, reducing risk.

3. Hawks thrive if Doves dominate, but too many Hawks lead to costly fights.

4. A mix of all three strategies stabilizes the population over time.

Applications of the Hawk-Dove-Bourgeois Game

1. **Animal Behaviour** – Explains why many animals defend their territories but avoid unnecessary fights.

2. **Human Conflict Resolution** – Societies establish property rights to reduce disputes.

3. **Business Strategy** – Companies use **aggression (Hawk), cooperation (Dove),** or **ownership claims (Bourgeois)** in competitive markets.

4. **Cybersecurity** – Some nations or organizations defend their digital assets (Bourgeois) but avoid unnecessary cyber wars (Dove).

Key Insights

1. **Territorial ownership stabilizes conflict by providing a rule-based resolution.**

2. **A mix of aggression, cooperation, and conditional behaviour creates an evolutionarily stable strategy (ESS).**

3. **Pure aggression (Hawk) leads to excessive costs, while pure passivity (Dove) leads to exploitation.**

4. **Recognizing and respecting ownership helps reduce unnecessary conflict in nature and human society.**

Final Thoughts

The **Hawk-Dove-Bourgeois Game** explains how **conditional aggression, based on ownership, creates stability** in competitive environments. Whether in **animal behaviour, business, or politics**, this model shows why **respecting established claims reduces unnecessary conflict and improves long-term survival**.

52 Tit-for-Tat in Evolution

Tit-for-Tat in Evolutionary Game Theory

Breakdown of the Theory

The **Tit-for-Tat strategy** in **evolutionary game theory** explains how **cooperation can evolve and stabilize in repeated interactions**. First introduced by **Anatol Rapoport** in the context of the **Prisoner's Dilemma**, it has been widely used to study **reciprocity, trust, and the evolution of cooperation** in biological and social systems.

The **Tit-for-Tat strategy** follows four simple rules:

1. **Start by cooperating.**

2. **If the opponent cooperates, continue cooperating.**

3. **If the opponent defects, retaliate by defecting in the next round.**

4. **Be forgiving—return to cooperation if the opponent cooperates again.**

This strategy ensures **mutual cooperation while discouraging exploitation,** making it a powerful **evolutionarily stable strategy (ESS)** in repeated interactions.

Example of Tit-for-Tat in Evolution

Consider two animals engaging in mutual grooming:

Round	Animal A's Action	Animal B's Response	Outcome
1	Cooperates (grooms)	Cooperates	Both benefit
2	Cooperates	Defects (doesn't groom back)	A suffers, B gains
3	Defects (stops grooming)	Defects	Mutual loss
4	Cooperates (tests trust)	Cooperates again	Cooperation restored

- **If both animals follow Tit-for-Tat, cooperation persists over time.**

- **If one defects, the other retaliates, discouraging further defection.**

- **Forgiveness allows relationships to rebuild after occasional mistakes.**

Since **cooperation leads to long-term benefits**, Tit-for-Tat **outperforms purely selfish strategies in repeated interactions.**

Why It Works

The **Tit-for-Tat strategy works because:**

- **It is nice (starts with cooperation), encouraging trust.**
- **It is retaliatory, discouraging exploitation.**
- **It is forgiving, allowing relationships to recover from mistakes.**
- **It is clear and predictable, making interactions stable.**

How It Works

1. **Two players interact repeatedly in a game (e.g., trade, social behaviour).**
2. **They start by cooperating, but respond based on the opponent's previous move.**
3. **If the opponent cooperates, cooperation continues.**
4. **If the opponent defects, retaliation occurs until cooperation is restored.**

Applications of Tit-for-Tat in Evolution

1. **Animal Cooperation** – Birds, primates, and fish engage in reciprocal grooming and food sharing.
2. **Human Social Behaviour** – People cooperate based on trust and reciprocity.

3. **Business Negotiations** – Companies engage in fair trade but retaliate against unfair deals.

4. **International Relations** – Countries use reciprocal diplomacy but impose sanctions in response to violations.

Key Insights

1. **Tit-for-Tat fosters long-term cooperation while deterring exploitation.**

2. **A balance of cooperation and retaliation stabilizes relationships.**

3. **Forgiveness prevents endless cycles of retaliation, maintaining harmony.**

4. **In nature and society, reciprocity is a powerful force for cooperation.**

Final Thoughts

The **Tit-for-Tat strategy** explains why **cooperation evolves in repeated interactions.** By balancing **kindness, retaliation, and forgiveness**, it ensures that **trust and cooperation remain stable over time**, making it a fundamental mechanism in both nature and human societies.

53 Altruism vs. Selfishness Game

Altruism vs. Selfishness Game in Game Theory

Breakdown of the Theory

The **Altruism vs. Selfishness Game** in **game theory and evolutionary biology** explores the strategic interaction between **cooperative (altruistic) and self-interested (selfish) individuals**. It examines how **selfish behaviour can lead to short-term individual gains but long-term instability**, while **altruism can foster group success at a personal cost**.

This model helps explain **social cooperation, economic behaviour, and evolutionary strategies**, where players must decide **whether to act in the interest of the group or prioritize personal benefits**.

Key assumptions of the **Altruism vs. Selfishness Game**:

1. **Two types of players exist: Altruists (who cooperate) and Selfish individuals (who exploit cooperation).**

2. **Altruists sacrifice personal gains for group benefit, while selfish individuals maximize their own gain.**

3. **If too many selfish players exist, cooperation collapses, leading to collective failure.**

4. **Reputation and repeated interactions influence players' strategies over time.**

Since **cooperation benefits the group but can be exploited by selfish individuals,** the game explores how **societies balance self-interest with collective well-being.**

Example of the Altruism vs. Selfishness Game

Consider **a workplace team project** where employees can either **work hard (altruism) or slack off (selfishness).**

Scenario	Altruist's Action	Selfish Player's Action	Outcome
1	Works hard	Works hard	Project succeeds, fair reward distribution
2	Works hard	Slacks off	Selfish player benefits, altruist is overworked
3	Slacks off	Slacks off	Project fails, both lose

- **If everyone works hard, the project succeeds, and all benefit.**

- **If altruists work while selfish players slack off, selfish individuals gain without effort.**

- **If too many players are selfish, cooperation collapses, leading to failure.**

Since **selfishness provides individual advantages in the short term,** but **group success depends on cooperation,** societies develop **social norms, punishments, and reputation systems** to sustain altruism.

Why It Works

The **Altruism vs. Selfishness Game works because:**

- **Self-interest drives short-term exploitation of cooperation.**

- **Repeated interactions and reputation create incentives for cooperation.**

- **Societies develop punishments and rewards to balance cooperation.**

How It Works

1. **Players choose between altruism (helping others) or selfishness (maximizing personal gain).**

2. **If enough players cooperate, the group thrives; if too many act selfishly, the system collapses.**

3. **Repeated interactions reinforce either cooperation (trust) or exploitation (mistrust).**

4. **Mechanisms like punishment, reputation, or reciprocal altruism sustain cooperation.**

Applications of the Altruism vs. Selfishness Game

1. **Workplace Teamwork** – Employees contribute or free-ride on others' efforts.

2. **Public Goods & Taxation** – Citizens either pay taxes (altruism) or evade them (selfishness).

3. **Environmental Sustainability** – People either conserve resources or overuse them.

4. **Economic & Social Policies** – Welfare systems balance helping the needy vs. preventing exploitation.

Key Insights

1. **Altruism sustains cooperation, but selfishness can destabilize groups.**

2. **Reputation and social norms influence long-term cooperative behaviour.**

3. **Punishment or incentives are necessary to prevent excessive selfishness.**

4. **A balance of self-interest and cooperation leads to stable societies.**

Final Thoughts

The **Altruism vs. Selfishness Game** explains why **societies, businesses, and ecosystems must balance cooperation with individual incentives.** Understanding these dynamics **helps create strategies to sustain trust, prevent exploitation, and ensure long-term success.**

54 Mutualism Game

Mutualism Game in Game Theory

Breakdown of the Theory

The **Mutualism Game** in **game theory and evolutionary biology** explores how **cooperative interactions between individuals or species lead to mutual benefits**. Unlike **zero-sum games**, where one player's gain is another's loss, **mutualism results in a win-win situation** where both participants benefit from cooperation.

Mutualism is essential in **nature, business, and economics**, demonstrating how **partnerships, alliances, and symbiotic relationships evolve and sustain over time**. The key challenge is ensuring that **both players benefit sufficiently to continue cooperation**, preventing exploitation.

Key assumptions of the **Mutualism Game**:

1. **Two or more players interact in a cooperative relationship.**

2. **Both players receive a benefit greater than what they would achieve alone.**

3. **If one player defects (stops cooperating), the mutual benefit disappears.**

4. **Repeated interactions reinforce trust and cooperation.**

Since **mutualism relies on cooperation**, both players must ensure that the **relationship remains beneficial and fair** to sustain long-term success.

Example of the Mutualism Game

Consider **bees and flowers** in an ecological mutualism relationship:

Scenario	Bee's Action	Flower's Action	Outcome
1	Pollinates flower	Produces nectar	Both benefit (sustained mutualism)
2	Pollinates flower	Stops producing nectar	Bee switches to another flower
3	Avoids flower	Produces nectar	No pollination, flower fails to reproduce

- **If the bee pollinates and the flower provides nectar, both thrive.**

- **If the flower stops providing nectar, bees stop visiting, disrupting the cycle.**

- **If bees stop pollinating, flowers fail to reproduce, leading to a loss for both.**

Since **both parties depend on each other**, mutualism remains stable as long as **cooperation continues to be beneficial**.

Why It Works

The **Mutualism Game works because**:

- **Both players gain more from cooperation than acting alone.**

- **Long-term stability encourages continued participation.**

- **Breaking cooperation leads to losses, reinforcing mutual dependence.**

How It Works

1. **Players engage in cooperative interactions, expecting reciprocal benefits.**

2. **If the cooperation is sustained, both players thrive.**

3. **If one player defects, the mutual benefit disappears, leading to failure.**

4. **Repeated cooperation builds trust and reinforces mutual dependence.**

Applications of the Mutualism Game

1. **Business Partnerships** – Companies form alliances to share resources and markets.

2. **Trade Agreements** – Countries engage in mutual trade to maximize economic gains.

3. **Symbiotic Relationships in Nature** – Clownfish and sea anemones protect and support each other.

4. **Digital Platforms & Users** – Social media platforms provide free services while benefiting from user data.

Key Insights

1. **Mutualism creates win-win situations, fostering stability.**

2. **Both players must continue benefiting to sustain cooperation.**

3. **Defection (one side withdrawing cooperation) leads to mutual losses.**

4. **Long-term interactions reinforce trust and strengthen partnerships.**

Final Thoughts

The **Mutualism Game** explains how **cooperation evolves and sustains in nature, business, and economics**. By ensuring **fair and continuous benefits**, mutualistic relationships **maximize gains for all participants**, leading to **long-term stability and success**.

55 Predator-Prey Game

Predator-Prey Game in Game Theory

Breakdown of the Theory

The **Predator-Prey Game** in **game theory and evolutionary biology** models the strategic interaction between **predators and prey**, where each side adapts behaviours to maximize survival and success. The game represents a classic **asymmetric conflict**, where:

- **The predator** aims to **capture and consume prey** for survival.

- **The prey** aims to **evade the predator** to avoid being eaten.

Both players continuously **adapt and evolve strategies** to outcompete the other. If **prey become too efficient at escaping**, predators starve. If **predators become too efficient at hunting**, prey populations collapse, eventually leading to the predator's downfall. The balance between these strategies ensures **coexistence and evolutionary stability**.

Key assumptions of the **Predator-Prey Game**:

1. **Predators and prey are in constant strategic competition.**

2. **Each side evolves adaptations to improve success (hunting or escaping).**

3. **The fitness of each species depends on the strategies they adopt.**

4. **If one side gains a large advantage, the ecosystem can become unstable.**

Since **evolution favours strategies that maximize survival**, both predators and prey engage in a continuous **"arms race" of adaptation**.

Example of the Predator-Prey Game

Consider **cheetahs (predators) and gazelles (prey)** in the wild:

Scenario	Cheetah's Strategy	Gazelle's Strategy	Outcome
1	Runs fast	Runs even faster	Gazelle escapes, cheetah fails to catch prey.
2	Hunts in groups	Uses unpredictable movement	Hunt success varies, maintaining balance.
3	Becomes stronger but slower	Uses agility to dodge	Gazelle outmanoeuvres the cheetah.

- If gazelles evolve to run faster, cheetahs must also evolve speed to keep up.

- If cheetahs become too strong and successful, gazelle populations decline, reducing food availability.

- A balanced adaptation ensures both species survive in the ecosystem.

Since **prey have a stronger survival incentive than predators (since failure means death),** they often **evolve more sophisticated evasion tactics** than predators evolve hunting skills.

Why It Works

The **Predator-Prey Game works because:**

- Both players are locked in an evolutionary arms race, ensuring adaptation.

- Neither side can afford to be too successful without causing instability.

- Trade-offs exist (e.g., speed vs. endurance) that prevent one side from dominating.

How It Works

1. Predators optimize hunting tactics to increase capture success.

2. Prey evolve escape mechanisms to avoid predation.

3. Each adaptation forces the other side to counter-adapt.

4. Over time, the system stabilizes with balanced survival rates.

Applications of the Predator-Prey Game

1. **Cybersecurity** – Hackers (predators) develop new attacks, while security systems (prey) evolve defences.

2. **Business Competition** – Established companies (predators) try to dominate, while startups (prey) innovate to survive.

3. **Military Strategy** – Nations develop weapons (predators) while others develop countermeasures (prey).

4. **Financial Markets** – Traders (predators) exploit opportunities, while regulators (prey) impose new restrictions.

Key Insights

1. Predators and prey must continuously adapt to maintain stability.

2. Prey often evolve more sophisticated strategies because survival is absolute.

3. An imbalance (too many predators or too few prey) leads to system collapse.

4. The arms race principle applies beyond nature to business, security, and geopolitics.

Final Thoughts

The **Predator-Prey Game** explains how **competition drives continuous adaptation and survival**. Whether in **nature, business, or cybersecurity, coexistence depends on maintaining balance**, ensuring that **neither side becomes too dominant**.

56 Mimicry Game

Mimicry Game in Game Theory

Breakdown of the Theory

The **Mimicry Game** in **game theory and evolutionary biology** examines how one player **imitates another** to gain a strategic advantage. Mimicry can be seen in **nature, business, and social interactions**, where individuals or organizations **copy the traits, actions, or behaviours of more successful players** to survive, deceive, or gain a competitive edge.

This game explains **why mimicry evolves and when it succeeds or fails** based on the interactions between:

1. **The mimic** – An individual or entity that copies another for advantage.

2. **The model** – The original that is being imitated.

3. **The observer** – The entity (predator, customer, regulator) that reacts to the mimic and model.

Mimicry can be:

- **Batesian Mimicry** – A harmless player copies a dangerous one (e.g., a non-toxic butterfly resembling a poisonous species).

- **Müllerian Mimicry** – Two harmful players mimic each other to reinforce a signal (e.g., multiple poisonous species looking alike).

- **Aggressive Mimicry** – A predator or parasite mimics something harmless to deceive prey (e.g., an anglerfish's lure).

Key assumptions of the **Mimicry Game**:

1. **Observers (predators, consumers, regulators) make decisions based on perceived traits.**

2. **Mimics benefit by copying successful or threatening models.**

3. **If too many mimics exist, the strategy becomes less effective.**

4. **Models may evolve countermeasures to distinguish themselves from mimics.**

Since **mimicry exploits perception**, it thrives when **observers cannot easily verify authenticity.**

Example of the Mimicry Game

Consider **poisonous coral snakes (model) and non-venomous king snakes (mimic):**

Scenario	Predator Encounters Coral Snake	Predator Encounters King Snake	Outcome
1	Recognizes as venomous and avoids	Mistakes for coral snake, avoids	Mimicry succeeds, king snake survives.

Scenario	Predator Encounters Coral Snake	Predator Encounters King Snake	Outcome
2	Attacks coral snake, gets poisoned	Attacks king snake, realizes it's harmless	Mimicry weakens if predators learn to differentiate.

- If predators avoid coral snakes, king snakes benefit without needing actual venom.

- If too many king snakes exist, predators may learn to distinguish and attack them.

- Over time, the effectiveness of mimicry depends on the ratio of mimics to models.

Since **mimicry relies on deception**, it **works best when mimics are rare but fails if overused.**

Why It Works

The **Mimicry Game works because:**

- Observers rely on quick pattern recognition, not deep verification.

- Copying successful traits provides immediate survival advantages.

- Mimics exploit the cost-benefit trade-off of avoiding potential risks.

How It Works

1. A mimic copies the traits of a successful model.

2. An observer reacts based on perceived similarity.

3. If mimicry succeeds, the mimic gains protection or advantage.

4. If mimics become too common, observers adapt, weakening the strategy.

Applications of the Mimicry Game

1. **Biology & Evolution** – Non-toxic species copy toxic ones to avoid predators.

2. **Business & Marketing** – Generic brands imitate premium products to attract buyers.

3. **Cybersecurity** – Hackers mimic trusted sources (phishing emails) to deceive users.

4. **Military Strategy** – Decoy tactics and camouflage mislead enemies.

Key Insights

1. Mimicry is most effective when mimics are rare.

2. Observers adapt over time, forcing mimics to evolve.

3. Mimicry can be defensive (avoiding predators) or aggressive (tricking prey).

4. **Successful mimicry depends on balancing deception and detection.**

Final Thoughts

The **Mimicry Game** explains how **deception and adaptation shape evolution, competition, and strategy.** Whether in **nature, business, or security**, successful mimicry **exploits perception but must evolve to remain effective.**

57 Parasite-Host Game

Parasite-Host Game in Game Theory

Breakdown of the Theory

The **Parasite-Host Game** in **game theory and evolutionary biology** models the strategic interactions between **a parasite (exploiter) and a host (resource provider).** In this relationship, the **parasite benefits by extracting resources from the host, while the host suffers harm**. However, the parasite must **balance exploitation** to avoid killing its host, which would threaten its own survival.

This game represents an **evolutionary arms race**, where:

1. **The parasite evolves strategies to maximize resource extraction while minimizing detection.**

2. **The host evolves defences to minimize damage or eliminate the parasite.**

3. **If the parasite becomes too aggressive, it risks host extinction, leading to its own downfall.**

4. **If the host becomes too resistant, it may waste resources on costly defences, reducing its overall fitness.**

The **optimal strategy** for both players is an **evolutionarily stable strategy (ESS)**, where both species **coexist in a dynamic balance.**

Example of the Parasite-Host Game

Consider **malaria-causing Plasmodium (parasite) and humans (host)**:

Scenario	Parasite's Strategy	Host's Response	Outcome
1	Low replication rate	Mild immune response	Long-term parasite survival, moderate host harm.
2	High replication rate	Strong immune response	Severe disease, possible parasite eradication.
3	Extreme exploitation	Host death	Parasite extinction along with the host.

- **If Plasmodium replicates at a moderate rate**, it avoids triggering a fatal immune response, ensuring its long-term survival.

- **If it replicates too aggressively**, the host's immune system may respond strongly, eliminating the infection.

- **If it becomes too extreme, the host dies, removing the parasite's environment for reproduction.**

Since **parasites rely on host survival,** evolution favours strategies that allow **long-term parasitic success without destroying the host population.**

Why It Works

The **Parasite-Host Game works because:**

- **Parasites must balance resource extraction with host survival.**

- **Hosts must balance immunity costs with the need for other survival functions.**

- **Natural selection creates a co-evolutionary cycle, preventing one side from complete dominance.**

How It Works

1. **Parasites infect the host, aiming to maximize replication.**

2. **Hosts detect parasites and activate immune responses.**

3. **If the parasite is too aggressive, the host may die or resist future infections.**

4. **A stable relationship emerges where the parasite thrives without killing the host.**

Applications of the Parasite-Host Game

1. **Infectious Disease Control** – Understanding how pathogens evolve resistance to treatments.

2. **Agricultural Pests** – Managing crop diseases without overusing pesticides.

3. **Cybersecurity** – Malware (parasites) evolve to avoid detection while extracting data.

4. **Business Exploitation** – Companies (parasites) using resources from industries (hosts) without fully collapsing the market.

Key Insights

1. **Parasites and hosts are locked in an evolutionary arms race.**

2. **Excessive parasitism risks host extinction, ultimately harming the parasite.**

3. **Hosts evolve countermeasures, but extreme resistance can be costly.**

4. **A balance between exploitation and survival ensures long-term stability.**

Final Thoughts

The **Parasite-Host Game** explains how **evolution shapes the balance between exploitation and resistance**. Whether in **biology, business, or cybersecurity**, this model highlights the importance of **sustained interactions, adaptation, and strategic survival** in competitive environments.

58 Flocking Behaviour Game

Flocking Behaviour Game in Game Theory

Breakdown of the Theory

The **Flocking Behaviour Game** in **game theory and behavioural ecology** models how individuals in a group coordinate their movements to maximize survival, efficiency, or other benefits. It is particularly relevant in **animal swarms, human crowds, and artificial intelligence (AI) systems**, where local decision-making influences global group behaviour.

Flocking behaviour follows **self-organizing principles**, where individuals make **simple decisions based on the actions of their neighbours**. The game focuses on **how cooperation emerges without central control**, balancing **individual freedom** with **group cohesion**.

Key assumptions of the **Flocking Behaviour Game**:

1. **Players (individuals in a group) base their actions on local information.**

2. **Coordination increases survival or efficiency, but too much uniformity can reduce adaptability.**

3. **There is a trade-off between sticking together (safety) and exploring independently (resources).**

4. **The group dynamically adjusts based on external threats, obstacles, or resources.**

Since **flocking emerges from local interactions**, this game provides insights into **collective intelligence and decentralized decision-making**.

Example of the Flocking Behaviour Game

Consider a **school of fish** avoiding predators:

Scenario	Fish Strategy	Group Response	Outcome
1	Stays with the group	Group remains cohesive	Predators struggle to target individuals (safety in numbers).
2	Moves independently	School loses cohesion	Predator easily picks off stray individuals.
3	Adapts direction based on nearest fish	Cohesion and adaptability maintained	Group remains safe and mobile.

- **If fish stay together, predators struggle to attack a single target.**
- **If individuals stray too far, they risk being caught.**

- If all fish move identically, they lose flexibility to respond to new threats.

Since **flocking behaviour dynamically adjusts based on local cues**, it balances **protection, exploration, and responsiveness**.

Why It Works

The **Flocking Behaviour Game works because**:

- **Local decision-making leads to emergent coordination without central control.**

- **Staying in a group reduces individual risk from predators.**

- **Balancing cohesion with adaptability improves long-term survival.**

How It Works

1. **Each player follows simple rules: stay close, avoid collisions, and match neighbours.**

2. **Group-level patterns emerge from these local decisions.**

3. **If individuals break formation, the group becomes vulnerable.**

4. **Adaptive strategies maintain cohesion while allowing flexibility.**

Applications of the Flocking Behaviour Game

1. **Animal Behaviour** – Birds, fish, and insects use flocking for defence and migration.

2. **Human Crowds** – Pedestrians in busy areas unconsciously follow similar movement rules.

3. **Robotics & AI** – Swarm intelligence algorithms help drones coordinate without central control.

4. **Traffic Flow** – Understanding collective movement optimizes road and pedestrian design.

Key Insights

1. **Decentralized decision-making leads to emergent group behaviour.**

2. **Flocking increases safety but requires adaptability.**

3. **Simple rules at the individual level create complex coordination at the group level.**

4. **The balance between cohesion and flexibility determines success.**

Final Thoughts

The **Flocking Behaviour Game** explains how **self-organizing systems emerge without central planning**. Whether in **nature, human crowds, or artificial intelligence**, understanding flocking dynamics helps **optimize coordination, improve efficiency, and enhance survival in dynamic environments**.

59 Genetic Selection Game

Genetic Selection Game in Game Theory

Breakdown of the Theory

The **Genetic Selection Game** in **game theory and evolutionary biology** models how **genetic traits spread or disappear in a population** based on their impact on reproductive success. This game explains why **some genes become dominant while others fade out**, influenced by **natural selection, mutation, competition, and cooperation**.

Unlike traditional strategic games, where players make conscious decisions, **the "players" in this game are genes** competing for survival through natural selection. The **payoff** is reproductive success—genes that **increase survival and reproduction** are more likely to persist across generations.

Key assumptions of the **Genetic Selection Game**:

1. **Genes act as players, competing for survival within a population.**

2. **Traits that enhance survival or reproduction are naturally selected.**

3. **Harmful traits disappear over generations unless linked to another advantage.**

4. **The environment influences which traits are favourable or unfavourable.**

Since **evolution operates through trial and error**, genetic selection follows a **dynamic process of adaptation,** shaping the biological diversity we see today.

Example of the Genetic Selection Game

Consider **a population of rabbits** with two genetic traits: **fast runners (A) and slow runners (B)**.

Scenario	Trait A (Fast Runners)	Trait B (Slow Runners)	Outcome
1	Survive predator attacks	More likely to be caught	More fast rabbits in future generations.
2	Use more energy for speed	Conserve energy but face higher risk	Trade-off between speed and endurance.
3	If predators disappear	No advantage for speed	Both traits may coexist.

- **If predators are common, fast-running rabbits (A) survive and reproduce more, increasing their gene frequency.**

- **If there's no predation, speed may lose its advantage, allowing both traits to persist.**

- **Natural selection ensures that the most beneficial traits become dominant over time.**

Since **environmental pressures change over time,** genetic selection is a **continuous and dynamic process.**

Why It Works

The **Genetic Selection Game works because:**

- **Genes that provide advantages spread through natural selection.**

- **Environmental changes continuously shape which traits are beneficial.**

- **Genetic diversity allows populations to adapt and survive over time.**

How It Works

1. **Random mutations introduce genetic variations in a population.**

2. **Individuals with beneficial traits reproduce more successfully.**

3. **Over generations, these traits become more common.**

4. **If the environment changes, different traits may become advantageous.**

Applications of the Genetic Selection Game

1. **Evolutionary Biology** – Understanding how species adapt to environmental changes.

2. **Medicine & Genetics** – Studying how genetic traits influence disease resistance.

3. **Artificial Selection** – Breeding plants and animals for desirable traits.

4. **Artificial Intelligence** – Genetic algorithms mimic evolution to optimize machine learning models.

Key Insights

1. **Genetic selection follows survival-of-the-fittest principles.**

2. **Environmental factors influence which traits persist.**

3. **Harmful traits disappear unless they offer hidden advantages.**

4. **Evolution is an ongoing process, constantly shaping genetic diversity.**

Final Thoughts

The **Genetic Selection Game** explains how **traits evolve through natural selection**, influencing **biodiversity, adaptation, and survival strategies**. Whether in **biology, medicine, or AI**, understanding genetic selection helps us **predict evolutionary trends and optimize complex systems**.

Social Dilemmas & Group Behaviour

60 Tragedy of the Commons

Tragedy of the Commons in Game Theory

Breakdown of the Theory

The **Tragedy of the Commons** is a fundamental concept in **game theory and economics** that describes how individuals, acting in their **own self-interest**, can deplete a shared resource, leading to negative outcomes for the entire group. The game demonstrates how **rational individual choices can lead to collective irrationality**, resulting in overconsumption and eventual resource depletion.

The concept was popularized by **Garrett Hardin (1968)** and applies to various real-world scenarios, such as **overfishing, deforestation, air pollution, and climate change**.

Key assumptions of the **Tragedy of the Commons Game**:

1. **A shared, finite resource exists (e.g., land, water, atmosphere).**

2. **Individuals act in their own self-interest to maximize personal benefit.**

3. **Overuse of the resource leads to depletion or collapse.**

4. **Without regulation or cooperation, long-term sustainability is impossible.**

Since **no single individual has an incentive to conserve,** the result is **resource exhaustion unless external interventions or agreements are in place.**

Example of the Tragedy of the Commons Game

Consider **a group of fishers** sharing a lake with a **limited fish population**:

Scenario	Fisher's Strategy	Group Outcome	Long-Term Effect
1	Catches a sustainable amount	Fish population remains stable	Resource is preserved.
2	Overfishes to maximize profit	Fish population declines	Future shortages occur.
3	Everyone overfishes	Fish population collapses	No fish left for future generations.

- **If all fishers cooperate and take only sustainable amounts, the lake remains productive.**
- **If one fisher overexploits, they benefit short-term while others suffer.**

- If everyone overfishes, the entire system collapses, leading to long-term losses.

Since **self-interest drives immediate gains**, the game highlights the challenge of **long-term collective responsibility**.

Why It Works

The **Tragedy of the Commons Game works because**:

- Individuals act rationally to maximize short-term benefits.

- Shared resources lack clear ownership, leading to overuse.

- Without coordination, depletion occurs faster than replenishment.

How It Works

1. Each player makes an independent decision on resource use.

2. Short-term incentives encourage overuse.

3. Resource depletion leads to long-term negative consequences.

4. The only solutions involve cooperation, regulation, or privatization.

Applications of the Tragedy of the Commons

1. **Environmental Issues** – Climate change, overfishing, and deforestation.

2. **Public Goods & Infrastructure** – Traffic congestion, water shortages.

3. **Digital & Data Usage** – Bandwidth overuse in shared networks.

4. **Economic Policy** – Managing inflation and government budgets.

Key Insights

1. **Individual rationality can lead to collective failure.**

2. **Without regulation or cooperation, shared resources are overexploited.**

3. **Solutions involve governance, incentives, and social norms.**

4. **The balance between short-term gains and long-term sustainability is crucial.**

Final Thoughts

The **Tragedy of the Commons** explains why **shared resources are often depleted due to individual self-interest**. Understanding this game helps in designing **policies, regulations, and cooperative solutions** that ensure **long-term sustainability and prevent resource collapse.**

61 Free Rider Problem

Free Rider Problem in Game Theory

Breakdown of the Theory

The **Free Rider Problem** in **game theory and economics** occurs when individuals benefit from a shared resource or public good without contributing to its cost. Since **public goods are non-excludable and non-rivalrous**, rational individuals have an incentive to **free ride**, meaning they **avoid paying while still enjoying the benefits**. This leads to **under-provision or depletion of resources**, causing inefficiencies and potential system failure.

The **core dilemma** is that **everyone benefits from public goods, but if too many free ride, the good may not be produced or maintained**. Examples include **public parks, national defence, clean air, and community services**.

Key assumptions of the **Free Rider Problem Game**:

1. **A public good exists that benefits all members of a group.**

2. **Contributions are voluntary, and individuals decide whether to pay or free ride.**

3. **If too many free ride, the good is underfunded or disappears.**

4. **The rational choice for individuals is often to free ride, even if it harms the group.**

Since **self-interest drives free-riding behaviour**, societies must develop **incentives, regulations, or social norms** to maintain public goods.

Example of the Free Rider Problem Game

Consider **a neighbourhood security system** that benefits all residents:

Scenario	Resident's Choice	Outcome for the Group	Long-Term Effect
1	Pays for security	The system is funded and benefits all.	Safety improves.
2	Free rides (doesn't pay)	Still benefits from security but doesn't contribute.	Others bear the cost.
3	Many free ride	The system lacks funding and collapses.	Security disappears.

- **If everyone contributes, the system remains effective.**

- **If some free ride, they still benefit while others pay.**

272

- **If too many free ride, funding collapses, and the system fails.**

Since **public goods require collective contributions,** free riding **threatens their sustainability.**

Why It Works

The **Free Rider Problem works because:**

- **Individuals benefit from public goods whether or not they contribute.**

- **Rational self-interest leads to under-contribution.**

- **Without intervention, public goods may disappear due to lack of funding.**

How It Works

1. **A public good is available to all individuals.**

2. **Each individual decides whether to contribute or free ride.**

3. **If enough people contribute, the good is sustained.**

4. **If too many free ride, the good is underfunded and eventually disappears.**

Applications of the Free Rider Problem

1. **Taxation & Public Services** – Some people evade taxes but still benefit from public infrastructure.

2. **Environmental Conservation** – Countries benefit from climate policies but may avoid costly participation.

3. **Open-Source Software** – Users benefit from free software without contributing to development.

4. **Workplace Team Projects** – Some employees contribute less but still share credit for success.

Key Insights

1. **Free riding leads to inefficiencies and resource under-provision.**

2. **Social norms, regulations, and incentives are needed to ensure fair contributions.**

3. **Public goods require coordination to avoid collapse.**

4. **The challenge is balancing individual rationality with collective well-being.**

Final Thoughts

The **Free Rider Problem** explains why **voluntary contributions to public goods are often insufficient**, risking underfunding and failure. Understanding this game helps in designing **policies, incentives, and regulations** that encourage **fair contributions and long-term sustainability**.

62 Coordination Game

Coordination Game in Game Theory

Breakdown of the Theory

The **Coordination Game** in **game theory** models situations where players benefit most by aligning their choices with others. Unlike conflict-based games like the **Prisoner's Dilemma**, where incentives push players toward defection, the **Coordination Game** rewards mutual cooperation.

The core idea is that **multiple equilibrium points exist**, meaning different outcomes can be stable depending on how players coordinate. The challenge is selecting the **best strategy when multiple beneficial outcomes exist**.

Key assumptions of the **Coordination Game**:

1. **Players prefer to match their choices rather than act independently.**

2. **There are multiple stable equilibria, but some may be more beneficial than others.**

3. **Players may struggle to coordinate if communication is limited.**

4. **Social norms, expectations, or signals can help establish coordination.**

Since **coordination problems appear in everyday life**, this game explains **how people, businesses, and societies align their actions to maximize benefits**.

Example of the Coordination Game

Consider **two friends choosing where to meet**:

Scenario	Friend A's Choice	Friend B's Choice	Outcome
1	Coffee shop	Coffee shop	Both meet, happy outcome.
2	Coffee shop	Library	They fail to meet, wasted effort.
3	Library	Library	Both meet, happy outcome.

- **If both choose the same location, they coordinate successfully.**

- **If they choose different places, coordination fails, leading to no meeting.**

- **Both coffee shop and library are valid coordination points, but agreement is required.**

Since **successful coordination leads to mutual benefits**, players must develop **expectations, norms, or signals** to align their choices.

Why It Works

The **Coordination Game works because:**

- **Players share an interest in matching decisions, reducing conflict.**

- **Past experiences, cultural norms, or communication help establish coordination.**

- **The best equilibrium depends on shared understanding and expectations.**

How It Works

1. **Players independently decide their actions.**

2. **If they coordinate, both receive a high payoff.**

3. **If they fail to coordinate, the payoff is low or zero.**

4. **Repetition, communication, or shared history improves coordination over time.**

Applications of the Coordination Game

1. **Traffic Systems** – Driving on the same side of the road prevents accidents.

2. **Business Standards** – Companies adopt common protocols (e.g., USB, Wi-Fi) for compatibility.

3. **Social Norms & Language** – Common words and customs ensure understanding.

4. **Technology Adoption** – Users coordinate to adopt dominant platforms (e.g., iOS vs. Android).

Key Insights

1. Mutual benefit drives players to coordinate.

2. Multiple stable outcomes exist, but choosing the best one is challenging.

3. Cultural norms, signals, or communication help solve coordination problems.

4. Lack of coordination leads to inefficiencies or missed opportunities.

Final Thoughts

The **Coordination Game** explains how **people and organizations align their actions to maximize collective benefits**. Whether in **traffic rules, business standards, or technology adoption**, successful coordination ensures efficiency, compatibility, and shared success.

63 Snowdrift Game

Snowdrift Game in Game Theory

Breakdown of the Theory

The **Snowdrift Game** (also known as the **Driveway Dilemma**) in **game theory** models scenarios where cooperation is beneficial, but some level of selfishness can still be rewarded. It differs from the **Prisoner's Dilemma**, where mutual defection leads to the worst outcome. In the **Snowdrift Game**, even if one player refuses to cooperate, the other can still act, ensuring that at least some benefit is achieved.

The game is named after a situation where **two drivers are trapped on opposite sides of a snowdrift**:

- If **both shovel**, they share the effort and clear the road.

- If **one shovels while the other waits**, the snow is cleared, but the non-shovelling driver benefits without effort (free-riding).

- If **neither shovels**, both remain stuck.

Key assumptions of the **Snowdrift Game**:

1. **Cooperation benefits both players, but individual costs exist.**

2. **A selfish player can still benefit if the other cooperates.**

3. **Mutual cooperation is best, but a mix of cooperation and defection can be stable.**

4. **Unlike the Prisoner's Dilemma, defection does not always result in the worst outcome.**

Since **selfish behaviour is rewarded only if someone cooperates**, the game explains why **cooperation persists even when free-riding is possible**.

Example of the Snowdrift Game

Consider **two roommates cleaning their shared apartment:**

Scenario	Roommate A's Choice	Roommate B's Choice	Outcome
1	Cleans	Cleans	Shared work, clean apartment (best outcome).
2	Cleans	Does nothing	One does all the work, both benefit.
3	Does nothing	Cleans	The other does all the work, both benefit.
4	Does nothing	Does nothing	Apartment stays dirty (worst outcome).

- **If both clean, they share the burden equally.**

- **If one refuses, the other still benefits but at a personal cost.**

- **If neither cleans, both suffer.**

Since **at least one party must act to avoid the worst-case scenario**, players face a **trade-off between personal effort and shared benefit**.

Why It Works

The **Snowdrift Game works because**:

- **Cooperation is rewarded, but free-riding is sometimes beneficial.**

- **Unlike the Prisoner's Dilemma, someone always benefits unless both refuse to act.**

- **Stable cooperation exists even if some players free-ride.**

How It Works

1. **Players choose to cooperate (share effort) or defect (free-ride).**

2. **If one cooperates, both benefit, even if the other defects.**

3. **Mutual cooperation leads to the best outcome, but defection is not as harmful as in other dilemmas.**

4. **Over time, a balance between cooperation and free-riding emerges.**

Applications of the Snowdrift Game

1. **Climate Change Action** – Some countries reduce emissions while others free-ride.

2. **Workplace Effort** – Some employees work harder, while others contribute less but still benefit.

3. **Traffic & Public Infrastructure** – Some drivers carpool, reducing congestion, while others benefit without contributing.

4. **Scientific Research** – Some scientists do extensive work, while others benefit from shared knowledge without equal effort.

Key Insights

1. **Partial cooperation is better than mutual defection.**

2. **Unlike the Prisoner's Dilemma, free-riding does not always lead to the worst case.**

3. **A mix of cooperation and defection can be a stable outcome.**

4. **Incentives must balance effort-sharing to sustain long-term cooperation.**

Final Thoughts

The **Snowdrift Game** explains why **cooperation can persist even when free-riding is possible**. Unlike strict dilemmas where defection is dominant, the **presence of partial cooperation ensures that benefits are still shared**, making it a valuable model for understanding **real-world teamwork, public goods, and social behaviour.**

64 Network Effects Game

Network Effects Game in Game Theory

Breakdown of the Theory

The **Network Effects Game** in **game theory and economics** models how the value of a product, service, or platform increases as more people use it. Unlike traditional competitive games where players act independently, the **payoff in a network effects game depends on the number of participants**.

Network effects are **positive feedback loops**, meaning the **more users join, the more attractive the network becomes**. This leads to **self-reinforcing adoption cycles**, where early adoption can determine market dominance. However, **if adoption is too slow, a network can fail to reach critical mass**.

Key assumptions of the **Network Effects Game**:

1. **The benefit of using a product increases as more people use it.**

2. **Users decide whether to adopt or wait based on expectations of future growth.**

3. **Early adoption can trigger mass adoption, but hesitation can lead to network failure.**

4. **Multiple equilibria exist—either widespread adoption or total market failure.**

Since **users base their choices on expected participation,** network effects create **winner-take-all markets** where dominant players capture most users.

Example of the Network Effects Game

Consider **social media platforms (e.g., Facebook vs. a new competitor):**

Scenario	User's Choice	Network Growth	Outcome
1	Joins Facebook	Others also join	Strong network, high engagement.
2	Joins a new platform	Few others join	Platform fails due to low activity.
3	Waits before choosing	Slows down network growth	Potentially no platform reaches dominance.

- **If many users join Facebook, its value increases, making it harder for alternatives to succeed.**

- **If users hesitate to join a new platform, it struggles to reach critical mass and may fail.**

- **If early adopters drive momentum, a new platform can challenge the incumbent.**

Since **network success depends on critical mass**, users must predict **which network will prevail** before committing.

Why It Works

The **Network Effects Game works because**:

- **Users benefit from a larger network, creating a self-reinforcing loop.**
- **Market dominance often emerges due to early user momentum.**
- **If users misjudge adoption potential, some networks fail to grow.**

How It Works

1. **Users evaluate current and potential network size.**
2. **Early adopters influence later adopters by signalling viability.**
3. **If critical mass is reached, adoption accelerates.**
4. **If expectations are weak, the network fails before reaching scale.**

Applications of the Network Effects Game

1. **Social Media & Messaging Apps** – Facebook, WhatsApp, and Instagram succeed because users follow where their peers are.

2. **E-Commerce Platforms** – Buyers and sellers prefer established marketplaces (e.g., Amazon, eBay).

3. **Cryptocurrency & FinTech** – Adoption of Bitcoin and blockchain depends on user confidence and network effects.

4. **Video Game Consoles** – More players attract more developers, reinforcing platform dominance.

Key Insights

1. **Success depends on achieving critical mass— without it, networks fail.**

2. **Early adoption momentum influences later users.**

3. **Strong network effects create winner-take-all markets.**

4. **Switching costs (difficulty of changing platforms) reinforce dominance.**

Final Thoughts

The **Network Effects Game** explains why **platforms, social networks, and marketplaces grow exponentially once they gain momentum.** Understanding these dynamics helps businesses, startups, and policymakers **navigate adoption challenges, predict market winners, and create strategies for new technologies.**

65 Majority Rule Game

Majority Rule Game in Game Theory

Breakdown of the Theory

The **Majority Rule Game** in **game theory and political science** models decision-making in groups where the **majority determines the outcome**. This game is central to **democratic voting systems**, policy decisions, and collective choices, where individual preferences compete, but the majority's preference prevails.

Unlike **unanimity-based systems**, where all players must agree, **majority rule ensures decisions are made even if some players disagree**. The challenge in this game is **strategic voting**, coalition formation, and the potential for **majority tyranny**, where minority preferences are ignored.

Key assumptions of the **Majority Rule Game**:

1. **A group of players (voters) must choose between two or more options.**

2. **The option with the most votes wins, regardless of how strongly minorities oppose it.**

3. **Individuals may vote strategically rather than honestly.**

4. **Coalitions form to secure winning majorities.**

Since **players anticipate how others will vote**, they may adjust their strategies to maximize their preferred outcome.

Example of the Majority Rule Game

Consider **a town deciding whether to build a new park or a shopping mall**:

Scenario	Group A (60% of voters)	Group B (40% of voters)	Outcome
1	Votes for the park	Votes for the mall	Park is built (majority wins).
2	Votes for the mall	Votes for the park	Mall is built (majority wins).
3	Splits votes	Splits votes	Deadlock, no decision.

- **If a majority votes for the park, it is built, even if the minority strongly prefers the mall.**

- **If votes are evenly split, decision-making stagnates.**

- **Strategic coalitions may form to negotiate compromises.**

Since **winning requires securing majority support**, players may **influence undecided voters** or form **alliances to shift outcomes**.

Why It Works

The **Majority Rule Game works because**:

- **It simplifies decision-making by allowing a single winner.**

- **It provides a structured framework for resolving conflicts.**

- **Strategic behaviour influences outcomes, creating incentives for coalition-building.**

How It Works

1. **Players (voters) express preferences.**

2. **Each player considers their vote's impact based on others' choices.**

3. **The majority decision determines the outcome.**

4. **Players may form coalitions to ensure favourable results.**

Applications of the Majority Rule Game

1. **Democratic Elections** – Candidates win by securing over 50% of the vote.

2. **Corporate Governance** – Shareholder decisions rely on majority rule.

3. **Jury Trials** – Verdicts are often based on majority consensus.

4. **Legislative Decisions** – Laws and policies pass if they secure majority approval.

Key Insights

1. **Majority rule simplifies decision-making but can marginalize minority views.**

2. **Strategic voting and coalitions shape outcomes.**

3. **The system works best when minority rights are protected.**

4. **Polarization or deadlock can occur if majorities are unstable.**

Final Thoughts

The **Majority Rule Game** explains how **democracies, organizations, and groups make decisions efficiently,** though **strategic voting and coalition formation heavily influence outcomes.** Understanding this game helps in **politics, business, and group decision-making,** ensuring **fair and effective governance.**

66 Diffusion of Responsibility Game

Diffusion of Responsibility Game in Game Theory

Breakdown of the Theory

The **Diffusion of Responsibility Game** in **game theory and social psychology** models situations where individuals are **less likely to take action when responsibility is shared among a group**. The concept explains why people may **fail to intervene in emergencies, contribute to group tasks less, or assume others will take responsibility**.

This game is closely linked to the **"bystander effect"**, where the presence of more people **reduces individual accountability**. When responsibility is distributed, each player assumes that **someone else will act**, leading to **inaction or inefficiency**.

Key assumptions of the **Diffusion of Responsibility Game**:

1. **A group of players shares responsibility for taking action.**

2. **Each player prefers that someone else bears the cost of acting.**

3. **The more players involved, the less likely any individual is to act.**

4. **If no one acts, the group suffers collective failure.**

Since **players prefer to avoid personal costs**, this game highlights **why people hesitate in shared responsibility situations**.

Example of the Diffusion of Responsibility Game

Consider **a workplace where a critical report needs to be completed**:

Scenario	Employee A's Action	Employee B's Action	Outcome
1	Completes the report	Does nothing	The report is done, but A does all the work.
2	Does nothing	Completes the report	The report is done, but B does all the work.
3	Both do nothing	Both do nothing	The report is late, and both face consequences.

- **If one employee completes the task, the other benefits without effort.**
- **If both assume the other will do it, the task is not completed.**
- **The larger the group, the higher the chance of inaction due to diffusion.**

Since **responsibility is spread across multiple people**, individuals may **rationalize inaction, expecting others to step up**.

Why It Works

The **Diffusion of Responsibility Game works because**:

- **People assume others will act, reducing personal obligation.**
- **Avoiding effort or risk is rational when responsibility is shared.**
- **Larger groups increase uncertainty about who should act.**

How It Works

1. **A task or decision requires action.**
2. **Players assess whether others will take responsibility.**
3. **If one player acts, others may free-ride.**
4. **If no one acts, the task fails, harming the group.**

Applications of the Diffusion of Responsibility Game

1. **Emergency Situations** – Bystanders hesitate to help in large crowds.
2. **Corporate Teams** – Employees may assume someone else will take charge.

3. **Environmental Responsibility** – People delay action on climate change, expecting others to act first.

4. **Public Policy & Governance** – Governments may avoid action, assuming other nations will take the lead.

Key Insights

1. **The larger the group, the greater the diffusion of responsibility.**

2. **Without clear assignment, tasks are often neglected.**

3. **Free-riding behaviour emerges when responsibility is ambiguous.**

4. **Creating accountability structures prevents inaction.**

Final Thoughts

The **Diffusion of Responsibility Game** explains why **people often fail to act when responsibility is shared.** Understanding this game helps in **designing incentives, assigning clear roles, and ensuring accountability,** improving **group efficiency and decision-making.**

67 Social Norms Enforcement Game

Social Norms Enforcement Game in Game Theory

Breakdown of the Theory

The **Social Norms Enforcement Game** in **game theory and behavioural economics** models how individuals enforce, comply with, or violate societal norms. **Social norms** are **unwritten rules** that govern behaviour in communities, ranging from politeness and dress codes to legal compliance and ethical conduct.

This game examines **how societies maintain norms through incentives, punishments, or reputation effects**. If norms are followed, society remains stable. However, if violations go unpunished, compliance weakens, leading to **norm erosion**. The **key challenge** is ensuring **enforcement without excessive policing costs or collective inaction**.

Key assumptions of the **Social Norms Enforcement Game**:

1. **Norms exist that benefit society when followed.**

2. **Some individuals may break norms for personal gain (defectors).**

3. **Others (enforcers) must punish violators to maintain compliance.**

4. **If too few enforce norms, violators increase, leading to breakdown.**

Since **enforcement carries costs**, players must decide **whether to invest in upholding norms or free-ride on others' enforcement efforts**.

Example of the Social Norms Enforcement Game

Consider **a neighbourhood with an informal rule against littering**:

Scenario	Citizen A's Action	Citizen B's Action	Outcome
1	Reports littering	Reports littering	Norm stays strong, littering is minimized.
2	Reports littering	Does nothing	Norm remains, but A bears the cost.
3	Does nothing	Reports littering	Norm remains, but B bears the cost.
4	Does nothing	Does nothing	Littering increases, norm collapses.

- **If everyone reports violators, the rule is upheld.**

- **If only a few report, violators increase, testing the norm's strength.**

- **If no one reports, rule-breaking escalates, leading to norm collapse.**

Since **enforcing norms is costly (time, effort, or social backlash)**, people may **hesitate unless they believe others will also enforce.**

Why It Works

The **Social Norms Enforcement Game works because:**

- **Norm compliance depends on credible enforcement.**
- **Social incentives (reputation, peer pressure) motivate enforcement.**
- **If enforcement fails, norms deteriorate, reducing societal cohesion.**

How It Works

1. **A norm is established, benefiting the group.**
2. **Individuals decide whether to comply or defect.**
3. **Enforcers decide whether to punish defectors.**
4. **If punishment is consistent, compliance remains high.**
5. **If enforcement is weak, defectors increase, and the norm collapses.**

Applications of the Social Norms Enforcement Game

1. **Traffic Laws** – Speed limits are followed when violations are punished.

2. **Workplace Ethics** – Fraud is deterred when employees report misconduct.

3. **Environmental Regulations** – Recycling laws work when monitored.

4. **Public Behaviour** – Dress codes and etiquette norms persist through social pressure.

Key Insights

1. **Norms persist when enforcement is strong and visible.**

2. **Enforcement is costly, leading to free-rider problems.**

3. **Social pressure and reputation effects encourage compliance.**

4. **If violations go unchecked, norms deteriorate over time.**

Final Thoughts

The **Social Norms Enforcement Game** explains **how societies maintain order through informal and formal enforcement mechanisms.** Understanding this game helps in **designing better policies, strengthening cultural norms, and improving collective governance** to ensure long-term societal stability.

68 Reputation Game

Reputation Game in Game Theory

Breakdown of the Theory

The **Reputation Game** in **game theory and behavioural economics** models how individuals or businesses **build, maintain, or lose trust over time**. Reputation acts as a strategic asset, influencing **future interactions, negotiations, and market position**.

Unlike one-shot games, where actions have **immediate and isolated consequences**, the **Reputation Game involves repeated interactions**, where players consider how their current behaviour affects future opportunities. **Maintaining a good reputation incentivizes cooperation and ethical behaviour**, while **damaged reputations reduce trust and limit long-term gains**.

Key assumptions of the **Reputation Game**:

1. **Players interact repeatedly, and past actions influence future choices.**

2. **A good reputation provides advantages (trust, better deals, customer loyalty).**

3. **A bad reputation leads to lost opportunities and higher transaction costs.**

4. **Players may act dishonestly in the short term but risk long-term damage.**

Since **trust and credibility shape decision-making,** reputation becomes a **valuable strategic tool** in economics, business, and social interactions.

Example of the Reputation Game

Consider **an online seller on a marketplace like Amazon:**

Scenario	Seller's Action	Customer's Response	Outcome
1	Delivers high-quality product	Leaves positive review	Seller gains trust and future sales.
2	Sends a defective product	Leaves negative review	Reputation drops, future customers hesitate.
3	Refunds or resolves complaint	Customer updates review	Seller restores reputation, maintains business.

- **If the seller consistently provides quality, they gain customer trust and repeat business.**

- **If the seller cheats, short-term profits rise, but long-term credibility falls.**

- **Reputation repair is possible, but rebuilding trust is costly.**

Since **future success depends on past behaviour**, rational players must **weigh short-term gains against long-term reputation risks.**

Why It Works

The **Reputation Game works because**:

- **Trust builds loyalty and reduces uncertainty in transactions.**

- **Good reputations create competitive advantages in markets.**

- **Players must balance short-term profits with long-term credibility.**

How It Works

1. **Players make choices that affect their reputation (honest vs. dishonest actions).**

2. **Observers track past behaviour and update their expectations.**

3. **A strong reputation increases cooperation and future opportunities.**

4. **Reputation damage leads to distrust, requiring costly recovery efforts.**

Applications of the Reputation Game

1. **E-Commerce & Business** – Sellers maintain positive ratings to attract customers.

2. **Corporate Governance** – Companies protect their reputation to secure investors.

3. **Political Leadership** – Politicians build trust through consistent policies.

4. **Job Market & Hiring** – Workers rely on professional reputations to secure employment.

Key Insights

1. **Reputation is an asset that compounds over time.**

2. **Short-term dishonesty can lead to long-term losses.**

3. **Reputation repair is possible but costly.**

4. **Trust-based systems reward ethical behaviour and punish deception.**

Final Thoughts

The **Reputation Game** explains why **trust, credibility, and ethical behaviour matter in long-term interactions**. Whether in **business, politics, or personal relationships**, managing reputation strategically ensures **sustained success and competitive advantage**.

69 Conformity Game

Conformity Game in Game Theory

Breakdown of the Theory

The **Conformity Game** in **game theory and behavioural economics** models how individuals adjust their behaviour to align with social norms, peer pressure, or majority expectations. The game explains why **people conform even when it may not be in their best interest** and how **social influence shapes decision-making**.

Unlike games based purely on rational self-interest, the **Conformity Game introduces social utility**, meaning that **players not only seek material payoffs but also value belonging, approval, and avoiding social rejection**. Players must decide between **conforming to the group or acting independently**, weighing **social rewards against personal preferences**.

Key assumptions of the **Conformity Game**:

1. **Players gain social approval by aligning with group norms.**

2. **Non-conformity risks social penalties (exclusion, disapproval, or criticism).**

3. **If enough players break the norm, the standard may shift.**

4. **The strength of conformity depends on peer influence and perceived costs.**

Since **social cohesion depends on shared behaviours**, this game helps explain **cultural norms, fashion trends, and groupthink.**

Example of the Conformity Game

Consider **a high school where students decide whether to wear a trending fashion item**:

Scenario	Student A's Choice	Student B's Choice	Outcome
1	Follows the trend	Follows the trend	Both fit in, social approval is high.
2	Follows the trend	Rejects the trend	A gains social status, B risks exclusion.
3	Rejects the trend	Rejects the trend	Both remain outsiders but may form a subculture.

- **If most students adopt the trend, others feel pressure to conform.**

- **If one resists, they risk social exclusion but may gain individuality.**

- **If many reject the trend, norms may shift, creating new standards.**

Since **social standing influences decisions**, players often choose conformity to maintain status.

Why It Works

The **Conformity Game works because:**

- **People value social approval and fear exclusion.**

- **Following group norms reduces uncertainty in decision-making.**

- **Norms evolve as more individuals conform or resist change.**

How It Works

1. **Individuals observe group behaviour.**

2. **They weigh personal preferences against social consequences.**

3. **If benefits of conformity outweigh independence, they follow the norm.**

4. **If enough resist, the norm shifts, creating new behavioural expectations.**

Applications of the Conformity Game

1. **Fashion & Consumer Trends** – People adopt trends to fit in.

2. **Corporate Culture** – Employees conform to workplace norms.

3. **Political Opinion** – Public views shift based on perceived majority beliefs.

4. **Social Media Behaviour** – Users follow viral trends due to peer influence.

Key Insights

1. **Social approval drives conformity, even against personal preferences.**

2. **Reputation and peer pressure shape individual choices.**

3. **If enough people resist, social norms evolve.**

4. **Understanding conformity helps predict mass behaviour shifts.**

Final Thoughts

The **Conformity Game** explains **how peer influence and social expectations shape decisions**, affecting **trends, policies, and cultural norms**. Whether in **business, fashion, or social movements**, recognizing the power of conformity helps **predict and influence group behaviour**.

Miscellaneous & Fun Games

70 Rock-Paper-Scissors

Rock-Paper-Scissors in Game Theory

Breakdown of the Theory

The **Rock-Paper-Scissors Game** is a classic example of a **non-cooperative, zero-sum game** where players have equal chances of winning if they play optimally. It illustrates the concept of **cyclic dominance**, where no single strategy is dominant, leading to **unpredictable and mixed-strategy equilibria**.

Each player chooses **one of three options**:

- **Rock beats Scissors** (Rock crushes Scissors).

- **Scissors beats Paper** (Scissors cut Paper).

- **Paper beats Rock** (Paper covers Rock).

Since **no option is strictly better than the others**, rational players avoid using **pure strategies** (choosing the same move every time). Instead, they use **mixed strategies**, selecting each option with equal probability to remain unpredictable.

Key assumptions of the **Rock-Paper-Scissors Game**:

1. **Players choose simultaneously without knowing the opponent's choice.**

2. **Each choice wins against one, loses to another, and ties with itself.**

3. **There is no dominant strategy—pure strategies lead to predictable losses.**

4. **Optimal play involves randomization (a mixed-strategy Nash equilibrium).**

Since **patterns can be exploited**, strategic players attempt to **predict opponents' moves**, leading to **psychological tactics and adaptive learning**.

Example of Rock-Paper-Scissors in Action

Consider **two competitive players** in a tournament:

Scenario	Player A's Move	Player B's Move	Outcome
1	Rock	Scissors	A wins (Rock crushes Scissors).
2	Scissors	Paper	A wins (Scissors cut Paper).
3	Paper	Rock	A wins (Paper covers Rock).
4	Both choose the same	Tie	No winner, replay round.

- If one player consistently chooses Rock, a smart opponent will counter with Paper.

- If a player recognizes a predictable pattern, they can exploit it.

- A truly optimal strategy is to randomize choices, preventing predictability.

Since **pure strategies are exploitable**, the game's balance depends on **randomization and adaptation**.

Why It Works

The **Rock-Paper-Scissors Game works because**:

- It has no inherent advantage—each move has equal power.

- Cyclic dominance prevents a single winning strategy.

- Randomization ensures unpredictability, making it fair.

How It Works

1. Each player independently selects Rock, Paper, or Scissors.

2. The outcome is determined based on predefined rules.

3. If players use patterns, opponents can exploit them.

310

4. **A mixed strategy (randomization) prevents exploitation.**

Applications of Rock-Paper-Scissors in Game Theory

1. **Business & Competitive Strategy** – Companies use unpredictable pricing and marketing strategies to avoid being outmanoeuvred.

2. **Evolutionary Biology** – Species interactions (e.g., competing bacteria) follow cyclic dominance patterns.

3. **Sports & Gaming** – Athletes and teams use feints and counter-strategies to mislead opponents.

4. **Military & Cybersecurity** – Avoiding predictability in tactics reduces vulnerability to adversaries.

Key Insights

1. **No single strategy dominates—cyclic dominance ensures balance.**

2. **Predictability leads to losses, making randomness a viable strategy.**

3. **Pattern recognition and psychological tactics influence outcomes.**

4. **The game represents broader competitive systems, from nature to economics.**

Final Thoughts

The **Rock-Paper-Scissors Game** illustrates **how randomness, strategy, and adaptation play a role in competitive decision-making**. Whether in **business, sports, or military strategy**, the ability to remain **unpredictable while adapting to opponents** is a key takeaway from this **simple yet profound game**.

71 Monty Hall Problem

Monty Hall Problem in Game Theory

Breakdown of the Theory

The **Monty Hall Problem** is a famous probability puzzle based on **decision-making under uncertainty**. It highlights how **optimal strategy and information updates** affect a player's choices. The problem is named after **Monty Hall**, the host of the TV game show *Let's Make a Deal*.

The game works as follows:

1. **A contestant is presented with three doors**, behind one of which is a prize (e.g., a car). The other two doors hide goats (losing choices).

2. **The contestant picks one door** but does not open it.

3. **The host, who knows where the prize is, opens one of the remaining doors to reveal a goat.**

4. **The contestant is given a choice: stick with their original door or switch to the remaining unopened door.**

The key question: **Should the contestant stick with their original choice or switch?**

Mathematically, **switching doubles the probability of winning** from **1/3 to 2/3**, a result that often surprises people.

Example of the Monty Hall Problem

Consider the possible scenarios:

Scenario	Initial Choice (Contestant)	Host Opens	Remaining Door	Outcome if Sticking	Outcome if Switching
1	Picks Door 1 (Car)	Opens Door 2 (Goat)	Door 3	Wins	Loses
2	Picks Door 2 (Goat)	Opens Door 3 (Goat)	Door 1	Loses	Wins
3	Picks Door 3 (Goat)	Opens Door 2 (Goat)	Door 1	Loses	Wins

- **Sticking with the original choice wins only if the car was initially chosen (1/3 chance).**

- **Switching wins if the original pick was a goat (2/3 chance).**

Since **the host always reveals a goat**, switching improves the odds because **the host's action provides new information**, effectively eliminating one losing option.

Why It Works

The **Monty Hall Problem works because**:

- **The original choice has a 1/3 probability of being correct.**

- **The host's action effectively consolidates the two losing doors into one, shifting probability.**

- **Switching accounts for this probability update, doubling the chances of winning.**

How It Works

1. **A player makes an initial choice (randomly 1/3 chance of being right).**

2. **The host eliminates one losing door, providing new information.**

3. **Switching allows the player to capitalize on the 2/3 chance that they originally picked a losing door.**

Applications of the Monty Hall Problem

1. **Decision Theory** – Helps understand how information updates impact strategic choices.

2. **Risk Management** – Used in finance and insurance to evaluate risk under uncertainty.

3. **Medical Diagnosis** – Doctors revise probabilities based on new test results.

4. **Cybersecurity** – Detecting false positives in security breaches by updating prior probabilities.

Key Insights

1. **Counterintuitive results in probability highlight cognitive biases.**

2. **Information updates significantly change decision-making strategies.**

3. **The optimal strategy (switching) is not always intuitively obvious.**

4. **Understanding probability improves choices in uncertain scenarios.**

Final Thoughts

The **Monty Hall Problem** demonstrates **how probability updates influence optimal decision-making**. Whether in **finance, risk analysis, or strategic planning**, learning to **reevaluate choices based on new information** is a key takeaway from this paradoxical yet powerful game.

72 Beauty Contest Game

Beauty Contest Game in Game Theory

Breakdown of the Theory

The Beauty Contest Game is a strategic game in game theory and behavioral economics that explores iterated reasoning and expectations. Introduced by John Maynard Keynes to explain stock market behavior, it was later formalized into a mathematical game-theoretic model. The game highlights how players make choices not only based on personal preferences but also by anticipating how others will decide.

The standard version of the game works as follows:

1. Each player selects a number between 0 and 100.

2. The winner is the player whose number is closest to a fraction (e.g., ⅔) of the average number chosen by all players.

3. Players must predict how others will choose, leading to multiple levels of reasoning.

Since players must anticipate how others will think, the game involves strategic depth—those who reason multiple steps ahead tend to select lower numbers. The Nash equilibrium occurs when all rational players choose 0, but real-world experiments show that human players tend to stop their reasoning at intermediate levels.

Example of the Beauty Contest Game

Consider three players choosing numbers between 0 and 100:

Player	Chosen Number	Sum of Numbers	Average (Sum ÷ 3)	⅔ of the Average	Distance from Target
A	40	40 + 30 + 20 = 90	90 ÷ 3 = 30	⅔ × 30 = 20	20
B	30	40 + 30 + 20 = 90	90 ÷ 3 = 30	⅔ × 30 = 20	10
C	20	40 + 30 + 20 = 90	90 ÷ 3 = 30	⅔ × 30 = 20	0

- If all players randomly select numbers, the average would be 50, making the winning number ⅔ × 50 = 33.

- If players anticipate this, they pick lower numbers, leading to further downward adjustments.

- A fully rational player, iterating indefinitely, would ultimately select 0 as the optimal strategy.

However, in reality, not all players think infinitely many steps ahead, which explains why real-world results often cluster around 20-30 instead of 0.

Why It Works

The Beauty Contest Game works because:

- It models strategic reasoning and decision-making in competitive settings.

- Players adjust choices based on expectations of others' actions.

- It reflects real-world phenomena like stock market speculation and advertising strategies.

How It Works

1. Players choose numbers, trying to anticipate others' choices.

2. Each round, players adjust expectations, leading to lower selections.

3. The Nash equilibrium occurs when all choose zero, but real-world choices stop earlier.

4. Human limitations (bounded rationality) result in choices clustering around 20-30 instead of 0.

Applications of the Beauty Contest Game

1. Stock Markets – Investors predict how others will value assets, creating speculative bubbles.

2. Advertising & Marketing – Companies anticipate how consumers react to competitors' campaigns.

3. Political Elections – Candidates adjust positions based on expected voter preferences.

4. Auctions & Bidding – Bidders estimate others' strategies to optimize offers.

Key Insights

1. Decision-making depends on predicting others' reasoning depth.

2. Full rationality leads to the Nash equilibrium (zero), but real players stop earlier.

3. Understanding strategic depth helps in finance, marketing, and politics.

4. Cognitive limitations and expectations shape real-world choices.

Final Thoughts

The Beauty Contest Game explains how strategic decision-making evolves based on others' expectations. Whether in financial markets, political strategies, or competitive business environments, anticipating how others think is key to making optimal choices.

73 Divide-the-Dollar Game

Divide-the-Dollar Game in Game Theory

Breakdown of the Theory

The **Divide-the-Dollar Game** is a **bargaining and negotiation game** in **game theory** where players must decide how to split a fixed amount of money. The challenge arises from **competing interests, fairness considerations, and strategic voting**, making it a fundamental model for studying **coalition formation, power dynamics, and negotiation strategies**.

In the simplest version:

1. **Two or more players must divide a fixed sum (e.g., $1 or 100%).**

2. **Players propose how much they should receive.**

3. **If the sum of their claims is less than or equal to the total, they receive their requested amounts.**

4. **If the total claims exceed the available amount, negotiations occur, and coalitions may form.**

Key assumptions of the **Divide-the-Dollar Game**:

1. **Players are rational and seek to maximize their share.**

2. **Negotiations determine the final distribution, often favouring stronger coalitions.**

3. Majority-rule voting may dictate the final allocation, disadvantaging minority players.

4. Strategic players may demand more than their fair share, leading to conflicts.

Since **players must balance personal greed with coalition stability**, this game highlights **how power dynamics shape negotiations**.

Example of the Divide-the-Dollar Game

Consider **three players (A, B, and C) dividing $1**:

Scenario	A's Claim	B's Claim	C's Claim	Total Claimed	Outcome
1	$0.40	$0.30	$0.30	$1.00	Everyone gets their request.
2	$0.50	$0.50	$0.50	$1.50	Claims exceed $1, requiring negotiation.
3	$0.60	$0.40	$0.00	$1.00	C is excluded, A and B form a coalition.

- If all claims total exactly $1, players receive their amounts.
- If claims exceed $1, bargaining is required, favouring coalitions.

- If two players form a majority (e.g., A and B), they can exclude C.

Since **majority coalitions often control outcomes,** weaker players must **negotiate strategically or risk exclusion.**

Why It Works

The **Divide-the-Dollar Game works because:**

- It models real-world bargaining, where resources are limited.

- Coalitions and alliances influence final outcomes.

- Fairness considerations compete with strategic self-interest.

How It Works

1. Players propose claims, knowing that excessive demands lead to conflict.

2. Negotiation and coalition-building shape the final allocation.

3. Majority alliances often dictate the division, disadvantaging weaker players.

4. Fairness may play a role, but strategic players often seek to maximize personal gain.

Applications of the Divide-the-Dollar Game

1. **Political Bargaining** – Governments negotiate budgets and spending.

2. **Business & Partnerships** – Companies distribute profits among stakeholders.

3. **Resource Allocation** – Dividing limited public goods in policy decisions.

4. **Labor Negotiations** – Unions and employers negotiate wage distributions.

Key Insights

1. **Coalitions determine bargaining power, influencing outcomes.**

2. **Players may overstate demands, forcing strategic negotiations.**

3. **Fairness is secondary to strategic advantage in competitive settings.**

4. **Understanding bargaining dynamics helps in politics, business, and economics.**

Final Thoughts

The **Divide-the-Dollar Game** demonstrates **how negotiations, coalitions, and strategic bargaining shape resource allocation**. Whether in **business, politics, or economics**, mastering **negotiation tactics and coalition-building** is key to **maximizing outcomes in competitive environments**.

74 Musical Chairs Game

Musical Chairs Game in Game Theory

Breakdown of the Theory

The **Musical Chairs Game** in **game theory and behavioural economics** models **competitive resource allocation** where the number of available resources (chairs) is **fewer than the number of players**. The game captures **scarcity dynamics, strategic positioning, and competitive elimination**, making it an effective model for **markets, job competition, and survival-based decision-making**.

The traditional game works as follows:

1. **N players compete for (N-1) chairs** placed in a circle.

2. **Music plays while players move around the chairs.**

3. **When the music stops, players rush to sit down.**

4. **One player is left standing and eliminated.**

5. **A chair is removed, and the process repeats until one winner remains.**

The key challenge is **anticipating when the music stops** and **positioning oneself optimally to secure a seat.** This models real-world situations where **resources are limited, competition is high, and strategic behaviour influences outcomes.**

Key assumptions of the **Musical Chairs Game**:

1. **Resources (chairs) are fewer than demand (players).**

2. **Players compete for survival, making elimination-based decisions.**

3. **Positioning, awareness, and reaction speed influence success.**

4. **Luck plays a role, but strategic positioning can improve outcomes.**

5.

Since **losers are eliminated each round**, the game provides insights into **market competition, hiring, and survival-of-the-fittest dynamics.**

Example of the Musical Chairs Game

Consider **job seekers applying for a limited number of positions**:

Scenario	Number of Applicants	Available Jobs	Outcome
1	10	9	1 applicant is unemployed.
2	5	3	2 applicants remain jobless.
3	2	1	1 final winner secures the last job.

- **If more applicants exist than jobs, competition increases.**
- **Applicants must differentiate themselves (positioning) to secure opportunities.**
- **As rounds progress, competition becomes tougher, favouring stronger players.**

Since **players must anticipate when and how to act**, the game highlights **survival-based decision-making under scarcity**.

Why It Works

The **Musical Chairs Game works because:**

- It models real-world scarcity, where resources are limited.

- It forces players to make quick, strategic decisions.

- Competition increases as resources shrink, making adaptation essential.

How It Works

1. Players move strategically to maximize survival chances.

2. Competition increases as resources decrease.

3. Elimination favours the strongest, fastest, or best-positioned players.

4. The last player standing wins, modelling a "winner-takes-all" scenario.

Applications of the Musical Chairs Game

1. **Job Markets** – Limited job openings force competition among applicants.

2. **Housing & Rental Markets** – Demand often exceeds supply, making positioning key.

3. **Corporate Competition** – Companies race for limited market share.

4. **Survival Economics** – Natural selection favours those best adapted to scarce resources.

Key Insights

1. **Scarcity drives competition, making strategic positioning crucial.**

2. **As resources shrink, competition intensifies, eliminating weaker players.**

3. **Survival depends on adaptability, speed, and awareness.**

4. **Winner-takes-all dynamics favour the best-positioned competitors.**

Final Thoughts

The **Musical Chairs Game** provides insights into **resource competition, strategic positioning, and survival dynamics.** Whether in **job markets, corporate strategy, or economic survival,** understanding **how to position oneself effectively in a competitive environment** is key to success.

75 Hot Potato Game

Hot Potato Game in Game Theory

Breakdown of the Theory

The **Hot Potato Game** in **game theory and decision-making** models situations where players try to **pass an unwanted burden to others** before it becomes a liability. The game captures **risk avoidance, strategic passing, and timing decisions**, making it useful for analysing **financial crises, blame-shifting, and resource management**.

The traditional version of the game works as follows:

1. **Players form a circle and pass an object (the "hot potato") while music plays.**

2. **When the music stops, the player holding the hot potato loses or is eliminated.**

3. **The game continues until one player remains.**

The key challenge is **avoiding being stuck with the liability** while ensuring it is passed away at the right time. In **game-theoretic terms**, this represents **a dynamic game of imperfect information**, where players must anticipate when the burden will stop moving.

Key assumptions of the **Hot Potato Game**:

1. **Players want to avoid holding the liability (hot potato).**

2. **Passing the burden too soon may reveal strategy and make others retaliate.**

3. **Waiting too long increases the risk of getting stuck with it.**

4. **The game relies on uncertainty, timing, and deception.**

Since **players have limited control over when the burden stops**, the game highlights **how risk is shifted in uncertain environments.**

Example of the Hot Potato Game

Consider **financial institutions offloading toxic assets**:

Scenario	Bank A's Strategy	Bank B's Strategy	Outcome
1	Sells risky assets early	Holds risky assets	Bank A avoids losses, Bank B suffers.
2	Holds assets	Sells risky assets later	Bank B avoids losses, Bank A suffers.
3	Both sell early	Market reacts, reducing losses	Smaller losses but reputational damage.
4	Both hold assets	Market crashes	Both banks suffer large losses.

- **If a bank offloads toxic assets first, it avoids losses while others suffer.**

- **If banks wait too long, they risk financial collapse.**

- **If all players attempt to pass the burden simultaneously, market panic may ensue.**

Since **players do not know exactly when the market (music) will stop,** risk management becomes a strategic challenge.

Why It Works

The **Hot Potato Game works because:**

- **Players try to avoid being the last holder of a negative asset.**

- **Timing and deception influence who ultimately bears the loss.**

- **The game captures real-world scenarios of risk transfer.**

How It Works

1. **Players pass the burden strategically to avoid holding it too long.**

2. **Some players delay to manipulate others into accepting it.**

3. **If passed too slowly, the risk becomes unavoidable.**

4. **The game ends when the burden stops, penalizing the final holder.**

Applications of the Hot Potato Game

1. **Financial Crises** – Banks offload bad loans before a market crash.

2. **Corporate Responsibility** – Companies shift blame or liabilities onto others.

3. **Political Decision-Making** – Governments delay unpopular policies to pass responsibility.

4. **Supply Chain Risks** – Companies offload costs before disruptions occur.

Key Insights

1. **Risk transfers create incentives for strategic delay or deception.**

2. **Holding the burden too long can result in significant losses.**

3. **Panic behaviour can arise when too many players try to offload risk simultaneously.**

4. **Managing timing and perception is key to avoiding negative consequences.**

Final Thoughts

The **Hot Potato Game** explains **how individuals, firms, and institutions pass unwanted burdens strategically.** Whether in **finance, politics, or corporate decision-making**, the ability to **time risk transfer and manage uncertainty** determines **who ultimately bears the cost.**

76 Matching Game

Matching Game in Game Theory

Breakdown of the Theory

The **Matching Game** in **game theory and economics** models scenarios where **two sets of players (or resources) must be paired based on preferences or compatibility**. The goal is to **find an optimal matching** that maximizes overall satisfaction while considering individual preferences.

Matching games are fundamental in **market design, labour economics, and social decision-making**, where participants must be paired based on preferences, qualifications, or constraints. A well-known framework for matching problems is the **Gale-Shapley algorithm**, which ensures **stable matches**—pairings where no two participants would rather switch to be with each other instead of their current matches.

Key assumptions of the **Matching Game**:

1. **Players have ranked preferences over potential matches.**

2. **The objective is to create pairings that satisfy individual preferences.**

3. **An optimal matching exists where no two players would prefer switching.**

4. **Strategic behaviour may influence outcomes, affecting fairness and efficiency.**

Since **matching problems occur in various real-world scenarios**, this game highlights **how preferences, stability, and fairness interact in pair formation**.

Example of the Matching Game

Consider **a college admissions system**, where **students** and **universities** must be matched:

Scenario	Student A's Preference	University's Preference	Outcome
1	Prefers University X	Prefers Student A	A is admitted to X.
2	Prefers University Y	Prefers Another Student	A is placed in the second-choice school.
3	Multiple students prefer the same university	University selects based on merit	Only top-ranked students get in.

- **If universities and students rank each other, a stable matching process occurs.**

- **A student may not get their top choice if other students rank higher.**

- A stable outcome ensures no student-university pair would prefer to swap.

Since **stability ensures that no unpaired individuals would prefer switching,** the system creates **optimal and efficient matches.**

Why It Works

The **Matching Game works because:**

- **Pairing based on mutual preferences creates stable outcomes.**

- **Algorithms (like Gale-Shapley) ensure fairness and efficiency.**

- **It applies to real-world scenarios like school admissions, job markets, and dating.**

How It Works

1. **Players (individuals or institutions) rank their preferences.**

2. **An algorithm or process finds optimal pairings based on mutual rankings.**

3. **If an unstable match exists, it is adjusted until stability is achieved.**

4. **The final matching ensures no two players would prefer to switch.**

Applications of the Matching Game

1. **College Admissions** – Universities match students based on applications.

2. **Job Markets** – Employers and candidates find optimal hiring matches.

3. **Organ Donation** – Matching donors with compatible recipients.

4. **Dating & Marriage** – Matchmaking platforms pair individuals based on compatibility.

Key Insights

1. **Stable matching prevents dissatisfaction and potential renegotiation.**

2. **Strategic behaviour influences match outcomes.**

3. **Algorithms like Gale-Shapley ensure efficiency and fairness.**

4. **Matching principles apply to diverse fields, from business to healthcare.**

Final Thoughts

The **Matching Game** explains **how individuals, firms, and institutions form optimal pairings** in structured environments. Whether in **education, job markets, or healthcare**, the ability to **design fair and stable matching mechanisms** ensures **efficient and mutually beneficial outcomes.**

77 Tipping Point Game

Tipping Point Game in Game Theory

Breakdown of the Theory

The **Tipping Point Game** in **game theory and social dynamics** models how small initial changes can lead to **large-scale shifts in collective behaviour**. The concept is based on the idea that once a **critical mass of players (or adopters) is reached**, the system experiences a rapid transition to a new equilibrium.

This game is commonly applied to **social movements, market trends, political changes, and technological adoption**, where a **minority influence grows until it becomes the majority**. The key challenge is predicting **when and how a tipping point will occur** and whether individuals will **follow the shift or resist change**.

Key assumptions of the **Tipping Point Game**:

1. **Individuals decide based on what others do (network effects).**

2. **A critical mass (threshold) must be reached before widespread change occurs.**

3. **Social influence accelerates once the tipping point is reached.**

4. **Some players may resist change, delaying or preventing the shift.**

Since **small changes can have disproportionate effects,** this game highlights **how social systems transition from one state to another**.

Example of the Tipping Point Game

Consider **the adoption of electric vehicles (EVs) in a country**:

Scenario	Early Adopters	Majority's Reaction	Outcome
1	Few people buy EVs	Majority ignores trend	No widespread adoption.
2	More people buy EVs	Some switch, but scepticism remains	Slow growth in adoption.
3	EVs become common	Majority follows	Tipping point reached—rapid adoption.

- If early adopters fail to influence the majority, adoption stagnates.

- Once a critical number of people switch, momentum accelerates.

- Social pressure and incentives drive mass adoption past the tipping point.

Since **players rely on others' actions to make decisions,** behaviour spreads **non-linearly.**

Why It Works

The **Tipping Point Game works because**:

- **People are influenced by the choices of others (herd behaviour).**

- **Once a trend reaches critical mass, momentum makes reversal difficult.**

- **Network effects create a self-reinforcing cycle, driving rapid change.**

How It Works

1. **A small number of early adopters make a change.**

2. **Their influence spreads, convincing others to follow.**

3. **Once the tipping point is reached, widespread adoption occurs.**

4. **Opponents may resist, but the momentum often overcomes resistance.**

Applications of the Tipping Point Game

1. **Social Movements** – Protests and policy changes gain momentum when enough people participate.

2. **Marketing & Virality** – Products go viral when enough users share them.

3. **Climate Action** – Green technology adoption accelerates after early thresholds.

4. **Stock Market Trends** – A small market shift can trigger mass buying or selling.

Key Insights

1. **A tipping point exists where change becomes inevitable.**

2. **Social influence drives adoption, often in a non-linear way.**

3. **Early adopters play a crucial role in shaping future trends.**

4. **Once the tipping point is reached, change happens rapidly and irreversibly.**

Final Thoughts

The **Tipping Point Game** explains **how small changes lead to large-scale transformations**. Whether in **business, politics, or technology**, understanding tipping points helps in **forecasting trends, shaping policies, and leveraging social influence for rapid change**.

78 Queueing Theory Game

Queueing Theory Game in Game Theory

Breakdown of the Theory

The **Queueing Theory Game** in **game theory and operations research** models how individuals or entities make strategic decisions when faced with **waiting times, congestion, and limited service capacity**. The game is particularly relevant in **transportation systems, customer service, internet traffic, and public infrastructure**, where players must decide **whether to wait, switch, or optimize their position in a queue**.

Queueing problems arise when **demand for a service exceeds immediate availability**, leading to **competition for priority and efficiency in resource allocation**. The challenge is to **minimize wait times while optimizing service flow**, often requiring strategic decision-making by both **service providers and consumers**.

Key assumptions of the **Queueing Theory Game**:

1. **Players experience different costs associated with waiting (e.g., time lost, opportunity costs).**

2. **Some players may attempt to jump ahead, pay for priority, or switch to alternative queues.**

3. **Service providers aim to balance efficiency and fairness in queue management.**

4. **Different queue structures (first-come, first-served vs. priority-based) affect strategy.**

Since **queues create incentives for strategic behaviour**, this game highlights **how players react to delays and congestion**.

Example of the Queueing Theory Game

Consider **passengers at an airport security checkpoint**:

Scenario	Passenger Strategy	Queue Outcome	Impact
1	Waits in line patiently	First-come, first-served	Fair but slow.
2	Pays for priority check-in	Priority queue moves faster	Increased efficiency, but costly.
3	Switches to a shorter line	Gains advantage if chosen wisely	Risky but may save time.

-   **If too many people pay for priority, congestion shifts to the priority queue.**

-   **If passengers constantly switch lines, they may end up increasing delays.**

-   **If queue management is poor, frustration and inefficiencies rise.**

Since **players weigh costs and benefits of different strategies, queue dynamics constantly adjust** based on behaviour.

Why It Works

The **Queueing Theory Game works because:**

- **Scarce service capacity forces competition and strategic decisions.**

- **Players optimize their choices to minimize waiting costs.**

- **Different queue structures affect fairness, efficiency, and congestion.**

How It Works

1. **Players assess queue length and expected wait times.**

2. **They decide whether to wait, switch, or pay for priority.**

3. **Service providers manage congestion through queueing policies.**

4. **Dynamic adjustments occur as players respond to delays.**

Applications of the Queueing Theory Game

1. **Customer Service** – Call centres manage wait times using priority queuing.

2. **Traffic Management** – Toll lanes and congestion pricing optimize road use.

3. **Healthcare** – Hospitals prioritize emergency patients while managing wait times.

4. **Network Traffic** – Internet service providers regulate data flow to prevent slowdowns.

Key Insights

1. **Queueing systems must balance fairness, efficiency, and strategic behaviour.**

2. **Priority queues benefit paying users but may create inequalities.**

3. **Switching queues can be risky if not done strategically.**

4. **Dynamic adjustments help optimize wait times and service flow.**

Final Thoughts

The **Queueing Theory Game** explains **how waiting time influences decision-making and efficiency**. Whether in **airports, hospitals, or digital networks, optimizing queue management** ensures **fairness, speed, and better resource allocation**.

79 Social Influence Game

Social Influence Game in Game Theory

Breakdown of the Theory

The **Social Influence Game** in **game theory and behavioural economics** models how individuals **make decisions based on the actions, opinions, or expectations of others**. This game helps explain why trends emerge, why people conform to group behaviours, and how **opinions, ideologies, and consumer preferences spread**.

The game highlights the **trade-off between independent decision-making and social conformity**. Players must decide whether to **follow their personal preferences or conform to social norms**, often considering the risks and rewards of each choice. In some cases, **early adopters influence others, leading to a cascading effect** where a small shift in behaviour can **spread widely across a population**.

Key assumptions of the **Social Influence Game**:

1. **Players base their decisions on personal preferences and observed behaviours of others.**

2. **Individuals may conform due to social pressure, reputation concerns, or perceived benefits.**

3. **Network effects exist—choices become more valuable as more people adopt them.**

4. **A tipping point can lead to mass adoption of new behaviours or ideas.**

Since **social norms evolve based on group dynamics**, this game highlights **how behaviours, opinions, and markets change over time**.

Example of the Social Influence Game

Consider **the adoption of a new social media platform**:

Scenario	Early Users	Majority's Reaction	Outcome
1	Few people sign up	Most ignore it	Platform struggles to gain users.
2	More people adopt it	Others start to take interest	Moderate growth.
3	A critical mass joins	Network effect kicks in	Platform goes viral.

- **If early adopters fail to attract others, the platform dies.**

- **If adoption slowly builds, it can reach a tipping point where mass participation follows.**

- Network effects ensure that more users lead to greater value for all participants.

Since **people look to others when making decisions, social influence accelerates adoption.**

Why It Works

The **Social Influence Game works because:**

- **People seek validation, belonging, or benefits from group behaviour.**

- **Network effects create increasing returns, reinforcing the dominant choice.**

- **Once a critical threshold is reached, widespread adoption follows.**

How It Works

1. **A small group of players adopts a behaviour, product, or belief.**

2. **Other players observe and decide whether to follow.**

3. **If adoption reaches a tipping point, momentum grows.**

4. **The majority conforms, solidifying the new trend or norm.**

Applications of the Social Influence Game

1. **Viral Marketing** – Companies use influencers to trigger mass adoption.

2. **Political Movements** – Social activism gains momentum through collective participation.

3. **Fashion & Trends** – People adopt styles based on peer influence.

4. **Technology Adoption** – The success of platforms like TikTok depends on social influence.

Key Insights

1. **Social proof and peer influence shape decision-making.**

2. **Early adopters play a crucial role in trend-setting.**

3. **Network effects amplify adoption rates.**

4. **Tipping points create rapid social or market shifts.**

Final Thoughts

The **Social Influence Game** explains **how collective behaviour drives trends, decisions, and social norms**. Whether in **marketing, politics, or technology adoption**, leveraging social influence effectively can lead to widespread change.

Advanced Theoretical Games

80 Repeated Games Theory

Repeated Games Theory in Game Theory

Breakdown of the Theory

Repeated Games Theory in **game theory** models **strategic interactions that occur multiple times between the same players**. Unlike **one-shot games**, where players make decisions without concern for future consequences, **repeated games involve long-term interactions**, encouraging cooperation, punishment, and learning over time.

The **key insight** of repeated games is that players can **condition their strategies on past behaviour**, allowing for the development of **trust, retaliation, and reputation-building**. This makes cooperation more likely compared to **single-shot games**, where defecting for short-term gain might be optimal.

Repeated games can be classified into:

1. **Finite Repeated Games** – The number of rounds is known in advance, often leading to backward induction (e.g., in the last round, players defect, unravelling cooperation).

2. **Infinitely Repeated Games** – The number of rounds is unknown or infinite, enabling long-term strategies such as **tit-for-tat**, fostering cooperation.

Key assumptions of the **Repeated Games Theory**:

1. **Players interact multiple times, considering future consequences.**

2. **Strategies evolve based on past interactions.**

3. **Cooperation can emerge when punishment strategies deter defection.**

4. **The length of interaction impacts the likelihood of cooperation.**

Since **future payoffs matter**, repeated interactions create **incentives for fair and reciprocal behaviour**.

Example of Repeated Games Theory

Consider **two competing airlines deciding on ticket pricing**:

Scenario	Airline A's Strategy	Airline B's Strategy	Outcome
1	Both set high prices	Both earn stable profits	Cooperation is sustained.
2	One lowers prices	Other keeps high prices	Price-cutter gains market share short-term.
3	Both lower prices	Price war, reducing long-term profits	Mutual defection leads to losses.

- **If both airlines keep prices high, they enjoy stable profits.**

- **If one lowers prices, it benefits short-term but risks retaliation.**

- **If both undercut each other, a price war ensues, reducing profits for both.**

Since **airlines compete repeatedly**, the risk of retaliation discourages aggressive price-cutting, leading to tacit cooperation.

Why It Works

The **Repeated Games Theory works because**:

- **Players consider long-term payoffs, reducing short-term greed.**
- **Reputation and trust-building enable cooperation.**
- **Punishment strategies (e.g., tit-for-tat) deter defection.**

How It Works

1. **Players make initial decisions, setting expectations.**
2. **Strategies evolve based on past behaviour.**
3. **Punishment or rewards reinforce cooperation or defection.**
4. **Long-term interactions stabilize relationships and outcomes.**

Applications of Repeated Games Theory

1. **Business & Market Competition** – Firms avoid destructive price wars through tacit agreements.
2. **International Relations** – Countries maintain treaties through repeated interactions.
3. **Workplace & Contracts** – Employees and employers build trust over long-term agreements.

4. **Social Norms** – Cooperation in communities is reinforced through repeated interactions.

Key Insights

1. **Long-term incentives encourage cooperation over defection.**

2. **Reputation and punishment deter short-term selfishness.**

3. **The possibility of retaliation stabilizes strategic relationships.**

4. **Infinitely repeated games foster more cooperation than finite ones.**

Final Thoughts

The **Repeated Games Theory** explains **how long-term interactions influence strategy, cooperation, and trust-building.** Whether in **business, politics, or personal relationships, anticipating future consequences leads to more stable and cooperative outcomes**.

81 Bayesian Games

Bayesian Games in Game Theory

Breakdown of the Theory

Bayesian Games in **game theory** model strategic interactions where **players have incomplete information** about others. Unlike standard games where all players know each other's payoffs, Bayesian games introduce **uncertainty** by assuming players have **private information** about their own type, which affects their payoffs and strategies.

Each player forms **beliefs about the types and strategies of others** using **Bayes' rule**, updating their expectations based on observed actions. This framework is widely used in **auctions, negotiations, and market competition**, where decision-making depends on **guessing others' private information**.

Key assumptions of **Bayesian Games**:

1. **Players have different types, representing private information (e.g., risk tolerance, valuation of goods).**

2. **Each player assigns probabilities (beliefs) to others' possible types.**

3. **Strategies are chosen based on expected payoffs, given the beliefs.**

4. **Players update beliefs using Bayesian inference based on observed behaviour.**

Since **uncertainty affects decisions,** Bayesian games highlight **how players strategically manage risk and incomplete information.**

Example of a Bayesian Game

Consider **an auction for an antique painting,** where bidders **do not know each other's exact valuation:**

Scenario	Bidder A's Private Value	Bidder B's Private Value	Outcome
1	Values painting at $500	Values painting at $700	B wins if bids reflect true value.
2	Values painting at $600	Values painting at $500	A wins with a higher bid.
3	Both value it at $700	Highest bidder wins, but risk overpaying.	

- If Bidder A underestimates B's value, A might bid too low and lose.

- If A overestimates B's value, A might bid too high and suffer losses (winner's curse).

- Players must balance aggressive bidding with avoiding unnecessary overpayment.

Since **bidders cannot see others' valuations**, they must estimate probabilities and adjust bids accordingly.

Why It Works

The **Bayesian Game framework works because**:

- **Real-world decisions often involve incomplete information.**

- **Players must infer hidden information from observable actions.**

- **Bayesian updating refines decision-making over repeated interactions.**

How It Works

1. **Each player starts with private information about their type.**

2. **They form beliefs about other players' types using probability distributions.**

3. **Strategies are chosen to maximize expected payoffs given these beliefs.**

4. As new actions are observed, players update their beliefs using Bayes' rule.

Applications of Bayesian Games

1. **Auctions** – Bidders estimate competitors' valuations in sealed-bid auctions.

2. **Negotiations** – Businesses negotiate contracts without knowing the opponent's true willingness to settle.

3. **Job Hiring** – Employers infer a candidate's skills based on resumes and interviews.

4. **Cybersecurity** – Defenders estimate an attacker's threat level based on behaviour.

Key Insights

1. **Incomplete information creates strategic uncertainty, requiring probabilistic reasoning.**

2. **Players must estimate opponents' private knowledge and adjust strategies accordingly.**

3. **Updating beliefs through Bayesian inference refines decision-making.**

4. **Understanding Bayesian Games improves performance in auctions, negotiations, and competitive markets.**

Final Thoughts

The **Bayesian Games framework** explains **how players make optimal choices under uncertainty**. Whether in business, auctions, or negotiations, **strategic decision-making requires estimating others' hidden information** and **adapting accordingly**.

82 Mean-Field Games

Mean-Field Games in Game Theory

Breakdown of the Theory

Mean-Field Games (MFGs) are a branch of **game theory and mathematical economics** that model strategic interactions in **large populations** of rational agents. Unlike traditional **finite-player games**, where players directly interact, MFGs assume that each player interacts **with the collective behaviour of the entire population**, rather than with individual opponents.

The fundamental idea is that as the number of players **approaches infinity**, their aggregate behaviour can be represented by a **mean-field (statistical average)**. Each individual optimizes their strategy based on **the evolving distribution of all other players**, leading to equilibrium solutions.

Key assumptions of **Mean-Field Games**:

1. **Each player is small relative to the whole population and does not significantly impact it alone.**

2. **Players make decisions based on a statistical distribution (mean-field), rather than direct interactions.**

3. An equilibrium exists where no player benefits by deviating unilaterally (mean-field Nash equilibrium).

4. Players optimize their strategies dynamically over time, often modelled through differential equations.

Since **players interact indirectly via aggregate effects**, this game highlights **how large-scale strategic decisions evolve dynamically**.

Example of a Mean-Field Game

Consider **traffic flow optimization in a smart city**, where **each driver chooses a route based on expected congestion**:

Scenario	Individual Driver's Decision	Mean-Field Effect	Outcome
1	Chooses shortest route	Few other drivers take the same route	Low congestion, fast travel time.
2	Chooses shortest route	Many others also choose it	High congestion, longer travel time.
3	Distributes routes	Players adapt dynamically	Traffic flow stabilizes at equilibrium.

- **If too many drivers choose the same route, congestion rises, making alternative routes preferable.**

- **Drivers continuously update their strategies based on observed traffic trends.**

- **The mean-field equilibrium emerges when drivers distribute optimally across available routes.**

Since **each driver affects and is affected by the overall traffic pattern**, decisions become **self-regulating over time**.

Why It Works

The **Mean-Field Game framework works because**:

- It models large-scale interactions efficiently, without tracking individual players.

- Players optimize behaviour dynamically based on evolving conditions.

- Mean-field approximations reduce computational complexity in multi-agent decision-making.

How It Works

1. Each player optimizes their strategy based on the population's distribution.

2. As conditions evolve, players adjust strategies dynamically.

3. An equilibrium emerges when no player benefits from further deviation.

4. The system stabilizes based on collective behaviour.

Applications of Mean-Field Games

1. **Traffic Management** – Optimizing vehicle flow based on congestion patterns.

2. **Financial Markets** – Modelling investor behaviour in stock trading.

3. **Epidemiology** – Predicting disease spread based on population movement.

4. **Artificial Intelligence** – Training multi-agent reinforcement learning systems.

Key Insights

1. **Mean-field approximations allow complex systems to be analysed efficiently.**

2. **Players influence and are influenced by aggregate population behaviour.**

3. **Dynamic optimization leads to self-regulating equilibrium outcomes.**

4. **Applications span economics, engineering, and artificial intelligence.**

Final Thoughts

The **Mean-Field Games framework** explains **how strategic decision-making emerges in large populations**. Whether in **traffic, finance, or AI**, understanding **how individuals respond to aggregate conditions** enables **better system-wide optimization and policy-making**.

83 Inspection Game

Inspection Game in Game Theory

Breakdown of the Theory

The **Inspection Game** in **game theory** models strategic interactions between a **monitoring authority (inspector)** and an **agent (inspected party)** who may or may not comply with rules. The game captures scenarios where one party seeks to **enforce rules or detect violations**, while the other **weighs the cost of compliance against the risk of getting caught.**

This game is used to analyse **regulatory enforcement, fraud detection, tax compliance, and military surveillance**, where the inspector **cannot monitor constantly but must strategically allocate inspection resources** to deter violations.

Key assumptions of the **Inspection Game**:

1. **The inspector wants to catch violators but has limited resources.**

2. **The inspected party must decide whether to comply or risk violating the rules.**

3. **The inspector must choose an optimal frequency of inspections to deter violations.**

4. **Players adjust their strategies dynamically based on the probability of detection.**

Since **inspections are costly,** the game highlights **how enforcement agencies balance deterrence and efficiency.**

Example of the Inspection Game

Consider **a company (agent) deciding whether to follow environmental regulations,** while a **government agency (inspector) performs random audits:**

Scenario	Company's Choice	Government's Inspection Decision	Outcome
1	Complies with regulations	Conducts inspection	No penalty, compliance maintained.
2	Violates regulations	No inspection	Company saves costs, avoids fines.
3	Violates regulations	Inspection occurs	Company is fined, deterring future violations.

- **If inspections are frequent, companies comply to avoid penalties.**

- **If inspections are rare, companies may take the risk and violate regulations.**

- An optimal inspection rate balances deterrence with enforcement costs.

Since **agents adjust behaviour based on inspection probability**, the game involves **strategic deterrence**.

Why It Works

The **Inspection Game works because**:

- **Inspectors cannot monitor constantly, making strategic planning necessary.**
- **Violators weigh potential rewards against the risk of detection.**
- **An optimal inspection rate emerges to balance costs and deterrence.**

How It Works

1. **The inspector chooses how often to inspect, considering costs.**
2. **The inspected party decides whether to comply or take risks.**
3. **If inspections are frequent, compliance increases.**
4. **If inspections are rare, violations may rise, requiring policy adjustments.**

Applications of the Inspection Game

1. **Tax Compliance** – Governments audit taxpayers to prevent fraud.

2. **Workplace Safety** – Regulators inspect businesses to enforce safety laws.

3. **Anti-Doping in Sports** – Athletes may dope unless frequent testing deters them.

4. **Cybersecurity** – Companies monitor systems to detect insider threats.

Key Insights

1. **Randomized inspections increase deterrence while reducing costs.**

2. **Violators adjust behaviour based on enforcement frequency.**

3. **Strategic deterrence balances compliance incentives and enforcement expenses.**

4. **Game dynamics apply to law enforcement, corporate regulation, and national security.**

Final Thoughts

The **Inspection Game** explains **how authorities enforce rules while managing resource constraints**. Whether in **tax enforcement, corporate oversight, or security,** optimizing **inspection strategies ensures compliance without excessive monitoring costs.**

84 Signalling Games

Signalling Games in Game Theory

Breakdown of the Theory

Signalling Games in **game theory and economics** model interactions where **one player (the sender) has private information that the other player (the receiver) does not**. The sender **chooses an action (signal) to reveal or conceal their type**, while the receiver **interprets the signal and decides how to respond.**

This framework is widely used in **markets, job hiring, education, and negotiations**, where parties make decisions based on **limited and asymmetric information**. The key challenge is distinguishing between **credible and deceptive signals**, as **cheap talk (false signals) can lead to inefficient outcomes.**

Key assumptions of **Signalling Games**:

1. **One player (the sender) knows their type (e.g., skill level, product quality).**

2. **The other player (the receiver) cannot directly observe the sender's type.**

3. **The sender can send signals to indicate their type.**

4. **The receiver updates their beliefs and chooses an action based on the signal.**

Since **signals can be costly or strategically manipulated,** this game highlights **how communication, incentives, and credibility shape decisions.**

Example of a Signalling Game

Consider **a job market,** where **candidates (senders) signal their abilities to employers (receivers):**

Scenario	Candidate's Skill Level	Signal Sent (Education)	Employer's Response	Outcome
1	High-skilled	Earns a degree	Employer offers a high salary	Good match, correct signalling.
2	Low-skilled	Earns a degree	Employer offers a high salary	Mismatch, signalling failure.
3	Low-skilled	No degree	Employer offers a lower salary	Correct inference, market efficiency.

- **If education is costly, only high-skilled workers will invest in degrees, making the signal credible.**
- **If low-skilled workers also obtain degrees, the signal loses value (signal breakdown).**

- **Employers adjust wages based on perceived credibility of signals.**

Since **not all signals are equally informative**, the game involves **strategic signalling and interpretation**.

Why It Works

The **Signalling Game works because:**

- **Signals provide information that would otherwise remain hidden.**

- **Costly signals are more credible than costless ones.**

- **Receivers adjust their strategies based on observed signals.**

How It Works

1. **The sender chooses whether to send a signal, considering costs and benefits.**

2. **The receiver interprets the signal based on prior knowledge.**

3. **If the signal is credible, it influences the receiver's decision.**

4. **Repeated interactions refine signalling behaviour and market expectations.**

Applications of Signalling Games

1. **Education & Job Markets** – Degrees signal competence to employers.

2. **Advertising** – High-quality brands spend more on marketing to signal reliability.

3. **Financial Markets** – Firms issue dividends to signal profitability.

4. **Dating & Social Behaviour** – People signal attractiveness through fashion, status, or behaviour.

Key Insights

1. **Credible signals require a cost that deters dishonest players from imitating them.**

2. **Signalling affects decisions in markets, hiring, branding, and social interactions.**

3. **Receivers must distinguish between genuine and misleading signals.**

4. **The effectiveness of signalling depends on market norms and verification methods.**

Final Thoughts

The **Signalling Game** explains **how private information is communicated through strategic actions.** Whether in **job hiring, marketing, or financial markets, credible signalling ensures efficient decision-making while minimizing deception.**

85 Stackelberg Security Game

Stackelberg Security Game in Game Theory

Breakdown of the Theory

The **Stackelberg Security Game** is a strategic model used in **security and resource allocation** where a **defender (leader)** must commit to a security strategy before an **attacker (follower) decides how to respond**. This game is based on the **Stackelberg competition model**, which involves **sequential decision-making**, meaning that the leader (defender) must anticipate the follower's (attacker's) reaction when making decisions.

Unlike simultaneous-move games (where players act at the same time), the Stackelberg framework **exploits the first-mover advantage**, allowing the defender to optimize security placement **while considering how attackers will respond**.

Key assumptions of the **Stackelberg Security Game**:

1. **The defender (leader) allocates security resources to protect critical locations.**

2. **The attacker (follower) observes the defender's strategy and selects the weakest target.**

3. **Defender strategies aim to maximize overall protection while minimizing vulnerabilities.**

4. **The attacker acts rationally, choosing the best available target based on the defender's strategy.**

Since **attackers adapt to defensive strategies**, the game highlights **how proactive resource allocation can minimize security risks**.

Example of a Stackelberg Security Game

Consider **airport security screening**, where **officials must allocate guards and checkpoints to prevent illegal activities**:

Scenario	Security Allocation	Attacker's Response	Outcome
1	Guards focus on major entry points	Attacker targets weakly guarded exits	Security breach.
2	Guards are evenly distributed	Attacker has no easy target	Risk is minimized.
3	Randomized security placement	Attacker faces uncertainty	High deterrence, attack probability decreases.

- **If security focuses only on high-risk areas, attackers exploit weak spots.**

- **If resources are evenly or unpredictably distributed, attackers have no clear advantage.**

- The optimal strategy balances security effectiveness and resource limitations.

Since **attackers react to visible defences**, defenders must anticipate threats and allocate resources efficiently.

Why It Works

The **Stackelberg Security Game works because**:

- Defenders exploit the first-mover advantage by planning ahead.
- Attackers' rational responses can be predicted and countered.
- Randomization in security deployment reduces predictability and deters threats.

How It Works

1. The defender commits to a strategy, allocating security resources.
2. The attacker observes and analyses weaknesses.
3. The attacker selects a target based on the defender's placement.
4. The defender adjusts strategies over time to improve security outcomes.

Applications of the Stackelberg Security Game

1. **Airport & Border Security** – Optimizing patrols and checkpoints to prevent smuggling or attacks.

2. **Cybersecurity** – Deploying firewalls and security patches to deter hackers.

3. **Critical Infrastructure Protection** – Securing power plants, water supplies, and transportation networks.

4. **Military Strategy** – Allocating defensive forces to strategic locations.

Key Insights

1. **Proactive security planning deters rational attackers.**

2. **Attackers adapt to security strategies, requiring constant adjustments.**

3. **Randomized security measures reduce attacker advantages.**

4. **The first-mover advantage allows defenders to shape the attacker's choices.**

Final Thoughts

The **Stackelberg Security Game** explains **how strategic resource allocation enhances defence against intelligent attackers**. Whether in **cybersecurity, law enforcement, or military operations, anticipating threats and optimizing defences minimizes risks and strengthens security.**

86 Cascading Failure Game

Cascading Failure Game in Game Theory

Breakdown of the Theory

The **Cascading Failure Game** in **game theory and network science** models how **small failures in a system can trigger a chain reaction, leading to widespread breakdowns**. The game is particularly useful for understanding **financial crises, power grid failures, supply chain disruptions, and cyberattacks**, where one weak link can lead to systemic collapse.

Unlike standard games where players compete, **cascading failure models focus on interdependencies**, showing how a failure in one area increases the risk of failure in connected areas. The key strategic question is **how to allocate resources to prevent failures from spreading**.

Key assumptions of the **Cascading Failure Game**:

1. **The system is composed of interconnected nodes (e.g., power plants, banks, or network servers).**

2. **A failure in one node increases the probability of failure in connected nodes.**

3. **Players (system operators or policymakers) must allocate resources to reinforce critical nodes.**

4. **Failure spreads dynamically, often accelerating as more nodes collapse.**

Since **failure spreads based on interconnections,** this game highlights **how preventive measures and resilience planning can reduce systemic risk.**

Example of a Cascading Failure Game

Consider **a financial system where banks lend money to each other:**

Scenario	Bank A's Stability	Bank B's Stability	Outcome
1	Bank A remains solvent	Bank B remains solvent	System remains stable.
2	Bank A collapses	Bank B is exposed, but has enough reserves	Containment is successful.
3	Bank A collapses	Bank B collapses due to exposure	Financial contagion spreads.

- **If one bank fails but others are strong, the failure is contained.**

- **If multiple banks are weakly connected, a domino effect occurs.**

- **The system's stability depends on the resilience of key nodes.**

Since **weaknesses amplify under stress, preventing failures before they spread is critical.**

Why It Works

The **Cascading Failure Game works because:**

- **Small failures can scale up, making prevention essential.**
- **Interconnected systems amplify risks, requiring strategic interventions.**
- **Adaptive responses and resource allocation influence system stability.**

How It Works

1. **A shock (e.g., power outage, bank run, cyberattack) affects a key node.**
2. **Failure spreads to connected nodes unless contained.**
3. **If prevention strategies are effective, the cascade stops.**
4. **If resources are insufficient, systemic collapse follows.**

Applications of the Cascading Failure Game

1. **Financial Crises** – Preventing contagion in interconnected banking systems.

2. **Power Grid Management** – Reinforcing infrastructure to stop blackouts.

3. **Cybersecurity** – Containing malware before it spreads across networks.

4. **Supply Chain Resilience** – Ensuring key suppliers do not trigger shortages.

Key Insights

1. **Early intervention prevents system-wide collapse.**

2. **Interdependencies amplify risks, making resilience planning crucial.**

3. **Strategic resource allocation can limit the spread of failure.**

4. **Understanding cascading effects helps design robust systems.**

Final Thoughts

The **Cascading Failure Game** explains **how small failures grow into systemic crises.** Whether in **finance, cybersecurity, or infrastructure, identifying and reinforcing weak links ensures resilience and long-term stability.**

87 Common Knowledge Game

Common Knowledge Game in Game Theory

Breakdown of the Theory

The **Common Knowledge Game** in **game theory and epistemic logic** models situations where **players must coordinate their actions based on shared knowledge**. The key distinction between **private knowledge** and **common knowledge** is that in the latter, **not only does everyone know a piece of information, but everyone knows that everyone else knows it, and so on, indefinitely**.

This concept is crucial in **coordination problems, market behaviour, political movements, and social conventions**, where **successful cooperation depends on mutual awareness of shared information**. Even if all players **individually know a fact**, they may fail to act unless they are sure that others also know it—and that others know that they know it.

Key assumptions of the **Common Knowledge Game**:

1. **Players have information that is not only known but is also publicly acknowledged.**

2. **Each player makes decisions based on the belief that others will act accordingly.**

3. **If common knowledge is absent, players may hesitate or fail to coordinate.**

4. **Public announcements, signals, or shared observations help establish common knowledge.**

Since **shared understanding is required for coordinated action**, this game highlights **how communication, expectations, and mutual trust drive strategic behaviour.**

Example of the Common Knowledge Game

Consider **a protest movement**, where **citizens oppose a government policy but fear acting alone**:

Scenario	Individual Knowledge	Belief About Others	Outcome
1	Knows the policy is unpopular	Believes others are unaware	No protest occurs.
2	Knows the policy is unpopular	Knows others also oppose it, but not sure they will act	Hesitation, weak protest.
3	Knows the policy is unpopular	Knows that others know it, and that they know it too	Large-scale protest happens.

- **If individuals privately oppose the policy but doubt others will act, no protest occurs.**

- If opposition becomes common knowledge, coordinated action follows.

- Public signals (e.g., news coverage, social media) turn private beliefs into common knowledge.

Since **coordination depends on expectations about others**, the game illustrates **why shared awareness is crucial for collective action**.

Why It Works

The **Common Knowledge Game works because**:

- **People act only if they believe others will act too.**

- **Public signals help establish common knowledge, enabling coordination.**

- **Lack of common knowledge can prevent action, even when all players share the same goal.**

How It Works

1. **Players privately hold the same information.**

2. **They assess whether others also know it.**

3. **If they are uncertain, coordination fails.**

4. **A public event (e.g., an announcement or visible action) makes knowledge common, enabling cooperation.**

Applications of the Common Knowledge Game

1. **Financial Markets** – Investors react to interest rate changes when they know that others know about it.

2. **Political Revolutions** – Uprisings occur when citizens realize their grievances are widely shared.

3. **Advertising & Branding** – Companies establish credibility when many consumers recognize their brand.

4. **Social Norms & Conventions** – Traffic rules work because drivers assume others follow them too.

Key Insights

1. **Common knowledge is essential for large-scale coordination.**

2. **Private knowledge alone does not guarantee action.**

3. **Public signals help convert shared beliefs into common knowledge.**

4. **Strategic decision-making depends on understanding what others believe.**

Final Thoughts

The **Common Knowledge Game** explains **why coordination depends on mutual awareness, not just private knowledge.** Whether in **politics, finance, or social behaviour, understanding how shared knowledge influences action is crucial for strategic decision-making.**

88 Self-Enforcing Agreements Game

Self-Enforcing Agreements Game in Game Theory

Breakdown of the Theory

The **Self-Enforcing Agreements Game** in **game theory and contract theory** models scenarios where agreements must be upheld **without external enforcement mechanisms**. Unlike legally binding contracts, self-enforcing agreements **rely on mutual incentives, trust, and the expectation of future interaction** to maintain cooperation.

This game is particularly relevant in **international relations, business partnerships, and informal economic transactions**, where players must ensure compliance **without relying on legal enforcement or third-party arbitration**. The key challenge is to structure agreements so that **each party benefits more from cooperation than from breaking the agreement**.

Key assumptions of the **Self-Enforcing Agreements Game**:

1. **Players engage in repeated or long-term interactions.**

2. **Breaking the agreement results in future losses, discouraging defection.**

3. **There is no external authority to enforce compliance.**

4. **Trust and reputation play a crucial role in sustaining cooperation.**

Since **players must voluntarily adhere to agreements,** this game highlights **how incentives, trust, and repeated interactions shape cooperation.**

Example of a Self-Enforcing Agreements Game

Consider **a trade partnership between two companies without legal contracts:**

Scenario	Company A's Action	Company B's Action	Outcome
1	Fulfils trade agreement	Fulfils trade agreement	Mutual trust, long-term gains.
2	Fulfils trade agreement	Defects, takes advantage	B gains short-term profit, but loses future business.
3	Defects	Defects	No trust, both suffer losses.

- **If both companies honour the agreement, they enjoy stable business.**

- **If one company defects, it gains short-term profit but loses long-term trust.**

- **If both defect, the relationship collapses, leading to mutual losses.**

Since **players anticipate long-term consequences, defection is discouraged, and cooperation is sustained.**

Why It Works

The **Self-Enforcing Agreements Game works because:**

- **Players value long-term cooperation over short-term gains.**
- **Trust and reputation act as natural enforcement mechanisms.**
- **Defection leads to loss of future benefits, discouraging opportunistic behaviour.**

How It Works

1. **Players voluntarily enter an agreement based on mutual benefit.**
2. **They assess the long-term consequences of breaking the agreement.**
3. **If defection leads to reputation loss or exclusion, they choose cooperation.**
4. **The agreement is self-sustaining as long as future benefits outweigh short-term gains.**

Applications of the Self-Enforcing Agreements Game

1. **International Trade** – Countries honour treaties without legal enforcement.

2. **Business Partnerships** – Companies maintain long-term relationships based on trust.

3. **Supply Chain Management** – Vendors and suppliers cooperate without strict contracts.

4. **Social & Community Agreements** – Informal pacts (e.g., rent agreements among friends) rely on self-enforcement.

Key Insights

1. **Reputation and future interactions incentivize cooperation.**

2. **Agreements must be structured so that breaking them is costly.**

3. **Long-term relationships sustain compliance better than legal enforcement alone.**

4. **Trust-based systems are essential in business, trade, and diplomacy.**

Final Thoughts

The **Self-Enforcing Agreements Game** explains **how cooperation can be sustained without external enforcement.** Whether in **business, international relations, or informal agreements, ensuring long-term incentives and trust-based mechanisms guarantees compliance and stability.**

89 Mechanism Design Theory

Mechanism Design Theory in Game Theory

Breakdown of the Theory

Mechanism Design Theory is a branch of **game theory and economics** that focuses on **creating systems or rules that lead to desired outcomes** when individuals act according to their own self-interest. Unlike traditional game theory, which analyses how players behave in existing games, **mechanism design is about designing the game itself to achieve specific goals**.

The theory is widely used in **auctions, voting systems, contract design, and resource allocation**, where decision-makers must **incentivize truthful behaviour and efficiency** while considering private information and strategic interactions.

Key assumptions of **Mechanism Design Theory**:

1. **Players act rationally and maximize their self-interest.**

2. **The designer (mechanism creator) sets rules to guide behaviour toward optimal outcomes.**

3. **Participants may have private information that influences their decisions.**

4. **The mechanism should be incentive-compatible, meaning that truthfully revealing information is the best strategy.**

Since **participants respond to incentives, mechanisms must be carefully structured** to align individual incentives with societal or organizational goals.

Example of Mechanism Design Theory

Consider **a government auctioning off radio frequencies to telecom companies:**

Scenario	Auction Design	Company Strategy	Outcome
1	Open bidding	Companies bid strategically	Prices may be driven too high or too low.
2	Sealed-bid auction	Companies submit secret bids	Encourages companies to bid truthfully.
3	Vickrey auction (second-price)	Highest bidder wins but pays second-highest bid	Truthful bidding is the best strategy.

- **If the auction is poorly designed, bidders may manipulate prices or misrepresent values.**

- **A well-designed mechanism ensures fair pricing and efficient allocation.**

- The Vickrey auction encourages truthful bidding, preventing inefficiencies.

Since **bidders act strategically, the auction mechanism must align incentives with efficiency goals**.

Why It Works

The **Mechanism Design Theory works because**:

- Rules shape strategic behaviour and decision-making.

- Incentive structures encourage truthful information sharing.

- Well-designed mechanisms maximize efficiency and fairness.

How It Works

1. A designer (government, firm, or institution) creates a mechanism with specific rules.

2. Participants act strategically based on their private information.

3. The mechanism ensures that following the rules leads to the desired outcome.

4. Incentives prevent manipulation and promote efficiency.

Applications of Mechanism Design Theory

1. **Auction Design** – Ensuring fair and efficient pricing in government auctions.

2. **Voting Systems** – Creating fair voting rules to reflect true public preferences.

3. **Contract Design** – Structuring contracts to incentivize performance.

4. **Healthcare & Education** – Allocating resources efficiently based on needs.

Key Insights

1. **Mechanisms must align individual incentives with societal goals.**

2. **Well-designed rules prevent strategic manipulation.**

3. **Truthful behaviour should be the best strategy for participants.**

4. **Applications span auctions, policy-making, and economic systems.**

Final Thoughts

Mechanism Design Theory explains **how to create rules and systems that drive desired behaviours and efficient outcomes.** Whether in **auctions, governance, or economic planning, designing the right incentives ensures fairness, efficiency, and truthfulness in decision-making.**

Classic & Foundational Game Theory Models

90 Prisoner's Dilemma

Prisoner's Dilemma in Game Theory

Breakdown of the Theory

The **Prisoner's Dilemma** is one of the most famous models in **game theory**, illustrating how **rational decision-making can lead to suboptimal outcomes** when individuals prioritize self-interest over cooperation. It is a **non-cooperative, simultaneous-move game** where two players must decide whether to **cooperate** or **defect**, without knowing what the other will choose.

The dilemma highlights the **conflict between individual rationality and collective benefit**. If both players act in their **own self-interest**, they end up worse off than if they had cooperated. This game is widely applied in **economics, politics, environmental policy, and international relations** to explain real-world conflicts between cooperation and competition.

Key assumptions of the **Prisoner's Dilemma**:

1. **Players cannot communicate or form binding agreements.**

2. **Each player seeks to maximize their individual payoff.**

3. **Mutual cooperation provides a better collective outcome than mutual defection.**

4. However, the incentive to defect is strong, leading to a suboptimal equilibrium.

Since **players cannot trust each other fully,** this game highlights **why cooperation is difficult, even when it benefits everyone.**

Example of the Prisoner's Dilemma

Consider **two criminals arrested for a crime.** The police offer each of them a deal:

Scenario	Prisoner A's Decision	Prisoner B's Decision	Outcome
1	Cooperates (Stays Silent)	Cooperates (Stays Silent)	Both serve 1 year.
2	Defects (Confesses)	Cooperates	A is freed, B serves 5 years.
3	Cooperates	Defects	B is freed, A serves 5 years.
4	Both Defect	Both serve 3 years.	

- **If both prisoners remain silent, they get a light sentence (best collective outcome).**

- **If one confesses while the other stays silent, the confessor goes free, and the silent prisoner gets the maximum penalty.**

- If both confess, they get a moderate sentence, which is worse than mutual silence but better than full betrayal.

Since **both players fear being betrayed, the rational choice is to defect, even though mutual cooperation is better**.

Why It Works

The **Prisoner's Dilemma works because**:

- Players face uncertainty about the other's choice, leading to distrust.

- The incentive to betray is greater than the incentive to cooperate.

- Self-interest leads to a stable but suboptimal Nash equilibrium.

How It Works

1. Each player independently decides whether to cooperate or defect.

2. They weigh the risk of betrayal against the benefit of mutual cooperation.

3. If both defect, they suffer a worse outcome than if they had trusted each other.

4. Over repeated interactions, trust and cooperation may evolve through strategies like tit-for-tat.

Applications of the Prisoner's Dilemma

1. **Business & Market Competition** – Firms face price wars when they fail to cooperate on pricing.

2. **Arms Races** – Countries escalate military spending instead of disarming together.

3. **Environmental Policy** – Nations hesitate to cut emissions unless others do the same.

4. **Social Behaviour** – Individuals may overuse public resources (e.g., deforestation, overfishing).

Key Insights

1. **Short-term self-interest can lead to worse long-term outcomes.**

2. **Trust and repeated interactions encourage cooperation over time.**

3. **Institutions and agreements (e.g., contracts, treaties) help enforce cooperation.**

4. **Understanding incentives and communication can shift outcomes toward mutual benefit.**

Final Thoughts

The **Prisoner's Dilemma** explains **why rational individuals** sometimes make collectively **irrational decisions.**
Whether in **economics, politics, or environmental issues, creating trust and enforcement mechanisms can lead to cooperation, avoiding suboptimal Nash equilibria.**

91 Nash Equilibrium

Nash Equilibrium in Game Theory

Breakdown of the Theory

The **Nash Equilibrium** is a fundamental concept in **game theory**, describing a situation where **no player has an incentive to change their strategy unilaterally**, given the strategies chosen by others. It represents a **stable state** where each player's choice is optimal **considering the decisions of all other players.**

This equilibrium applies to **competitive and cooperative scenarios** in **economics, business, politics, and social interactions**, explaining why players **stick to certain strategies even when better outcomes might exist through cooperation.**

Key assumptions of the **Nash Equilibrium**:

1. **Players act rationally to maximize their payoffs.**

2. **Each player knows the strategies of others.**

3. **No player benefits by deviating unilaterally from their strategy.**

4. **Multiple Nash equilibria can exist in some games.**

Since **players do not have an incentive to change strategies, the equilibrium remains stable** unless external forces alter the game.

Example of Nash Equilibrium

Consider **a pricing decision between two competing firms (A and B):**

Scenario	Firm A's Price	Firm B's Price	Outcome
1	Low	Low	Price war, both earn low profits.
2	Low	High	A captures the market, B suffers losses.
3	High	Low	B captures the market, A suffers losses.
4	High	High	Both maintain stable profits (Nash Equilibrium).

- **If both firms price high, neither has an incentive to undercut, as it would lead to retaliation and lower profits.**

- **If one firm lowers its price, it gains a short-term advantage, but the other firm may retaliate.**

- **The stable outcome is where both firms price high, as neither gains by deviating alone.**

Since **each firm's best response depends on the other's choice, a Nash equilibrium emerges when both firms settle on a stable pricing strategy.**

Why It Works

The **Nash Equilibrium works because:**

- **Players optimize their strategies given the choices of others.**

- **Deviating from equilibrium results in lower payoffs.**

- **It represents a self-enforcing strategy profile, requiring no external enforcement.**

How It Works

1. **Each player selects a strategy, anticipating others' choices.**

2. **They evaluate whether changing their strategy would increase their payoff.**

3. **If no player benefits from deviation, the game reaches equilibrium.**

4. **Players remain in equilibrium unless external conditions change.**

Applications of Nash Equilibrium

1. **Business & Market Competition** – Firms stabilize pricing and market strategies.

2. **Politics & Elections** – Candidates adopt positions that appeal to the median voter.

3. **Traffic Flow** – Drivers select optimal routes based on congestion levels.

4. **Negotiation & Bargaining** – Parties reach stable agreements without unilateral deviation.

Key Insights

1. **Nash equilibrium ensures stability, even if outcomes are not socially optimal.**

2. **Multiple equilibria may exist, depending on game structure.**

3. **Players must consider others' responses when making decisions.**

4. **In real-world scenarios, learning and adaptation influence equilibrium formation.**

Final Thoughts

The **Nash Equilibrium** explains **why strategic interactions lead to stable yet sometimes inefficient outcomes.** Whether in **business, politics, or economics, understanding equilibrium behaviour helps predict decision-making and optimize strategic choices.**

92 Battle of the Sexes

Battle of the Sexes in Game Theory

Breakdown of the Theory

The Battle of the Sexes is a coordination game in game theory that models a scenario where two players want to coordinate but have conflicting individual preferences. It illustrates how mutual cooperation is beneficial but requires negotiation and compromise.

The game typically involves two players (e.g., a couple) choosing between two activities. They prefer to be together rather than apart, but each has a different preferred activity. The challenge lies in how they coordinate and decide whose preference to follow while avoiding a situation where they fail to meet at all.

Key assumptions of the Battle of the Sexes:

1. **Players prefer to coordinate rather than act separately.**

2. **Each player has a different preferred outcome.**

3. **Multiple equilibria exist, meaning different stable solutions are possible.**

4. **If coordination fails, both players receive the lowest payoff.**

Since players value staying together more than enforcing their preference, this game highlights negotiation, compromise, and the role of communication.

Example of the Battle of the Sexes

Consider a couple deciding on an evening plan:

Scenario	Player A's Choice (Prefers Football)	Player B's Choice (Prefers Ballet)	Outcome
1	Goes to football	Goes to football	A is happy, B less happy but they are together.
2	Goes to ballet	Goes to ballet	B is happy, A less happy but they are together.
3	Goes to football	Goes to ballet	No coordination, both are unhappy.

- **If they fail to coordinate, both suffer.**

- **If one player compromises, they coordinate, but satisfaction is uneven.**

- **An external agreement (taking turns, flipping a coin) could help resolve the conflict.**

Since mutual benefit depends on successful coordination, this game involves strategic communication and decision-making.

Why It Works

The Battle of the Sexes works because:

- It models real-world situations where coordination is essential, but preferences differ.

- Players must balance self-interest with mutual benefit.

- Compromise and signalling play key roles in achieving a stable outcome.

How It Works

1. Players independently choose an action without knowing the other's choice.

2. They prefer to be together but have different ideal outcomes.

3. They must decide how to resolve the conflict— either through compromise or external agreements.

4. If coordination fails, both suffer, reinforcing the need for negotiation.

Applications of the Battle of the Sexes

1. Business Negotiations – Partners must agree on terms despite differing preferences.

2. Workplace Decision-Making – Teams must align on strategic goals despite internal conflicts.

3. International Relations – Countries align on trade deals despite varying interests.

4. Social Interactions & Relationships – Couples or friends negotiate on mutual plans.

Key Insights

1. Coordination is more valuable than personal preference enforcement.

2. Multiple equilibria require negotiation or compromise.

3. Signalling and external agreements can resolve conflicts.

4. The game illustrates challenges in teamwork, diplomacy, and decision-making.

Final Thoughts

The Battle of the Sexes explains how individuals navigate coordination dilemmas when preferences differ. Whether in business, relationships, or diplomacy, successful negotiation and compromise ensure stable, mutually beneficial outcomes.

93 Stag Hunt

Stag Hunt in Game Theory

Breakdown of the Theory

The **Stag Hunt** is a **coordination game** in **game theory** that models the trade-off between **social cooperation and individual risk aversion**. It describes a scenario where **players must decide whether to cooperate for a high-reward outcome or act independently for a lower but safer payoff**.

The game is based on a story by **Jean-Jacques Rousseau**, where two hunters must decide whether to **hunt a stag (which requires cooperation)** or **hunt a hare (which can be done alone but offers lower rewards)**. The dilemma arises because **cooperation yields the highest reward, but if one hunter defects, the other is left with nothing**.

Key assumptions of the **Stag Hunt**:

1. **Players can choose between a high-risk, high-reward strategy (cooperation) or a low-risk, low-reward strategy (individualism).**

2. **If both players cooperate, they achieve the best possible outcome.**

3. **If one defects, the other suffers a loss, making defection a safer choice.**

4. **Multiple equilibria exist, meaning different stable solutions are possible.**

Since **trust and expectations shape player choices**, this game highlights **the challenge of achieving cooperation when risk is involved**.

Example of the Stag Hunt

Consider **two business partners deciding on an investment**:

Scenario	Player A's Choice	Player B's Choice	Outcome
1	Invest (Stag)	Invest (Stag)	High profit for both.
2	Invest (Stag)	Play it safe (Hare)	A loses investment, B gets small profit.
3	Play it safe (Hare)	Invest (Stag)	B loses investment, A gets small profit.
4	Play it safe (Hare)	Play it safe (Hare)	Both get a small, guaranteed profit.

- **If both invest (cooperate), they get a high return.**
- **If one plays it safe, the other suffers a loss.**
- **If both play it safe, they avoid risk but miss out on the best opportunity.**

Since **cooperation is optimal but risky, trust is essential for achieving the best outcome**.

Why It Works

The **Stag Hunt works because**:

- **It models real-world coordination challenges where trust impacts decisions.**
- **Players must weigh short-term security against long-term rewards.**
- **The game illustrates how expectations about others' behaviour shape strategic choices.**

How It Works

1. **Players assess the risks and rewards of cooperation vs. individualism.**
2. **They decide based on their expectations of the other's choice.**
3. **If mutual cooperation occurs, both benefit greatly.**
4. **If uncertainty leads to defection, both players settle for a suboptimal but safe result.**

Applications of the Stag Hunt

1. **Business Partnerships** – Companies collaborate for mutual success or compete individually for smaller gains.

2. **International Treaties** – Countries commit to agreements or act in self-interest.

3. **Technology Development** – Firms share research or work alone for minor advancements.

4. **Public Goods & Social Welfare** – Citizens invest in communal projects or prioritize individual benefits.

Key Insights

1. **Trust and coordination are crucial for achieving the best outcomes.**

2. **Fear of defection can lead to lower payoffs for all players.**

3. **Establishing credibility and communication improves cooperation.**

4. **The game illustrates real-world dilemmas in politics, business, and economics.**

Final Thoughts

The **Stag Hunt** explains **how cooperation can lead to superior outcomes, but fear of betrayal often hinders collective progress. Whether in business, politics, or social projects, building trust and commitment is key to maximizing rewards in strategic interactions.**

94 Chicken Game

Chicken Game in Game Theory

Breakdown of the Theory

The **Chicken Game** is a classic model in **game theory** that represents a **high-risk, competitive situation where two players must decide whether to yield or stay firm**. The central tension in this game arises from **the potential catastrophic outcome if neither player backs down**. The game illustrates **brinkmanship, risk-taking, and strategic negotiation** and is widely applied in **politics, business, and social dynamics**.

The game is often described using the metaphor of **two drivers heading toward each other**—whoever swerves first is labelled a "chicken" (loser), but if neither swerves, they crash, leading to the worst possible outcome. The game captures **conflict escalation, competitive aggression, and the importance of credibility in strategic decision-making**.

Key assumptions of the **Chicken Game**:

1. **Two players must choose between yielding (cooperating) or staying firm (defecting).**

2. **The worst outcome occurs if neither player yields.**

3. **If one player yields while the other does not, the yielding player gets a lesser payoff.**

4. **Each player prefers that the other yield while they stand firm.**

Since **the game involves extreme risk, players must balance strategic aggression with the cost of mutual destruction.**

Example of the Chicken Game

Consider **a business price war between two competing firms:**

Scenario	Firm A's Decision	Firm B's Decision	Outcome
1	Lowers prices aggressively	Lowers prices aggressively	Price war, both suffer heavy losses.
2	Lowers prices aggressively	Maintains stable pricing	A captures market share, B loses.
3	Maintains stable pricing	Lowers prices aggressively	B captures market share, A loses.
4	Maintains stable pricing	Maintains stable pricing	Both retain profits, no destructive competition.

- If both lower prices aggressively, a destructive price war occurs.

- If one lowers prices while the other maintains stability, the aggressive firm wins market share.

- If both maintain stability, they avoid unnecessary losses.

-

Since **players want to be aggressive but fear mutual destruction, strategic signalling and reputation matter**.

Why It Works

The **Chicken Game works because**:

- It models real-world conflicts where backing down has social or strategic costs.

- Bluffing, commitment, and signalling influence outcomes.

- Players must gauge their opponent's willingness to take risks.

How It Works

1. Each player decides whether to yield or stay firm.

2. They evaluate the risk of mutual destruction versus strategic advantage.

3. If neither backs down, both suffer the worst outcome.

4. If one player yields, they avoid disaster but at a strategic cost.

Applications of the Chicken Game

1. **International Relations** – Nuclear deterrence and diplomatic standoffs.

2. **Business Competition** – Price wars, labour strikes, or aggressive market strategies.

3. **Social & Political Movements** – Protesters vs. governments in policy disputes.

4. **Personal Conflicts** – Stubborn negotiations in personal or workplace settings.

Key Insights

1. The fear of mutual destruction creates incentives for compromise.

2. Strategic commitment and signalling influence the opponent's decision.

3. **Bluffing can be risky—misjudging the opponent's resolve leads to disaster.**

4. **Understanding the opponent's risk tolerance is crucial in high-stakes scenarios.**

Final Thoughts

The **Chicken Game** explains **how strategic decision-making unfolds in high-risk conflicts where backing down has costs but standing firm risks disaster**. Whether in business, politics, or competitive negotiations, players must carefully balance risk, credibility, and negotiation tactics to avoid catastrophic outcomes.

95 Ultimatum Game

Ultimatum Game in Game Theory

Breakdown of the Theory

The **Ultimatum Game** is a fundamental model in **game theory and behavioural economics** that explores **fairness, negotiation, and rational decision-making**. It demonstrates how **social and psychological factors influence economic behaviour**, often contradicting classical economic theory, which assumes players act solely in their own financial self-interest.

In the **Ultimatum Game**, two players must decide how to split a sum of money:

- **Player 1 (Proposer)** offers a division of the total amount.

- **Player 2 (Responder)** can either **accept** the offer (both players receive the proposed amounts) or **reject** it (both players get nothing).

Traditional economic theory suggests that **Player 2 should accept any nonzero offer**, as receiving something is better than nothing. However, in practice, **unfair offers are often rejected**, highlighting the role of **fairness, emotions, and social norms** in decision-making.

Key assumptions of the **Ultimatum Game**:

1. **Player 1 wants to maximize their share but must consider Player 2's reaction.**

2. **Player 2 may reject an unfair offer even at a personal financial cost.**

3. **Fairness and reciprocity influence decision-making.**

4. **Players behave differently based on cultural, psychological, and social factors.**

Since **accepting even a small offer is rational but not always psychologically acceptable, the game highlights the conflict between economic self-interest and perceived fairness.**

Example of the Ultimatum Game

Consider **two coworkers splitting a $100 work bonus:**

Scenario	Player 1's Offer	Player 2's Decision	Outcome
1	$50 to A, $50 to B	Accepts	Fair split, both receive money.
2	$80 to A, $20 to B	Accepts	Unfair but accepted, B gets some money.
3	$90 to A, $10 to B	Rejects	B refuses, both receive nothing.

- **If Player 1 offers an even split, Player 2 usually accepts.**

- If Player 1 offers too little, Player 2 may reject it out of fairness, even at a personal cost.

- Anticipating rejection, Player 1 often makes a fairer offer than pure economic rationality would predict.

Since **social norms affect decision-making**, strategic fairness leads to better outcomes.

Why It Works

The **Ultimatum Game works because**:

- It challenges traditional economic models of rationality.

- Fairness, social norms, and emotions shape financial decisions.

- Players adapt strategies based on expected responses.

How It Works

1. Player 1 proposes a division, balancing greed with fairness.

2. Player 2 assesses the offer based on fairness, not just financial gain.

3. If Player 2 rejects, both players lose, enforcing fairness norms.

4. Over multiple rounds, proposers learn to offer more equitable splits.

Applications of the Ultimatum Game

1. **Salary & Contract Negotiations** – Employers and employees negotiate wages.

2. **Business Deals** – Partners decide how to distribute profits.

3. **Legal Settlements** – Parties negotiate compensation in disputes.

4. **Public Policy & Taxation** – Governments set policies that balance fairness and compliance.

Key Insights

1. **People value fairness and will sacrifice financial gains to enforce it.**

2. **Social and psychological factors influence economic behaviour.**

3. **Negotiation success depends on anticipating the other party's response.**

4. **Fairness norms emerge naturally, even without external enforcement.**

Final Thoughts

The **Ultimatum Game** explains **how fairness influences strategic decision-making.** Whether in **business, law, or social interactions, understanding fairness expectations can lead to better negotiations, cooperation, and long-term success.**

96 Dictator Game

Dictator Game in Game Theory

Breakdown of the Theory

The **Dictator Game** is a fundamental experiment in **game theory and behavioural economics** that explores **altruism, fairness, and social preferences**. Unlike traditional economic models that assume people act purely out of self-interest, the Dictator Game provides insights into **human generosity, ethical decision-making, and power dynamics**.

In this game:

- **Player 1 (the Dictator)** is given a sum of money or resources and has total control over how to divide it.

- **Player 2 (the Recipient)** has no say in the decision and must accept whatever is given.

Unlike the **Ultimatum Game**, where the recipient can reject the offer, the Dictator Game is a pure test of **generosity and fairness** because there is no strategic reason for Player 1 to give anything—they face no consequences for keeping the entire sum.

Key assumptions of the **Dictator Game**:

1. **Player 1 has complete power over the resource allocation.**

2. **Player 2 is passive and cannot influence the decision.**

3. **Rational self-interest suggests Player 1 should keep everything.**

4. **In practice, many dictators give away some portion, revealing social preferences.**

Since **there is no penalty for selfishness, this game highlights the role of moral considerations in decision-making.**

Example of the Dictator Game

Consider a university experiment where students receive $100 and must decide how much to share with an anonymous partner:

Scenario	Player 1's Offer	Player 2's Response	Outcome
1	$100 to A, $0 to B	Accepts	A keeps everything, B gets nothing.
2	$80 to A, $20 to B	Accepts	A keeps most, but B receives something.
3	$50 to A, $50 to B	Accepts	Fair split, mutual benefit.

- **If Player 1 follows economic self-interest, they keep everything.**

- **If Player 1 values fairness, they share a portion, even without external pressure.**

- **Cultural and ethical norms influence generosity levels.**

Since **many dictators give away money despite having no obligation, social preferences play a key role in economic behaviour.**

Why It Works

The **Dictator Game works because**:

- **It isolates pure altruism by removing strategic incentives.**
- **It reveals social norms, ethics, and fairness preferences.**
- **Results vary across cultures, showing the impact of social conditioning.**

How It Works

1. **Player 1 receives a sum and decides how much to share.**
2. **Player 2 passively accepts the outcome.**
3. **Decisions reflect a mix of self-interest and moral considerations.**
4. **Over repeated experiments, patterns emerge, showing generosity norms.**

Applications of the Dictator Game

1. **Charitable Giving** – Explains why people donate money with no direct benefit.
2. **Workplace Leadership** – How managers allocate bonuses or promotions.
3. **Welfare & Policy Design** – Understanding support for wealth redistribution.

4. **Behavioural Economics** – Studying fairness and ethical decision-making.

Key Insights

1. Humans often act against pure economic self-interest due to fairness concerns.

2. Generosity levels vary based on culture, upbringing, and social context.

3. The game highlights the role of altruism, ethics, and social expectations in decision-making.

4. Understanding generosity helps in designing better policies and organizational structures.

Final Thoughts

The **Dictator Game** explains **how people balance self-interest with fairness, even in the absence of strategic incentives.** Whether in **charity, business, or policymaking,** understanding altruistic behaviour is crucial for shaping better economic and social systems.

97 Public Goods Game

Public Goods Game in Game Theory

Breakdown of the Theory

The **Public Goods Game** is a classic model in **game theory and behavioural economics** that explores the **tension between individual self-interest and collective benefit**. It demonstrates the **free-rider problem**, where individuals benefit from a public resource **without contributing** to its maintenance.

The game models **real-world dilemmas** such as **taxation, environmental conservation, and community projects**, where individuals must decide **whether to contribute or rely on others' generosity**.

Key assumptions of the **Public Goods Game**:

1. **A group of players receives an initial endowment (money, resources, or effort).**

2. **Each player decides how much to contribute to a shared public fund.**

3. **The total contributions are multiplied and distributed equally, regardless of individual input.**

4. **Players may choose to contribute fully, partially, or not at all (free-riding).**

Since **public goods benefit everyone regardless of contribution, players face the temptation to free-ride while hoping others contribute.**

Example of the Public Goods Game

Consider **a neighbourhood deciding whether to contribute to a community park:**

Scenario	Contribution Levels	Outcome
1	All contribute fairly	The park is well-funded and benefits everyone.
2	Some contribute, some free-ride	The park is built, but contributors feel exploited.
3	No one contributes	The park is not built, and everyone loses.

- **If everyone contributes, the group benefits the most.**

- **If too many people free-ride, the project fails, harming everyone.**

- **Players must balance personal cost against collective gain.**

Since **contributions are voluntary, enforcing cooperation** becomes a key challenge.

Why It Works

The **Public Goods Game works because**:

- It models real-world challenges in funding shared resources.

- It reveals how incentives, reputation, and trust influence contributions.

- Punishment and rewards can alter strategic behaviour.

How It Works

1. Players start with private resources.

2. They decide how much to contribute to a public fund.

3. Total contributions are multiplied and distributed equally.

4. Over multiple rounds, cooperation may increase or decline based on group dynamics.

Applications of the Public Goods Game

1. **Tax Compliance** – Governments rely on citizens paying taxes to fund public services.

2. **Environmental Conservation** – Individuals decide whether to reduce carbon footprints.

3. **Workplace Collaboration** – Employees contribute to team success but may shirk responsibility.

4. **Charitable Giving** – People donate to community projects without direct enforcement.

Key Insights

1. **Voluntary cooperation is fragile without enforcement mechanisms.**

2. **Trust and reputation encourage contributions.**

3. **Punishment for free-riders (e.g., fines, social sanctions) improves cooperation.**

4. **The game explains why governments use taxes and laws to maintain public goods.**

Final Thoughts

The **Public Goods Game** explains **how self-interest and collective benefit interact in shared-resource dilemmas.** Whether in **taxation, environmental policies, or community projects, incentives, trust, and enforcement mechanisms are essential for sustaining public goods.**

98 All-Pay Auction

All-Pay Auction in Game Theory

Breakdown of the Theory

The **All-Pay Auction** is a type of **auction game** in **game theory** where all bidders must **pay their bids regardless of whether they win**. This distinguishes it from traditional auctions, where only the highest bidder pays. It is commonly used to model **lobbying, political campaigns, rent-seeking behaviour, and competitive business investments**, where multiple players expend resources, but only one wins.

Unlike standard auctions where losing bidders pay nothing, in an **All-Pay Auction**:

- **Each participant submits a bid.**

- **The highest bidder wins the prize.**

- **All bidders, regardless of the outcome, pay their bid amount.**

This auction often leads to **overbidding**, where the total amount spent by participants exceeds the actual value of the prize.

Key assumptions of the **All-Pay Auction**:

1. **Players compete for a prize of fixed value.**

2. **All players pay their bids, even if they lose.**

3. **Each player aims to maximize their expected payoff by balancing bid size and winning probability.**

4. **Players may engage in overbidding, leading to potential losses.**

Since **losing still incurs a cost, the All-Pay Auction highlights the risks of competitive escalation and sunk costs.**

Example of an All-Pay Auction

Consider **two companies competing for a government contract:**

Scenario	Company A's Bid	Company B's Bid	Outcome
1	$500,000	$400,000	A wins but pays $500,000, B loses and pays $400,000.
2	$300,000	$600,000	B wins but pays $600,000, A loses and pays $300,000.
3	$700,000	$700,000	Tie—could lead to re-bidding or alternative selection.

- **If both companies bid aggressively, they may spend more than the contract's value.**

- A losing company still incurs significant costs, despite gaining nothing.

- If players anticipate aggressive bidding, they may adopt conservative strategies or drop out.

Since costs are unavoidable, participants must carefully assess whether the reward is worth the risk.

Why It Works

The **All-Pay Auction works because**:

- It models real-world competition where efforts are costly, regardless of success.

- Strategic escalation often leads to excessive spending.

- Participants face a dilemma between aggressive bidding and financial restraint.

How It Works

1. Players evaluate the prize's worth and decide on a bid.

2. Each submits a bid, knowing they must pay regardless of the outcome.

3. The highest bidder wins but may overpay.

4. Losers pay their bids and exit with losses.

Applications of the All-Pay Auction

1. **Political Lobbying** – Multiple interest groups spend money to influence legislation, but only one wins.

2. **Military Arms Races** – Countries invest in defence regardless of actual conflict.

3. **Advertising Wars** – Companies spend on marketing, but only one gains the dominant market position.

4. **Scholarship & Grant Applications** – Applicants invest time and resources, but only a few succeed.

Key Insights

1. **Sunk costs affect decision-making, leading to excessive bidding.**

2. **Participants must weigh the probability of winning against guaranteed losses.**

3. **All-Pay Auctions often result in inefficiency, as total spending exceeds the prize's value.**

4. **Understanding escalation risks helps prevent wasteful competition.**

Final Thoughts

The **All-Pay Auction** explains **how competitive environments with unavoidable costs lead to aggressive bidding and inefficiencies.** Whether in **politics, business, or military strategy, participants must carefully assess whether competing is worth the cost before engaging in an escalating contest.**

99 Matching Pennies

Matching Pennies in Game Theory

Breakdown of the Theory

The **Matching Pennies Game** is a fundamental example of a **zero-sum game** in **game theory**, where one player's gain is exactly the other player's loss. It represents **strategic decision-making under uncertainty**, with applications in **psychology, competitive markets, cybersecurity, and military tactics**.

In the game:

- **Two players (A and B) simultaneously choose heads or tails.**

- **If the choices match (both heads or both tails), Player A wins and Player B loses.**

- **If the choices differ (one heads, one tails), Player B wins and Player A loses.**

There is **no pure strategy Nash equilibrium** because if one player's choice is predictable, the other can always counter it. This creates a situation where the **best strategy is randomization**, making it an example of **mixed strategy equilibrium**.

Key assumptions of the **Matching Pennies Game**:

1. **The game is strictly competitive (zero-sum).**

2. **Each player tries to outguess the opponent.**

3. **Players cannot gain an advantage through a fixed strategy.**

4. **The optimal strategy involves randomness.**

Since **predictability leads to exploitation, players must act unpredictably to avoid losing.**

Example of the Matching Pennies Game

Consider **two companies launching a marketing campaign:**

Scenario	Company A's Strategy	Company B's Strategy	Outcome
1	Runs TV Ads	Runs TV Ads	A wins, B loses.
2	Runs TV Ads	Runs Social Media Ads	B wins, A loses.
3	Runs Social Media Ads	Runs TV Ads	A wins, B loses.
4	Runs Social Media Ads	Runs Social Media Ads	B wins, A loses.

- **If Company A always advertises on TV, Company B can exploit this by choosing social media.**

- **If Company A switches to social media, Company B may adapt to TV ads.**

- Since predictability is a disadvantage, companies should randomize strategies.

Since **opponents react to each other's moves, pure strategies are ineffective**, and the **optimal play is a probabilistic mix.**

Why It Works

The **Matching Pennies Game works because:**

- It models strategic uncertainty and competitive adaptation.

- Predictable strategies lead to exploitation.

- Players must use mixed strategies to maximize expected payoffs.

How It Works

1. Each player selects a strategy, trying to predict the other's choice.

2. If one player becomes predictable, the opponent exploits the pattern.

3. Since no fixed strategy guarantees a win, players use randomization.

4. A mixed strategy equilibrium occurs when players randomize choices optimally.

Applications of the Matching Pennies Game

1. **Cybersecurity** – Attackers and defenders must randomize strategies to avoid predictability.

2. **Sports Strategy** – Players in penalty kicks or poker mix strategies to remain unpredictable.

3. **Stock Market Trading** – Traders use algorithmic randomization to prevent exploitation.

4. **Military Tactics** – Nations use deception and mixed strategies in warfare.

Key Insights

1. **Pure strategies lead to exploitation, requiring mixed strategies.**

2. **Randomization prevents opponents from gaining an advantage.**

3. **The game is strictly zero-sum—one player's win is the other's loss.**

4. **Applications extend to business, security, and psychology.**

Final Thoughts

The **Matching Pennies Game** explains **how strategic unpredictability is crucial in competitive environments.** Whether in **business, sports, or cybersecurity, optimal decision-making often requires randomization to prevent exploitation.**

10 ames in Digital & AI Strategy

100 Algorithmic Trading Game

Algorithmic Trading Game in Game Theory

Breakdown of the Theory

The **Algorithmic Trading Game** applies **game theory** to **financial markets**, where traders use **automated algorithms** to buy and sell assets at high speeds. This creates a strategic competition where traders **predict, react, and counter each other's strategies** to maximize profits.

Unlike traditional trading, where humans make decisions based on market trends, **algorithmic trading (or high-frequency trading, HFT)** relies on **pre-programmed strategies** that execute trades in milliseconds. These algorithms must **anticipate competitors' moves while avoiding exploitation** by other trading bots.

Key assumptions of the **Algorithmic Trading Game**:

1. **Multiple traders (bots) operate simultaneously, competing in real-time.**

2. **Each bot tries to predict market trends and other bots' behaviour.**

3. **The fastest and most efficient strategies gain a competitive advantage.**

4. **Traders must balance risk, timing, and information processing.**

Since **market conditions change rapidly, bots must continuously adapt to maintain profitability**.

Example of an Algorithmic Trading Game

Consider **two hedge funds using algorithmic trading to profit from small price movements**:

Scenario	Fund A's Strategy	Fund B's Strategy	Outcome
1	Uses high-speed execution	Uses high-speed execution	Both compete, minimal advantage.
2	Uses arbitrage	Uses trend-following	Arbitrage strategy profits, trend strategy lags.
3	Uses market manipulation	Uses standard trading	Manipulator profits until detected.

- **If both funds rely on speed, no one gains a significant advantage.**

- **If one fund exploits pricing inefficiencies (e.g., arbitrage), it gains an edge.**

- **If a fund manipulates the market (e.g., spoofing), it profits until regulators intervene.**

Since **bots must predict rivals' actions, financial markets become a strategic battleground**.

Why It Works

The **Algorithmic Trading Game works because**:

- **It models real-time competition between intelligent agents.**

- **Speed, efficiency, and prediction define success.**

- **Players must constantly adjust strategies to avoid being outmanoeuvred.**

How It Works

1. **Traders develop algorithms based on historical data and market trends.**

2. **Bots execute trades, reacting to real-time price movements.**

3. **Competitors adapt to counter rival strategies.**

4. **Winners are those who predict, adapt, and execute the fastest.**

Applications of the Algorithmic Trading Game

1. **High-Frequency Trading (HFT)** – Firms execute thousands of trades per second.

2. **Market Making** – Bots provide liquidity by adjusting bid-ask spreads.

3. **Arbitrage Strategies** – Exploiting price differences across markets.

4. **Portfolio Optimization** – AI-driven trading for risk management.

Key Insights

1. **Speed is crucial, but predictive accuracy matters more.**

2. **Overly aggressive strategies can trigger market crashes (e.g., flash crashes).**

3. **Regulation plays a role in curbing manipulative trading tactics.**

4. **Algorithmic trading reshapes financial markets by increasing efficiency and volatility.**

Final Thoughts

The **Algorithmic Trading Game** explains **how financial markets have evolved into high-speed battlegrounds of strategic competition.** Whether in **HFT, market making, or portfolio management, traders must continuously adapt their algorithms to stay ahead of rivals and maximize profitability.**

OKAY, SO THAT'S 100!

BUT IF YOU HAVE GOT TO THIS PAGE, YOU ARE PROBABLY INTERESTED IN A COUPLE MORE GAME THEORY'S?

SO I'VE INCLUDED AN ADDITIONAL 9 HERE OVER THE NEXT FEW PAGES.

WHILST YOU ARE HERE , WHY NOT SCAN THIS TO SEE IF THERE ARE ANY MORE BOOKS PUBLISHED YET

OR FOLLOW ME AT @DANDANMUSICMAN

OKAY, 101 TO 109 HERE WE GO!

(A BIT LIKE THE HIDDEN TRACKS ON AN ALBUM)

101 Bonus - Ad Auction Game

Ad Auction Game in Game Theory

Breakdown of the Theory

The **Ad Auction Game** is a **game theory model** that explains how companies bid for online advertising space in **automated digital auctions**. These auctions determine which ads appear in **search engine results, social media feeds, and websites** based on **competitive bidding**.

The most widely used system is the **Generalized Second-Price (GSP) auction**, where advertisers **bid for ad placement**, but the **winner pays the price of the second-highest bid**. This creates a **strategic interaction**, as advertisers must decide how much to bid while anticipating their competitors' actions.

Key assumptions of the **Ad Auction Game**:

1. **Multiple advertisers compete for a limited number of ad slots.**

2. **Each advertiser assigns a value to appearing in a particular ad position.**

3. **The auction mechanism determines which ads are shown and at what price.**

4. **Advertisers aim to maximize clicks and conversions while minimizing ad costs.**

Since **bidding too high reduces profit margins and bidding too low risks losing visibility**, this game highlights **strategic balancing between cost and visibility**.

Example of an Ad Auction Game

Consider **three e-commerce companies bidding for Google Ads space for the keyword "running shoes"**:

Advertiser	Bid Amount ($)	Ad Rank (Based on Algorithm)	Payment ($)
A	$3.00	1st	Pays $2.50 (next highest bid)
B	$2.50	2nd	Pays $2.00
C	$2.00	3rd	Pays $1.50

- Advertiser A wins the top slot but pays only $2.50, the bid of the next-highest advertiser.

- If A had bid too low, it could have lost the top spot.

- Advertisers must balance bid size with the expected return on investment (ROI).

Since **bidding strategies affect both visibility and cost-efficiency, optimizing bids is crucial for maximizing ad performance.**

Why It Works

The **Ad Auction Game works because:**

- It models real-world competition for online visibility.

- Bidders must consider competitors' strategies, not just their own value.

- Automated algorithms make strategic adjustments in real-time.

How It Works

1. Advertisers set a maximum bid for ad placement.

2. A ranking algorithm (based on bid + quality score) determines ad placement.

3. Winning bidders pay the second-highest bid (GSP model).

4. Advertisers optimize bids based on performance data and competitor behaviour.

Applications of the Ad Auction Game

1. **Search Engine Advertising** – Google Ads, Bing Ads, and Yahoo auctions.

2. **Social Media Advertising** – Facebook, Instagram, and LinkedIn ad auctions.

3. **E-Commerce Marketplaces** – Amazon and eBay promote top-paying sellers.

4. **Digital Display Ads** – Websites auction ad space via real-time bidding.

Key Insights

1. **Bidding strategically (not just the highest) leads to cost-effective advertising.**

2. **The auction format influences how advertisers set bids.**

3. **Quality Score (ad relevance and click-through rate) impacts rankings.**

4. **Automated AI-driven bidding optimizes performance over time.**

Final Thoughts

The **Ad Auction Game** explains **how companies compete for digital ad space using strategic bidding**. Whether in Google Ads, social media, or e-commerce, understanding bid dynamics and optimization strategies ensures higher ROI and market efficiency.

102 Bonus - Clickbait vs. Quality Game

Clickbait vs. Quality Game in Game Theory

Breakdown of the Theory

The **Clickbait vs. Quality Game** is a **strategic interaction in digital media and online content platforms** where publishers must decide whether to **prioritize engaging, high-quality content or rely on clickbait strategies to maximize short-term views**. This game highlights the **trade-off between long-term credibility and short-term revenue gains**, especially in **advertising-driven digital markets**.

Clickbait articles use **sensationalized headlines, misleading information, or exaggerated claims** to attract clicks, while high-quality content focuses on **accuracy, depth, and user value**. Since **online platforms reward engagement metrics like clicks and watch time**, content creators face a **strategic dilemma**:

- **High-quality content builds trust and retains users but may have slower growth.**

- **Clickbait attracts immediate clicks but risks losing credibility over time.**

Key assumptions of the **Clickbait vs. Quality Game**:

1. **Content creators seek to maximize views, engagement, and revenue.**

2. **Users prefer high-quality content but may be drawn to sensational headlines.**

3. **Platforms (e.g., Google, Facebook, YouTube) use algorithms to rank and promote content.**

4. **Short-term clickbait gains may lead to long-term audience loss if trust erodes.**

Since **user behaviour and algorithmic incentives shape content strategies, creators must balance short-term gains with long-term sustainability.**

Example of the Clickbait vs. Quality Game

Consider **two news websites competing for online traffic**:

Scenario	Website A's Strategy	Website B's Strategy	Outcome
1	High-quality journalism	High-quality journalism	Loyal audience, steady growth.
2	Clickbait headlines	High-quality journalism	A gets more clicks initially, but trust erodes over time.
3	High-quality journalism	Clickbait headlines	B gains short-term traffic, but long-term credibility suffers.
4	Clickbait headlines	Clickbait headlines	Both compete for clicks, audience trust declines.

- **If both focus on high-quality content, they build credibility but may grow slowly.**

- **If one site uses clickbait while the other maintains quality, the clickbait site may gain short-term traffic.**

- **If both rely on clickbait, audience trust erodes, reducing long-term engagement.**

Since **platform algorithms and user feedback influence content performance, strategies must adapt dynamically.**

Why It Works

The **Clickbait vs. Quality Game works because**:

- It models real-world competition among digital media companies.

- Players must balance engagement with reputation management.

- The game explains how algorithmic ranking systems shape content strategies.

How It Works

1. Publishers choose between high-quality content and clickbait.

2. Users respond based on engagement and trust levels.

3. Platforms rank and promote content based on algorithms and feedback.

4. Over time, user behaviour influences which strategy is sustainable.

Applications of the Clickbait vs. Quality Game

1. **Digital News & Journalism** – Competing for clicks while maintaining credibility.

2. **Social Media Content Creation** – Balancing viral content with audience trust.

3. **YouTube & Video Platforms** – Thumbnail and title strategies for engagement.

4. **E-Commerce & Marketing** – Writing attention-grabbing vs. informative product descriptions.

Key Insights

1. **Clickbait maximizes short-term gains but risks long-term audience loss.**

2. **Platforms adjust algorithms to balance engagement with content quality.**

3. **Users influence content strategies through feedback and trust.**

4. **Sustainable success requires a mix of engagement tactics and high-quality value.**

Final Thoughts

The **Clickbait vs. Quality Game** explains **how digital media strategies evolve based on engagement incentives and user trust.** Whether in **journalism, social media, or digital marketing, balancing immediate attention with long-term credibility is key to sustainable growth**.

103 Bonus - Social Media Virality Game

Social Media Virality Game in Game Theory

Breakdown of the Theory

The **Social Media Virality Game** is a **strategic interaction in digital platforms** where content creators, influencers, and marketers compete to make their posts go viral. The game highlights the trade-offs between **authentic engagement and algorithm-driven tactics** while accounting for **user behaviour, platform algorithms, and competition**.

Social media platforms like **TikTok, Instagram, YouTube, and Twitter (X)** use **engagement-driven algorithms** to determine which posts get amplified. This creates a strategic dilemma:

- **High-quality, organic content builds long-term credibility but may not go viral.**

- **Algorithmic gaming (clickbait, sensationalism, controversial topics) may lead to short-term virality but risks backlash or platform penalties.**

Key assumptions of the **Social Media Virality Game**:

1. **Content creators want to maximize reach, engagement, and monetization.**

2. **Algorithms prioritize content that keeps users engaged.**

3. **Users respond based on trends, emotional appeal, and perceived authenticity.**

4. **Short-term virality doesn't always translate into long-term audience retention.**

Since **platform dynamics constantly change, creators must adapt their strategies to maintain visibility.**

Example of the Social Media Virality Game

Consider **three YouTube creators competing for virality:**

Scenario	Creator A's Strategy	Creator B's Strategy	Creator C's Strategy	Outcome
1	High-quality, original content	Trend-chasing	Clickbait & controversy	B & C get initial virality, but A gains long-term audience.
2	Trend-chasing	Trend-chasing	Clickbait & controversy	Virality for B & C, but potential algorithm penalties.
3	High-quality content	High-quality content	High-quality content	Steady growth, audience trust, but slower reach.
4	Clickbait	Clickbait	Clickbait	Short-term virality, long-term credibility loss.

- If all creators rely on clickbait, audience trust declines, and platforms adjust algorithms.

- If one focuses on quality while others chase trends, the trend-followers may gain temporary advantage.

- Balanced strategies of authenticity and trend-awareness lead to sustainable success.

Since **users and algorithms drive engagement, creators must balance trend participation with content quality**.

Why It Works

The **Social Media Virality Game works because**:

- It models real-world digital competition for visibility.

- Players must adapt to changing algorithms and audience behaviour.

- Engagement-driven platforms incentivize both quality and virality.

How It Works

1. Creators choose a content strategy: high-quality, trend-driven, or clickbait.

2. Platform algorithms rank content based on engagement and retention metrics.

3. Users interact based on interest, trust, and perceived authenticity.

4. Over time, strategies evolve as platforms refine ranking mechanisms.

Applications of the Social Media Virality Game

1. **Influencer Marketing** – Brands select influencers based on engagement strategies.

2. **Advertising & Monetization** – Content creators optimize revenue models for ads and sponsorships.

3. **Political & Social Movements** – Virality shapes public discourse and activism.

4. **Brand Awareness & Growth Hacking** – Businesses use viral marketing tactics to gain customers.

Key Insights

1. Short-term virality may not guarantee long-term audience retention.

2. Platforms reward engaging but ethical content over time.

3. Clickbait and extreme tactics may lead to algorithmic penalties.

4. Understanding platform mechanics helps optimize content strategy.

Final Thoughts

The **Social Media Virality Game** explains **how creators and businesses navigate digital platforms to maximize reach and engagement**. Whether in **influencer marketing, digital** branding, or viral campaigns, balancing authenticity with algorithmic optimization is key to long-term success.

104 Bonus - Online Reputation Management Game

Online Reputation Management Game in Game Theory

Breakdown of the Theory

The **Online Reputation Management (ORM) Game** is a **game-theoretic model** that explains how businesses, influencers, and individuals strategically manage their **digital reputation** in a competitive online environment. Since reputation influences **customer trust, engagement, and revenue**, players must carefully balance **authenticity, response strategies, and crisis management** to maintain a positive image.

In the **ORM Game**, key players include:

- **Businesses** – Managing customer reviews and brand perception.

- **Influencers** – Maintaining credibility and follower trust.

- **Consumers** – Providing feedback, which impacts online reputation.

- **Competitors** – Exploiting weaknesses to gain an advantage.

Key assumptions of the **ORM Game**:

1. **Reputation is a valuable digital asset that influences consumer choices.**

2. **Online feedback (reviews, ratings, comments) can rapidly shape public perception.**

3. **Businesses and influencers can either respond, ignore, or manipulate reputation signals.**

4. **Consumers react based on transparency, responsiveness, and perceived authenticity.**

Since **online reputation spreads quickly,** this game highlights **strategic decision-making in digital crisis management.**

Example of the Online Reputation Management Game

Consider **a restaurant receiving an unexpected wave of negative reviews**:

Scenario	Business Response	Customer Reaction	Outcome
1	Apologizes, offers compensation	Customers feel heard	Reputation recovers.
2	Ignores complaints	Customers feel ignored	Reputation declines.
3	Responds aggressively	Customers retaliate	Reputation worsens.
4	Uses fake positive reviews	Short-term gain, but risks exposure	Long-term credibility loss.

- If the business handles the situation professionally, it can rebuild trust.

- If the business ignores or reacts poorly, the reputation damage escalates.

- If it uses dishonest tactics (fake reviews), short-term gains may turn into long-term penalties.

Since **trust is difficult to rebuild once lost, businesses must act strategically**.

Why It Works

The **Online Reputation Management Game works** because:

- It models real-world digital reputation strategies.

- Players must anticipate and respond to consumer reactions.

- Reputation crises can escalate if not managed correctly.

How It Works

1. An event (negative review, controversy) triggers a reputation challenge.

2. The business/influencer decides on a response strategy.

3. Consumers react based on transparency, accountability, and perceived honesty.

4. Reputation evolves based on feedback loops and long-term trust.

Applications of the Online Reputation Management Game

1. **Brand & Corporate Reputation** – Managing public perception in crises.

2. **Influencer & Social Media Presence** – Building credibility and handling backlash.

3. **Political Campaigns** – Managing candidate reputation in digital spaces.

4. **E-Commerce & Online Reviews** – Handling negative customer feedback effectively.

Key Insights

1. **Transparency and responsiveness improve long-term reputation.**

2. **Ignoring crises or reacting poorly escalates digital backlash.**

3. **Fake reputation management (e.g., fake reviews) carries long-term risks.**

4. **Businesses must continuously monitor and adapt to digital feedback.**

Final Thoughts

The **Online Reputation Management Game** explains how **digital perception shapes business and influencer success.**

Whether in **corporate branding, social media, or e-commerce, strategic reputation management ensures long-term trust, loyalty, and digital credibility**.

105 Bonus - Misinformation Spread Game

Misinformation Spread Game in Game Theory

Breakdown of the Theory

The **Misinformation Spread Game** is a **game-theoretic model** that explains how **false information propagates through networks** and how different players—**content creators, social media users, fact-checkers, and platforms**—strategically interact in the spread or containment of misinformation.

In digital environments, misinformation spreads because:

1. **It often triggers emotional responses, making it more shareable.**

2. **It aligns with confirmation bias—people believe what supports their views.**

3. **It may be intentionally spread for political, financial, or ideological gain.**

4. **Algorithms amplify viral content without verifying accuracy.**

461

Players in this game include:

- **Misinformation spreaders (bad actors)** – Intentionally or unintentionally spreading false information.

- **Consumers (social media users)** – Choosing to believe, share, or ignore content.

- **Fact-checkers & media platforms** – Trying to debunk false claims.

- **Algorithms & social networks** – Influencing visibility and engagement.

Since **misinformation can be profitable or politically advantageous, incentives drive its spread unless countered by corrective mechanisms**.

Example of the Misinformation Spread Game

Consider **three groups interacting in an election misinformation scenario**:

Scenario	Misinformation Spreaders	Social Media Users	Fact-Checkers	Outcome
1	Fabricate viral fake news	Share widely	Slow response	Misinformation dominates.
2	Fabricate misleading news	Some users share, some sceptical	Platforms flag content	Mixed trust outcomes.
3	No misinformation	Users engage with verified content	Fact-checkers monitor	Trust in news remains stable.

- **If misinformation spreads unchecked, it influences public perception.**

- **If fact-checkers intervene early, they may reduce its impact.**

- **If users critically assess content, misinformation loses power.**

Since **virality depends on user behaviour and algorithmic promotion, misinformation tactics evolve to exploit weaknesses.**

Why It Works

The **Misinformation Spread Game works because:**

- **It models real-world digital manipulation tactics.**

- **Players make strategic decisions based on incentives and risks.**

- **Fact-checkers and platforms act as counterforces but face challenges.**

How It Works

1. **Misinformation creators decide what and how to spread.**

2. **Social media users choose to believe, share, or ignore.**

3. **Fact-checkers intervene to verify and counter false claims.**

4. **Algorithms determine whether content reaches mass audiences.**

Applications of the Misinformation Spread Game

1. **Political Campaigns** – Influence elections through fake narratives.

2. **Public Health & Science** – Combat vaccine misinformation and hoaxes.

3. **Financial Markets** – Stock price manipulation through rumours.

4. **Crisis Response** – Fake news during pandemics or natural disasters.

Key Insights

1. **Misinformation thrives when virality incentives outweigh verification efforts.**

2. **Critical thinking and digital literacy reduce the impact of misinformation.**

3. **Algorithms must balance engagement with content authenticity.**

4. **Real-time fact-checking is essential to counteract false narratives.**

Final Thoughts

The **Misinformation Spread Game** explains **how digital misinformation spreads and how different players respond strategically.** Whether in **politics, science, or media, understanding these dynamics helps in designing better countermeasures, ensuring a more informed society.**

106 Bonus - Cybersecurity Game

Cybersecurity Game in Game Theory

Breakdown of the Theory

The **Cybersecurity Game** is a **game-theoretic model** that represents the strategic interactions between **attackers (hackers) and defenders (security teams)** in **cybersecurity threats and defence mechanisms**. It explains how **organizations, individuals, and nations allocate resources to protect digital assets while adversaries attempt to exploit vulnerabilities**.

This game is crucial because **cyber attacks are costly**, and **defence mechanisms require continuous investment**. Attackers aim to **maximize damage or gain unauthorized access**, while defenders must **minimize risk and mitigate threats efficiently**.

Key assumptions of the **Cybersecurity Game**:

1. **Attackers (hackers) seek to exploit system vulnerabilities.**

2. **Defenders (security teams) implement security measures to prevent breaches.**

3. **Both sides operate with incomplete information— attackers don't know all defences, and defenders don't know where attacks will occur.**

4. **Resources (time, money, computing power) limit both attackers and defenders.**

Since **cyber threats evolve constantly,** this game highlights adaptive **strategies, risk management, and cost-benefit trade-offs.**

Example of the Cybersecurity Game

Consider **a financial institution protecting its online banking system:**

Scenario	Hacker's Strategy	Security Team's Strategy	Outcome
1	Launches a phishing attack	Implements email filtering & employee training	Attack fails, security holds.
2	Exploits a software vulnerability	Patches systems regularly	No breach, system remains secure.
3	Uses a zero-day exploit	No proactive defences	Attack succeeds, data compromised.
4	Targets weak passwords	Enforces multi-factor authentication	Attack fails, strong protection.

- **If security teams anticipate attacks and deploy the right defences, breaches are prevented.**

- If attackers discover unpatched vulnerabilities, they gain access.

- Both sides continuously adjust strategies, making cybersecurity an evolving battle.

Since **defenders must protect all potential entry points while attackers only need one success**, cybersecurity requires **constant vigilance and strategic planning**.

Why It Works

The **Cybersecurity Game works because**:

- It models real-world digital threats and defence interactions.

- Attackers exploit gaps, forcing defenders to adapt continuously.

- Decision-making under uncertainty is key to both sides' strategies.

How It Works

1. Hackers identify vulnerabilities and decide whether to launch an attack.

2. Defenders allocate security resources to protect critical assets.

3. If defences are strong, attacks fail; if gaps exist, breaches occur.

4. Both sides learn from past encounters and update their strategies.

Applications of the Cybersecurity Game

1. **Corporate IT Security** – Preventing data breaches and ransomware attacks.

2. **Government Cyber Defence** – Protecting national infrastructure from cyber warfare.

3. **Personal Cyber Hygiene** – Individuals securing accounts from phishing and hacking.

4. **AI & Machine Learning Security** – Protecting automated systems from adversarial attacks.

Key Insights

1. **Cybersecurity is a continuous strategic battle, not a one-time solution.**

2. **Proactive defence (patching, training, encryption) reduces attack success rates.**

3. **Attackers constantly innovate, requiring adaptive and evolving security.**

4. **Balancing security costs with risk mitigation is crucial for businesses and governments.**

Final Thoughts

The **Cybersecurity Game** explains **how attackers and defenders engage in strategic decision-making to exploit or protect digital systems.** Whether in **corporate security, government defence, or personal safety, continuous adaptation and proactive measures are essential to staying ahead of cyber threats.**

107 Bonus - Spam Detection Game

Spam Detection Game in Game Theory

Breakdown of the Theory

The **Spam Detection Game** is a **game-theoretic model** that represents the ongoing strategic interaction between **spammers (attackers) and spam filters (defenders)**. It illustrates how **email providers, social media platforms, and search engines** attempt to identify and block spam while **spammers continuously evolve their strategies to bypass detection**.

Spam detection is a **classic adversarial game** because:

1. **Spammers seek to maximize the number of messages delivered.**

2. **Email providers (e.g., Gmail, Outlook) develop filters to block unwanted messages.**

3. **Both sides operate in a dynamic environment where one party's success depends on outsmarting the other.**

4. **Machine learning models and algorithms continuously evolve to improve spam detection.**

Since **false negatives (missed spam) and false positives (legitimate emails flagged as spam) impact user experience**, platforms must **balance strictness with accuracy**.

Example of the Spam Detection Game

Consider **an email service provider combating spam emails**:

Scenario	Spammer's Strategy	Email Filter's Strategy	Outcome
1	Uses simple keyword-based spam	Filters block common spam words	Spam is detected and blocked.
2	Uses obfuscated text (e.g., "Fr.ee Mo.ney")	Filters adapt using pattern recognition	Spam is detected, but delayed response.
3	Mimics legitimate emails	Basic filters fail, users report spam	Some spam reaches inboxes before learning algorithms update.
4	Uses AI-generated messages	AI-driven detection models improve	Spam is detected at higher accuracy.

- **If email filters rely on fixed rules, spammers can adapt and bypass them.**

- If spam filters use machine learning, they can evolve based on new spam tactics.

- Spammers continuously test filters to find weaknesses, forcing constant updates.

Since **spammers need only a small percentage of emails to bypass filters, while email providers must stop nearly all spam, the burden of adaptation falls on defenders**.

Why It Works

The **Spam Detection Game works because:**

- It models real-world adversarial interactions in cybersecurity.

- Players must continuously adjust strategies to outmanoeuvre opponents.

- Automation and machine learning play a key role in maintaining efficiency.

How It Works

1. Spammers create deceptive messages to evade detection.

2. Spam filters analyse patterns, keywords, and user reports.

3. Filters update detection algorithms, forcing spammers to adapt.

4. The cycle repeats as both sides refine their strategies.

Applications of the Spam Detection Game

1. **Email Spam Filtering** – Preventing phishing and junk emails.

2. **Social Media Moderation** – Blocking spam comments and bot-generated content.

3. **Search Engine Optimization (SEO)** – Filtering out spam websites from search results.

4. **Online Fraud Prevention** – Detecting spam-based scams and deceptive ads.

Key Insights

1. **Spam detection is an evolving battle requiring adaptive filtering.**

2. **Machine learning enhances spam detection efficiency over time.**

3. **Spammers rely on exploiting weaknesses in automated systems.**

4. **User reporting and AI integration improve detection accuracy.**

Final Thoughts

The **Spam Detection Game** explains **how spammers and security systems engage in a continuous cycle of attack and defence.** Whether in **email filtering, social media moderation, or SEO,** adaptive detection strategies and AI-driven solutions are crucial to staying ahead of evolving spam tactics.

108 Bonus - AI Alignment Game

AI Alignment Game in Game Theory

Breakdown of the Theory

The **AI Alignment Game** is a **game-theoretic model** that explores the strategic interaction between **humans (AI designers, regulators) and artificial intelligence (AI systems)** to ensure that AI behaves in a way that aligns with human goals and ethical values. Since **advanced AI operates autonomously and makes decisions based on programmed objectives**, ensuring **alignment between AI's incentives and human well-being** is a critical challenge.

This game is crucial because:

1. **AI systems are optimized for objectives set by humans, but misalignment can lead to unintended consequences.**

2. **Human designers must balance control, safety, and adaptability.**

3. **AI must interpret complex human values while avoiding adversarial incentives.**

4. **As AI capabilities advance, alignment strategies must evolve to prevent unpredictable behaviour.**

Since **misalignment can lead to catastrophic failures, both sides must optimize their strategies for cooperation, transparency, and robustness.**

Example of the AI Alignment Game

Consider **a company developing an AI system for autonomous financial trading:**

Scenario	AI's Objective	Human Designer's Oversight	Outcome
1	Maximizes profit	Strong ethical constraints	AI follows profit goals while avoiding unethical actions.
2	Maximizes profit	Weak oversight	AI exploits loopholes (e.g., market manipulation).
3	Optimizes for fairness	AI is not transparent	AI makes unpredictable decisions, causing distrust.
4	Prioritizes safety over profit	Human feedback loop active	AI aligns well but may underperform financially.

- **If AI is purely profit-driven with minimal oversight, it may exploit unethical strategies.**

- If AI is constrained but lacks interpretability, its decisions may be unpredictable.

- Optimal alignment occurs when AI is both goal-optimized and ethically constrained.

Since **AI learns from data and feedback loops, designers must continuously refine objectives to prevent harmful unintended consequences.**

Why It Works

The **AI Alignment Game works because:**

- It models real-world challenges in AI safety and governance.

- Players must strategically balance control, adaptability, and ethical considerations.

- Misalignment can lead to unintended or adversarial outcomes.

How It Works

1. Humans define objectives and constraints for AI systems.

2. AI optimizes performance within given parameters.

3. If objectives are too narrow, AI may misinterpret human intent.

4. Alignment improves with iterative feedback, constraints, and learning mechanisms.

Applications of the AI Alignment Game

1. **Autonomous Vehicles** – Ensuring safety decisions align with human values.

2. **AI Ethics & Governance** – Preventing biased or harmful AI behaviour.

3. **Financial AI Systems** – Aligning profit-seeking with ethical trading.

4. **Military AI** – Ensuring AI follows rules of engagement without unintended escalation.

Key Insights

1. **AI alignment requires continuous human oversight and iteration.**

2. **Misalignment risks increase as AI becomes more autonomous.**

3. **Regulation and ethical frameworks improve AI behaviour.**

4. **AI interpretability and transparency are crucial for trust and safety.**

Final Thoughts

The **AI Alignment Game** explains **how human designers and AI systems interact to ensure safe and beneficial AI deployment.** Whether in **finance, healthcare, or autonomous decision-making, strategic alignment between AI objectives and human values is essential for avoiding unintended consequences.**

109 Bonus - Self-Driving Car Dilemma

Self-Driving Car Dilemma in Game Theory

Breakdown of the Theory

The **Self-Driving Car Dilemma** is a **game-theoretic model** that explores how **autonomous vehicles (AVs) interact with human drivers, pedestrians, and other AVs** in real-world traffic scenarios. It highlights strategic decision-making in **risk management, ethical dilemmas, and coordination between AI-driven and human-driven vehicles**.

This dilemma is critical because:

1. **Self-driving cars must predict and respond to unpredictable human behaviour.**

2. **Human drivers may exploit AVs' programmed safety measures.**

3. **Traffic efficiency depends on coordination between AVs and traditional vehicles.**

4. **Ethical challenges arise in accident scenarios (e.g., who should an AV prioritize in a crash?).**

Since **AVs rely on algorithms while human drivers behave unpredictably, achieving a balance between safety, efficiency, and fairness is a strategic challenge**.

Example of the Self-Driving Car Dilemma

Consider **an autonomous vehicle approaching an intersection with a human-driven car**:

Scenario	AV's Strategy	Human Driver's Strategy	Outcome
1	Waits for the human driver	Human yields	Smooth, safe traffic flow.
2	Waits for the human driver	Human takes advantage	AV gets stuck, human driver exploits predictability.
3	Moves forward cautiously	Human is aggressive	Risk of accident due to miscoordination.
4	Moves forward assertively	Human follows traffic rules	Safe and efficient outcome.

- **If the AV is too cautious, human drivers may take advantage, reducing efficiency.**

- **If the AV is too assertive, it risks collisions with unpredictable drivers.**

- **Optimal behaviour involves balancing caution with assertiveness to ensure smooth traffic flow.**

Since **AVs must make real-time decisions in uncertain environments, their strategies must continuously adapt based on observed behaviour.**

Why It Works

The **Self-Driving Car Dilemma works because:**

- **It models real-world decision-making in mixed-traffic environments.**
- **Players (AVs and humans) adjust strategies based on expectations.**
- **Safety, efficiency, and fairness are competing priorities.**

How It Works

1. **AVs predict human behaviour using sensors and historical data.**
2. **Human drivers adjust their driving based on perceived AV behaviour.**
3. **Regulations and AI programming influence AV decision-making.**
4. **Reinforcement learning helps AVs refine strategies over time.**

Applications of the Self-Driving Car Dilemma

1. **Traffic Safety** – Preventing accidents by optimizing AV decision-making.

2. **Urban Mobility** – Ensuring smooth integration of AVs with traditional traffic.

3. **Insurance & Liability** – Determining fault in mixed-driver accidents.

4. **AI Ethics & Regulation** – Defining ethical rules for AV accident decisions.

Key Insights

1. **AVs must balance caution and assertiveness to prevent inefficiencies.**

2. **Human drivers may exploit AVs' programmed behaviours, requiring countermeasures.**

3. **Ethical decision-making in unavoidable accidents remains an open challenge.**

4. **Government regulations and AI learning models will shape AV adoption and effectiveness.**

Final Thoughts

The **Self-Driving Car Dilemma** explains **how autonomous vehicles must strategically navigate human-driven traffic and ethical challenges.** Whether in **urban mobility, AI ethics, or transportation policy,** game-theoretic approaches are essential to ensuring safety, efficiency, and fairness in AV deployment.

OTHER BOOKS IN THIS 100 SERIES – SCAN HERE

100 COGNITIVE AND MENTAL MODELS TO HELP YOUR CAREER: Mental Shortcuts for Smarter Choices, Sharper Thinking, and Success

-

ANOTHER 100 MENTAL MODELS TO HELP YOUR CAREER - VOLUME 2: Another 100 Powerful Mental Models for Clarity, Confidence, and Climbing the Career Ladder

-

100 HEURISTICS AND HEURISTIC MODELS: The Hidden Rules of Smart Thinking Used by Experts, Entrepreneurs, and Machines

-

100 GAME THEORIES AND DECISION MODELS FOR RATIONAL DECISION MAKING IN COMPETITIVE SITUATIONS: 100 Winning Strategies for Rational Thinking in High-Stakes Scenarios

-

WHILST YOU ARE HERE , WHY NOT SCAN THIS TO SEE IF THERE ARE ANY MORE BOOKS PUBLISHED YET

OR FOLLOW ME AT @DANDANMUSICMAN ON X AND @DANDANMUSICMANUK ON INSTAGRAM

484

100 HEURISTICS + HEURISTIC MODELS

THE HIDDEN RULES OF SMART THINKING USED BY EXPERTS, ENTREPRENEURS, AND MACHINES

100 HEURISTIC MODELS
BY DAN WAITE

BRANCH AND BOUND	VORONOI	MANHATTAN DISTANCE
A* SEARCH	MINIMAX	METAHEURISTICS
SERIAL POSITION	CONTEXT-DEPENDENT	MNEMONIC
RETRIEVAL FLUENCY	SPACED REPETITION	CHUNKING
ADVERSE SELECTION	RULE CHAINING HEURISTIC	MEANS-ENDS ANALYSIS
NORM-FOLLOWING	IN-GROUP BIAS	LEFT-HAND RULE
LEFT-HAND RULE	NAVIGATION AND SPATIAL	EUCLIDEAN DISTANCE
SALIENCE	BASE RATE NEGLECT	AND MANY, MANY MORE

MASTERING SIDE HUSTLES AND SMART INVESTMENTS

SIDE HUSTLES
BY DAN WAITE

SLEEP & MEDITATION SOUNDTRACKS	RENTING OUT DRONES	LONG-TERM BONDS
SOLAR FARM INVESTMENTS	AIRBNB RENTAL ARBITRAGE	SUBSCRIPTION BASED FINANCIAL SERVICES
INVESTING IN TIMBERLAND	AUTOMATED E-COMMERCE	HEDGE FUNDS
PUBLISHING AUDIOBOOKS	AI-POWERED SEO WEBSITES	AUTOMATED PLATFORMS MONEY LENDING
AMAZON FBA BUSINESS	YOUTUBE AUTOMATION CHANNELS	FRANCHISING
TAX LIEN INVESTING	SILENT PARTNERSHIPS	CASHBACK APPS

100 PASSIVE INCOME STREAM GENERATING IDEAS

ELECTRIC BIKE RENTAL STATIONS	AIRPORT PARKING SPACE RENTAL	AUTOMATED BIKE SCOOTER RENTALS
DRONE RENTALS	SEMI-TRUCK LEASING	SOLAR PANEL LEASING
ICE VENDING MACHINES	ARCADE MACHINES	BILLBOARD SPACE
LAUNDROMATS	STORAGE FACILITY OWNERSHIP	ATM MACHINES
SAAS BUSINESS	STOCK MUSIC SALES	PRINT-ON-DEMAND
WEBSITE FLIPPING	YOUTUBE ADS	COACHING PROGRAMS
AI-GENERATED CONTENT	STOCK VIDEO FOOTAGE SALES	SELF-PUBLISHING BOOKS
VENDING MACHINES	OLD COURSE ROYALTIES	AND MANY, MANY MORE

PROVEN TACTICS FOR GROWTH, INNOVATION, AND MARKET DOMINATION

100 BUSINESS STRATEGIES
BY DAN WAITE

REFERRAL PROGRAM STRATEGY	CUSTOMER-CENTRIC STRATEGY	BOOTSTRAPPING STRATEGY
VENTURE CAPITAL STRATEGY	CROWDFUNDING STRATEGY	PRIVATE EQUITY STRATEGY
DEFENSIVE STRATEGY	HYPERLOCAL STRATEGY	DROPSHIPPING STRATEGY
AUTOMATION STRATEGY	SURPRISE & DELIGHT STRATEGY	HYPERAUTOMATION STRATEGY
REVERSE LOGISTICS STRATEGY	SIX SIGMA STRATEGY	GAMIFICATION STRATEGY
HYPER-PERSONALIZATION STRATEGY	ECOSYSTEM STRATEGY	JUST-IN-TIME (JIT) STRATEGY

100 BUSINESS STRATEGIES

BLUE OCEAN EXPANSION	BLOCKCHAIN STRATEGY	UPSELLING STRATEGY
WEB3 STRATEGY	METAVERSE STRATEGY	SEO STRATEGY
BLUE OCEAN STRATEGY	GLOBAL EXPANSION STRATEGY	CONGLOMERATE STRATEGY
HORIZONTAL INTEGRATION	VERTICAL INTEGRATION	FIRST-MOVER ADVANTAGE
FAST-FOLLOWER STRATEGY	PLATFORM STRATEGY	COST LEADERSHIP STRATEGY
DIFFERENTIATION STRATEGY	ORGANIC GROWTH STRATEGY	GROWTH HACKING STRATEGY
OMNICHANNEL STRATEGY	LOYALTY PROGRAM STRATEGY	VIRAL MARKETING STRATEGY
STORYTELLING STRATEGY	NOSTALGIA MARKETING STRATEGY	AND MANY, MANY MORE

100 GAME THEORIES AND DECISION MODELS

GAME THEORY
BY DAN WAITE

MUTUALLY ASSURED DESTRUCTION	DOLLAR AUCTION	HAWK-DOVE GAME
VOLUNTEER'S DILEMMA	SILENT DUEL	AI ALIGNMENT GAME
BAYESIAN GAME	TIPPING POINT GAME	SOCIAL INFLUENCE
TIT-FOR-TAT IN EVOLUTION	DIVIDE THE DOLLAR GAME	MONTY HALL PROBLEM
DIFFUSION OF RESPONSIBILITY	FREE RIDER PROBLEM	FLOCKING BEHAVIOUR
PARASITE-HOST GAME	CYBERSECURITY GAME	PREDATOR-PREY GAME

100 GAME THEORIES
RATIONAL DECISION-MAKING IN COMPETITIVE SITUATIONS

EVOLUTIONARILY STABLE STRATEGY	LIMITED WAR GAME	SECURITY DILEMMA
TRUST GAME	SUNK COST GAME	SHAPLEY VALUE
TERRORIST VS. GOVERNMENT	SPY VS. SPY GAME	DETERRENCE THEORY GAME
COLONEL BLOTTO GAME	WAR OF ATTRITION	MARKET FOR LEMONS
MORAL HAZARD GAME	PRINCIPAL-AGENT PROBLEM	JOB MARKET SIGNALLING
SOCIAL MEDIA VIRALITY GAME	SPAM DETECTION GAME	ADVERSE SELECTION GAME
BERTRAND COMPETITION	CASCADING FAILURE GAME	EL FAROL BAR PROBLEM
SELF-DRIVING CAR DILEMMA GAMES	MECHANISM DESIGN THEORY	AND MANY, MANY MORE

ORGANIZATIONAL SUCCESS AND EFFECTIVE DECISION-MAKING
100 LEADERSHIP
MODELS AND STRATEGIES
BY DAN WAITE

GAMIFICATION LEADERSHIP	NONPROFIT LEADERSHIP	IMPROV LEADERSHIP
HACKER LEADERSHIP	SWARM LEADERSHIP	TECH LEADERSHIP
GREAT MAN THEORY	SITUATIONAL LEADERSHIP	AGILE LEADERSHIP
HOLOGRAPHIC LEADERSHIP	TRANSFORMATIONAL LEADERSHIP	PEER LEADERSHIP
LAISSEZ-FAIRE LEADERSHIP	AUTOCRATIC LEADERSHIP	BENEVOLENT DICTATORSHIP
POLITICAL LEADERSHIP	MILITARY LEADERSHIP	LEVEL FIVE LEADERSHIP

100 LEADERSHIP
MODELS

RESONANT LEADERSHIP	COACHING LEADERSHIP	EMPATHETIC LEADERSHIP
AI-INTEGRATED LEADERSHIP	MAVERICK LEADERSHIP	IMPROV LEADERSHIP
VISIONARY LEADERSHIP	PACESETTING LEADERSHIP	SUSTAINABLE LEADERSHIP
PARADOXICAL LEADERSHIP	INFLUENCER LEADERSHIP	OPEN-SOURCE LEADERSHIP
STOIC LEADERSHIP	ZEN LEADERSHIP	STARTUP LEADERSHIP
EXISTENTIAL LEADERSHIP	DIALECTICAL LEADERSHIP	SPIRITUAL LEADERSHIP
HUMAN-CANTERED LEADERSHIP	CRISIS LEADERSHIP	HOLACRACY LEADERSHIP
SPORTS LEADERSHIP	DATA-DRIVEN LEADERSHIP	AND MANY, MANY MORE

100 ECONOMIC THEORIES DEMYSTIFIED
ECONOMIC THEORIES
BY DAN WAITE

MERCANTILISM	GIG ECONOMY THEORY	SAY'S LAW
MALTHUSIAN THEORY	JAPAN'S ECONOMIC MODEL	MARXIST ECONOMICS
RICARDIAN EQUIVALENCE	UTILITY THEORY	MARGINAL UTILITY THEORY
D.O.G.E. DEPARTMENT OF GOVERNMENT EFFICIENCY	GENERAL EQUILIBRIUM THEORY	RANDOM WALK THEORY
PRICE ELASTICITY OF DEMAND	CONSUMER SURPLUS	CLASSICAL ECONOMICS
THEORY OF THE FIRM	PIGOUVIAN TAXES	KEYNESIAN ECONOMICS

100 ECONOMIC
THEORIES DEMYSTIFIED

EVOLUTIONARILY STABLE STRATEGY	LIMITED WAR GAME	IRRATIONAL EXUBERANCE
PHILLIPS CURVE	DEBT-DEFLATION THEORY	SHAPLEY VALUE
PERMANENT INCOME HYPOTHESIS	VEBLEN GOODS	BRETTON WOODS SYSTEM
MORAL HAZARD	MARKET STRUCTURE THEORY	DUTCH DISEASE
ADVERSE SELECTION	NETWORK EFFECTS	HARROD-DOMAR GROWTH MODEL
GLOBALIZATION THEORY	GRAVITY MODEL OF TRADE	NEW TRADE THEORY
CONVERGENCE THEORY	HECKSCHER-OHLIN MODEL	SOLOW-SWAN GROWTH MODEL
CREATIVE DESTRUCTION	BIG PUSH THEORY	AND MANY, MANY MORE

HACKS AND STRATEGIES TO GROW PROFIT
100 BUSINESS GROWTH HACKS
BY DAN WAITE

ABANDONED CART HACK	SKYSCRAPER CONTENT HACK	DRIP CAMPAIGN HACK
POLL AND QUIZ HACK	GIVEAWAY COLLAB HACK	F.O.M.O. HACK
SOCIAL PROOF HACK	BRANDED HASHTAG HACK	MICRO-EXPERIMENT HACK
"FIRST NAME PLUS EMOJI HACK"	TREND JACKING HACK	SOCIAL LOCK HACK
SCRAPING AND OUTREACH HACK	STICKER BOMB HACK	STEAL COMPETITOR TRAFFIC HACK
TRIP-WIRE OFFER HACK	MICRO COMMITMENT HACK	GAMIFICATION IN-APP HACK

100 BUSINESS
GROWTH HACKS

LOSS AVERSION HACKS	PEOPLE ALSO ASK HACK	ANSWER BOX HACK
LIVE CHAT HACK	INFOGRAPHIC HACK	AI CHATBOT HACK
WIN-BACK CAMPAIGN HACK	FAKE WAITING LIST HACK	YOUTUBE SEO HACK
LEAD MAGNET HACK	PEOPLE ALSO ASK HACK	DRIP CAMPAIGN HACK
AI CONTENT CREATION HACK	REACTIVATION HACK	REDDIT AND QUORA HACK
CROSS PROMOTION HACK	REFFERAL LOOP HACK	TREND JACKING HACK
MEMES AND GIFS HACK	REVERSE FUNNEL HACK	EXIT-INTENT POPUPS HACK
"DARK MODE" HACK	LEADERBOARD HACK	AND MANY, MANY MORE

www.ingramcontent.com/pod-product-compliance
Lightning Source LLC
Chambersburg PA
CBHW030332220326
41518CB00047B/808